CELEBRATIONS
AROUND THE WORLD

CELEBRATIONS
AROUND THE WORLD

A Multicultural Handbook

Carole S. Angell

fulcrum resources

Fulcrum Publishing
Golden, Colorado

Illustrations © Geoffrey M. Smith (pages 1, 5, 6, 7, 8, 9, 11, 12,
19, 26, 31, 33, 36, 41, 45, 53, 61, 71, 72, 83, 95, 96, 105, 108,
111, 112, 116, 121, 134, 135, 147, 148, 152)
Book design by Deborah Rich

Library of Congress Cataloging-in-Publication Data

Angell, Carole S.
    Celebrations around the world : a mulitcultural handbook /
Carole S. Angell.
        p.   cm.
    Includes bibliographical references and index.
    ISBN 1-55591-945-6 (pbk.)
    1. Holidays—Cross-cultural studies.   2. Festivals—Cross-
cultural studies.   3. Fasts and feasts—Cross-cultural studies.
    4. Multiculturalism.   I. Title.
GT3933.A59   1996
394.2'6—dc20   96-14473
                                                                    CIP

Printed in the United States of America

0 9 8 7 6 5 4 3 2 1

Fulcrum Publishing
350 Indiana Street, Suite 350
Golden, Colorado 80401-5093
(800) 992-2908 • (303) 277-1623

Dedicated to my father, who taught me how to celebrate,
and to the students of Glen Forest Elementary School,
who taught me how to be a citizen of the world.

Contents

Preface   ix
Acknowledgments   xi
Introduction   xiii

• • • •

Holidays with Nonfixed Dates   1

1

• • • •

January Holidays   7
Nonfixed Dates   8
Fixed Dates   11

2

• • • •

February Holidays   19
Nonfixed Dates   20
Fixed Dates   25

3

• • • •

March Holidays   31
Nonfixed Dates   32
Fixed Dates   34

4

• • • •

April Holidays   41
Nonfixed Dates   42
Fixed Dates   46

5

• • • •

May Holidays   53
Nonfixed Dates   54
Fixed Dates   60

6

• • • •

June Holidays   71
Nonfixed Dates   72
Fixed Dates   75

7

• • • •

July Holidays   83

Nonfixed Dates   84

Fixed Dates   85

8

• • • •

August Holidays   95

Nonfixed Dates   96

Fixed Dates   98

9

• • • •

September Holidays   105

Nonfixed Dates   106

Fixed Dates   113

10

• • • •

October Holidays   121

Nonfixed Dates   122

Fixed Dates   127

11

• • • •

November Holidays   135

Nonfixed Dates   136

Fixed Dates   139

12

• • • •

December Holidays   147

Nonfixed Dates   148

Fixed Dates   149

Appendix A: Trade Books Arranged According to Topic   161

Appendix B: Recipes   177

Appendix C: Music   191

Bibliography   195

Index of Holidays   199

Index of Activities   215

Preface

The United States has long been known as the "melting pot" and now, more than ever, has become a veritable microcosm of the world. People from nearly all nations, religions, cultures, and backgrounds make up our citizenry. It is essential that we learn to live together and to accept each other. What better place to start than with the children?

Life should be a joy, and learning about the lives of others can truly be a celebration. By learning about and participating in the celebrations of different peoples, students of all ages can understand the cultures, religions, customs, beliefs, traditions, and rituals of others. We can learn to appreciate our differences and, more importantly, to recognize the innumerable similarities that exist between all cultures.

For some years I have tried to espouse this philosophy in my classroom. My students—who come from all corners of the world, speak many different languages in their homes, and bring with them a rich variety of cultural backgrounds—have been my teachers. In order to meet their needs and my own I have done extensive research over the years and have collected a fascinating clutter of information, ideas, and materials. This book is my attempt to organize all of that and to share it with you.

Whether you are a teacher, a parent, a scout leader, or just an aging child yourself this book is for you, and with it I give you permission to make every day of your life a celebration!

Acknowledgments

Without the help and support of many special people this book would never have been written. Thanks to Mary Ann Carr, fellow author and educator, who initially convinced me that I was capable of tackling this project and who bullied and dared me until I finally got tired of listening to her and started writing. Thanks to the fine library staff of Fairfax County, Virginia; to "Chef" Minnie Wingert who tested and tasted all of the enclosed recipes; to Dick Ward, Lynn Schug, and Barbara Payne; and to the dozens of employees of various embassies who helped me with my research. Thanks also to Lisa Horst, Linda Rashidi, Nancy Skornik, Rosemary McKillips, Jamila Gary, Fran Jackson, and the many other teachers of Glen Forest Elementary School who field-tested the ideas in the book and gave me much valuable input regarding its contents. And finally, special thanks to my husband, Jerry Angell, for his willingness to do research, cook meals, run errands, and work out my technical difficulties with the computer while I was engaged in writing. Without these people the material contained in this book would still be a disorderly heap of folders in my file cabinet. I offer my sincere gratitude to each and every one of them.

Introduction

A Guide for Choosing and Using Holidays for Classroom Instruction

THERE ARE SO MANY! HOW DO I CHOOSE?

With so many international holidays and celebrations it would be impossible to address all of them in the context of a 180-day school year. Selecting which events to include is of utmost importance and is a responsibility that can only be undertaken by the individual classroom teacher. Even holidays that may be designated as schoolwide celebrations, such as Black History Month, will require teachers to make decisions and prepare a sampling of activities appropriate for the students in their classes.

When first contemplating which holidays to include the teacher must take into careful account the following considerations:

1. the timing of the instruction,
2. the objectives of the instructional program and the ways in which the study of holidays of different cultures might enhance these objectives,
3. the importance of choosing a representative sampling of countries, cultures, and religions,
4. the needs, interests, backgrounds, and prior knowledge of the students in the class.

The easiest way to arrange the year is chronologically, studying holidays as they occur on the calendar. While this simplifies things, it is nevertheless not always possible or desirable. Religious beliefs will sometimes exclude certain students (Jehovah's Witnesses, for example) from lessons about holidays if they are undertaken on or near the date of that holiday. Another possible problem would be that a particular holiday or group of holidays fits perfectly with a unit of study but does not occur during the time of the year when that unit is scheduled to be covered.

In cases such as these the teacher should feel free to adjust instruction as needed. Holidays do not need to be studied on the day they occur, but can be discussed at the time most suited to the curriculum. During a science unit on plants or a health unit on nutrition a teacher may, for example, elect to teach about, compare, and contrast harvest festivals from different countries around the world.

Holidays may also be studied by theme. Freedom festivals, New Year's observances, and spring celebrations occur year-round and provide a sampling of customs and cultures from around the globe.

It must also be remembered that while the teacher has the power to decide which holidays to include in the program of study, with this power comes a double responsibility to the students and their cultural backgrounds. The teacher must be careful not to slight any students by neglecting to include their heritage at some time during the year. At the same time the teacher needs to be equally cautious not to include the study of a holiday or holidays simply because a student from that culture is a member of the class—the lesson must have a strong instructional basis. Through careful selection and planning the teacher can easily meet both of these criteria and assure that all students feel a sense of belonging and an eagerness to learn.

HOW TO HANDLE RELIGIOUS HOLIDAYS

Culture and religion go hand in hand; you cannot teach one without the other. To understand a culture, one needs to study and understand the religion(s) of the peoples who make up that culture. It is also not enough to simply touch on modern-day religious practices. We must go back through history and study the ancient religious beliefs—even back to pagan times—that have influenced culture and religion and given us the customs and traditions that we have today.

What about the separation of church and state? Doesn't the Constitution prohibit religion in public schools? Emphatically, no, it does not! In fact, school systems that exclude the study of religion are not in compliance with the Constitution. In 1962 and then again in 1963 the Supreme Court stated that the study of religion is not prohibited by the Constitution and that, in fact, education without religion is incomplete. A curriculum that ignores religion would appear to deny religion's historical importance.

While acknowledging that the study of religion is an important part of everyone's education and endeavoring to integrate it into the curriculum, we must be equally aware of the importance of maintaining religious neutrality. Schools are required to refrain from promoting any given religion and from showing preference for one religion over another. In other words we should strive to inform students about religion, but should never seek to have students conform to one set of religious beliefs. The key is to teach *about* religion while avoiding the teaching *of* religion in public schools.

You can feel comfortable and safe about including religion and religious holidays in your program of study if you consider and remain sensitive about the need to:

1. consider students' needs and feelings,
2. achieve balance,
3. remain personally neutral,
4. meet instructional objectives.

For the first item, we must take care to see that no child is ever made to feel uncomfortable about the lesson being taught. It is the teacher's role to obtain adequate and accurate information related to religious holidays and to present that information. Avoid embarrassing your students by asking them to explain their religious observances or beliefs. (Of course, if students volunteer information let them speak! It could be equally embarrassing to them to keep them from talking about a subject when they are the "experts"!)

Second, it is important to achieve a balance. For example, if you have made a decision to integrate the study of five religious holidays into your program, make sure that they are not all Christian holidays, but rather that they give insights into a variety of religious doctrines and beliefs.

Third, it is essential that teachers remain personally neutral. This is one area of the curriculum where teachers would do best not to discuss their personal beliefs or philosophy as this may be perceived as an influence on the students. "Some people believe ..." is a phrase that I have found most useful.

Finally, remember that any lesson that addresses religion or religious issues must be based in the curriculum and designed to meet educational objectives. This does not mean that your instructional program necessarily will or should contain specific goals regarding religion per se. What it does imply is that you cannot use classroom time to study holidays just for fun—they need to be tied in with your overall instructional program. Frequently such lessons fit nicely into the social studies curriculum, but the study of holidays, whether religious in nature or not, can also quite often complement other areas of the curriculum as you will see in later chapters.

INTEGRATING ACROSS THE CURRICULUM

Holidays are fun, and studying holidays makes learning fun. When students are enjoying academic lessons their motivation soars and as a result more learning takes place. As mentioned above it is important that lessons on holidays have strong links to the educational objectives of the program of study, but these links occur naturally and it is quite easy to find them once you start looking.

The following chapters give some ideas of ways to work holidays into the school day while meeting academic goals, but these are only a starting point. Use them as written if they suit your purpose, but realize that my main goal in presenting these ideas is to plant a seed in your imagination which will help your own creative thoughts blossom as you create individual ways to integrate holidays into the curriculum.

The sample activities span a variety of curricular areas. There are, however, three academic areas that generally can be made to apply to any and all of the holidays and for which I have included few distinct examples under specific holidays. This does not imply that these areas are less important than those I have addressed, but rather that they are more important. I have chosen not to list them under each specific holiday because they can be so universally applied that to do so would have been redundant. As you begin brainstorming and planning I would ask you to consider incorporating these three fundamental areas into your program on a daily basis. They are: literature, geography, and multisensory activities.

Literature

Trade books containing wonderful examples of children's literature are available for many holidays and I encourage you to use them regularly as part of your daily language arts program. Include trade books pertinent to the country and/or culture under study in addition to those that specifically deal with the holiday. Mythology and folktales as well as nonfiction books provide valuable insights for students, and can be used instructionally to teach many, if not all, of the required language arts skills of a given grade level. Appendix A of this book provides a partial listing of trade books appropriate for elementary-aged children, organized by country or holiday.

Geography

The second area to consider is geography. Map skills, topography, climate, resources, in short all geography skills can become an integral, practical part of your program and not a separate, disconnected subject. A world map is an excellent and necessary resource and can be used almost daily. One idea is simply to write the name of a holiday and its country on the chalkboard and watch to see how quickly intermediate grade students find the country on the map.

Or you may want to give clues—latitude, continent, neighboring countries, etc.—and have the students come up with the country's name. These are only a few suggestions. Think of your classroom, your students, and your curriculum and let your mind race. Within a few minutes you will probably have more ideas than you can fit into the day!

Multisensory Activities

When planning to integrate holidays into your program, do not forget to integrate the five senses as well. It is a fact that sounds, smells, and tastes aid in the retention and recall of information. When you are teaching about a culture, using the recipes included in Appendix B and the music listed in Appendix C will allow your students to experience a part of that culture firsthand. Eat some ethnic dishes, play environmental tapes or ethnic music in the background, and plan lots of hands-on activities. Multisensory activities not only help your students academically, but they are fun as well, and that is what this book is all about!

CELEBRATIONS AROUND THE WORLD

HOLIDAYS WITH NONFIXED DATES

NONFIXED DATES

Arbor Day	International
Ramadan	Muslim
Eid-ul-Fitr	Muslim
Seker Bayrami (Candy Festival)	Turkey
Eid-ul-Adhia	Muslim
Muharram	Muslim
Eid Milad-un-Nabi	Muslim

A significant number of holidays do not occur yearly on the same date on our Gregorian calendar. There are several reasons for this. Some holidays fall on a given day, but not a given date. Labor Day, for example, is always observed on the first Monday of September, Thanksgiving, on the fourth Thursday in November; but the actual dates of these celebrations will vary. The Jewish calendar is used to calculate the dates of Jewish holidays, so dates for these celebrations vary widely but usually occur near the same time each year. Chinese celebrations are determined by the lunar calendar, however, they, too, generally occur at about the same time each year. (Chinese New Year, for example, is nearly always sometime in January or February.) Because these holidays can be roughly situated within the framework of one or sometimes two months, for the purpose of this book they are listed under an appropriate month with more specific notations given as necessary.

Other holidays are not so easily classified within the context of our calendar. The dates of Islamic holidays, for example, are calculated by the Muslim or Hijra calendar, which is based on the lunar cycle but differs from the Chinese lunar calendar. Islamic holidays move forward about ten to twelve days each year and can fall during any season and month of our calendar. These holidays and others like them are listed in this section.

The slight inconvenience of establishing the time of the celebration of these holidays during a given year is not a valid reason for discounting them. Many of these are major observances for a large portion of our world community and I strongly urge that you take the time to refer to a calendar of religious and ethnic holidays and festivals at the start of each year to establish the dates of these celebrations so that they may be included in your program.

ARBOR DAY

• • • •

International

Background

The first Arbor Day took place on April 10, 1872, in the state of Nebraska when J. Sterling Morton, who believed that the state needed more trees, urged the state board of agriculture to declare a tree-planting day. On that first Arbor Day, counties in Nebraska that planted the most trees were awarded prizes. The event was such a success that it became an annual holiday. In honor of Morton the date was changed from the 10th of April to the 22nd, his birthday. The observance of Arbor Day spread to other states in the United States and to many other countries around the world. Officially the date set aside internationally for the celebration of Arbor Day is December 22, but because of varying climates and planting times different countries and different states in the United States observe the holiday at various times.

Activities

- Have children work in cooperative groups to brainstorm lists of the things we get from living trees (oxygen, fruits, maple syrup, etc.) and the things that can be made from trees that have been cut down (paper, wood products, etc.).

- For one day collect all of the paper used in your classroom. This should include worksheets, homework, notes, paper towels, milk cartons, tissues—everything! At the end of the day examine the pile and weigh it. Estimate how much paper was used by your entire school that day, and how much would be used in a week and a year. Brainstorm a list of ways in which you might conserve paper.

- Plant a tree!
- Have children gather samples of leaves and needles from trees. Compare/contrast the different samples. Learn to identify common trees in your area.
  Study the codependence of trees and animals in your part of the country or in the rain forest.

RAMADAN

• • • •

Muslim

Background

The Muslim faith is based on the Five Pillars of Islam. These include: (1) belief in Allah as the One God, (2) prayer, (3) giving to the poor and helping others, (4) fasting, and (5) making a pilgrimage to Mecca. Ramadan, the fifth month of the Muslim year, is considered particularly sacred because it was during this month that the Koran was sent down from Allah to Muhammad as guidance to his people.

During the entire 29 days of the month of Ramadan, Muslims fast as a means of spiritual discipline. The fast includes total abstinence from food, water, tobacco, and sex from sunrise to sunset of each day. Although there are other days during the year on which Muslims fast, none are thought to be as powerful or as important to the fulfillment of the Fourth Pillar of Islam as the fast of Ramadan. Pregnant women, nursing mothers, and people who are making long journeys as well as the young, aged, and sick are exempt from fasting, but those who are able are expected to make up the days of fasting that they missed as soon as possible.

Because the Muslim year is made up of twelve lunar months it is 354 days long, 12 days shorter than the Gregorian calendar year. Therefore, Ramadan, as well as all other Muslim holidays, moves all the way through all four seasons once in about every 33 years. (See also "Eid-ul-Fitr" below.)

Activities

- Prepare a chart that compares the similar elements of different religions. Across the top list "Christianity," "Islam," and "Judaism." Down the side list "holy writings" (Bible/Koran/Torah); "believe in ..." (God/ Allah/Jehovah); "fasting" (Lent/Ramadan/Yom Kippur); "days that break the fast" (Easter/Eid-ul-Fitr/ sundown of Yom Kippur). Have the children work together to complete and discuss the chart.

- Have children research and report on the benefits and disadvantages of fasting from a medical point of view.

EID-UL-FITR

• • • •

Muslim

Background

Eid-ul-Fitr falls on the day after the month of Ramadan (see above) and is a celebration of the end of the fasting. Preparations begin the night before. In Muslim countries the streets and public buildings are illuminated and hung with colorful pennants and buntings. On Eid day people bathe and perfume themselves before putting on new clothes bought specially for the holiday. Religious services are attended by all and a feeling of peace and brotherhood reigns. Old wrongs are forgiven and money is given to the poor. Special foods are prepared and friends or relatives are invited to share in the feasting. Gifts and greeting cards are exchanged and the children anxiously wait to receive their *Eidi* (gifts of money) and other presents from their relatives and elders. Although Eid is a happy and joyous occasion the underlying purpose of the holiday is to praise Allah and to give thanks unto him.

Activities

- Have children draw names then make Eid gifts for each other from construction paper, glue, paint or markers, and "junk" that has been collected from home (egg cartons, Styrofoam meat trays, cardboard tubes, etc.). Exchange gifts along with the greeting "Eid Mubarak."

- Ask children to skip breakfast on the morning of Eid, then, after "fasting" until about ten o'clock serve wheat cereal with milk, sugar, and choices of chopped dates, coconut, almonds, raisins, or pistachio nuts. (This has many of the ingredients of *sheer khurma*, a traditional breakfast dish served on Eid.) Discuss the origin of the word "breakfast" (the meal by which people break the fast after sleeping all night).

Seker Bayrami

• • • •

(Candy Festival)

Turkey

Background

In Turkey, Muslims celebrate the end of Ramadan, the month of fasting, with Seker Bayrami, the Candy Holiday or Day of Sweet Things. Preparations for the three days of celebration begin well in advance. New clothing is bought to be worn during Seker Bayrami and gifts of money or clothing are given to those less fortunate, particularly widows or orphaned children. The morning of the first day of Seker Bayrami begins with the men going to the mosque for holiday prayers. Upon their return home they are greeted by their wives who honor them by kissing their hands. The husband then kisses his wife on each cheek. The children of the household greet their parents and any other adults who are present by kissing, and then pressing their foreheads to, their hands. After the formal honoring and greeting has taken place the children are given fancy handkerchiefs with money wrapped in them, and plates of candy and other sweets are passed around. Families gather for dinner at the homes of the eldest member after which visits are made to relatives and friends where holiday greetings and lots of candy are exchanged. Other special foods that may be served are small cakes, sweetened coffee, and fruit. Children are taken to small amusement parks with puppet shows and rides that have been set up for the occasion. In the evening baklava, a pastry filled with honey and nuts, is served.

Activities

- Have the children make puppets, write scripts, and present their own puppet shows.

- Discuss forms of greetings, both formal and informal, verbal and nonverbal, and the appropriate use of different types of greetings.

- Use measurement skills to put together a Turkish dessert for the class to eat. (See Appendix B, "Turkey," for recipes.)

- Compare this Muslim holiday that breaks the fast of Ramadan to the Christian holiday of Easter that breaks the Lenten fast and also includes family feasts and lots of candy.

EID-UL-ADHIA

• • • •

Muslim

Background

The Fifth Pillar of Islam (see "Ramadan" above) is the hajj, the pilgrimage to Mecca, which every Muslim is required to make at least once during his life if he is financially and physically able. Hajj is undertaken between the 8th and the 13th of Dhul-Hijjah, the last month of the Muslim calendar. Among the rituals associated with this ceremony are: (1) the wearing of special garments; (2) making seven circuits of the Ka'aba (according to the Koran, the first house of worship ever established on Earth) while repeating the words of the prophet Abraham; (3) performing the Sa'ee, a walk, made seven times, between two hills near the Ka'aba, which symbolizes the search of Hagar, wife of Abraham, for water for her infant son, Ismael; (4) visiting Mina, Arafat, and Muzdalifa where the pilgrims meditate and praise Allah; (5) performing the Rami, during which small stones are thrown at Jumrat-ul-Aqba, a pillar representing Satan; and (6) offering the sacrifice of an animal. Animals are sacrificed on the 10th of Dhul-Hijjah, which is known as Eid-ul-Adhia or the Festival of Sacrifice, by all who can afford to do so. The sacrifice is made not in an effort to atone for sins, or to appease God, but rather is a symbolic expression of the Muslims' willingness to sacrifice anything, even their own lives, for Allah. The animals that are sacrificed actually are symbolic of the animal within man himself.

For persons who do not make the hajj, the celebration of Eil-ul-Adhia includes prayer services; a sermon centered on the prophet Abraham, his wife Hagar and son Ismael, and the sacrifices they made for God; and sacrifices of animals. The meat of the animals is shared with friends, family, and the poor. Skins of the slaughtered animals are sold and the profits given to charity. Feasting and festivities begin later in the Eid day and continue for two days afterward.

MUHARRAM

• • • •

Muslim

Background

Muharram is a solemn festival in honor of Hussain, the grandson of the prophet Muhammad, who was martyred along with a number of his family members and followers. Muharram lasts for ten days and is marked by the wearing of black clothing in mourning and speeches on the lives of Hussain and other martyrs.

Activities

- Study martyrs throughout history and their causes.

- Discuss traditions that surround death and/or the remembrance of those who have died.

- Every religion has its most holy sites and shrines. Use this opportunity to study the architecture of different mosques, temples, or cathedrals. Look at some floor plans. Discuss mathematically the problems of supporting some of these massive structures. Find their locations on a world map.

EID MILAD-UN-NABI

• • • •

Muslim

Background

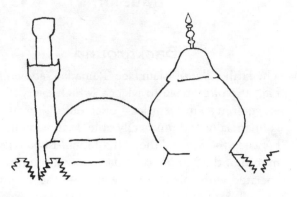

Eid Milad-un-Nabi is a time when Muslims commemorate the anniversary of the birth of the prophet Muhammad. In the mosques public meetings are held during which the story of the prophet's life is narrated in great detail and he is praised through songs, speeches, and chants. Because this date also commemorates the date of Muhammad's death, festivities are restricted and the occasion is generally solemn in nature.

1
JANUARY HOLIDAYS

NONFIXED DATES

New Year	China	January or February
Tet	Vietnam	January or February
Carnival	International	January of February
Martin Luther King Jr. Day	United States	Third Monday
Lantern Festival	China	January or February

FIXED DATES

January 1	New Year's Day	International
January 1	Emancipation Day	United States
January 1	Independence Day	Australia
January 1	Independence Day	Cameroon
January 1	Independence Day	Haiti
January 1	Independence Day	Sudan
January 1	Independence Day	Western Samoa
January 1	Junkanoo	Bahamas (see December 26)
January 4	Independence Day	Myanmar (Burma)
January 6	Epiphany	Christian
January 6	Día de los Reyes Magos (Three Kings Day)	Latin America
January 11–13	Makra Sankrant (Winter Festival)	India
January 13	St. Knut's Day	Sweden, Finland
January 26	Republic Day	India
January 31	Independence Day	Nauru

JANUARY HOLIDAYS WITH NONFIXED DATES

NEW YEAR

• • • •

January or February
China

Background

For centuries China used a lunar calendar and the Chinese New Year Festival was celebrated on the first day of the first lunar month. Following the revolution of 1911 China adopted the Gregorian calendar. At this time the name of the lunar new year was officially changed to the Spring Festival to distinguish it from the celebration of the solar new year, yet many people still think of this holiday as Chinese New Year.

The celebration actually lasts for most of a month. During the last month of the "old" year preparations are made. The house is scrubbed and cleaned, arguments and debts are settled, and all of the food that will be eaten during the main five days of the celebration is prepared in advance. Sweets are offered to Tsao-Chun, the kitchen god, and a week before the New Year begins the picture of Tsao-Chun that has hung in the kitchen all year is burned, sending him off to heaven to make a report on the household. (The hope is that the sweet treats offered earlier will put sweet words in his mouth when he makes his report!) On New Year's Eve Tsao-Chun returns and a new picture is hung to welcome him. Firecrackers and other noise-makers fill the air to scare away the old year and the evil spirits.

Families gather on New Year's Eve and New Year's Day to celebrate, feast, and exchange gifts. Money,

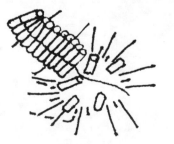

wrapped in red and gold packages, is given to the children to spend as they wish. The celebration continues for five full days during which stores and most businesses are closed. Starting on the third day and often continuing through the fifth there is much going on outdoors with dragon dancers, parades, firecrackers, lion dancers, and drumming. After the five "big" days of celebrating things return more or less to normal, but the Spring Festival is not really over until the Lantern Festival takes place at the time of the first full moon of the new year, about ten days later (see below).

In China the new year is always assigned to an animal. According to tradition, Buddha promised gifts to all animals who would pay him homage. Only twelve animals came to honor Buddha, so to favor these twelve animals each was given one of the twelve years of the Chinese zodiac. Persons born during a given animal's year are said to inherit the distinctive characteristics of that animal. The signs repeat every twelve years as follows:

Rat	ambitious, sincere	1960, 1972, 1984, 1996, 2008
Ox	bright, cheery, leader	1961, 1973, 1985, 1997, 2009
Tiger	courageous, sensitive	1962, 1974, 1986, 1998, 2010
Rabbit	talented, loving	1963, 1975, 1987, 1999, 2011
Dragon	robust, passionate	1964, 1976, 1988, 2000, 2012
Snake	wise, strong-willed	1965, 1977, 1989, 2001, 2013
Horse	attractive, popular	1966, 1978, 1990, 2002, 2014
Sheep	aesthetic, stylish	1967, 1979, 1991, 2003, 2015
Monkey	persuasive, smart	1956, 1968, 1980, 1992, 2004
Cock	pioneering spirit, wise	1957, 1969, 1981, 1993, 2005
Dog	generous, loyal	1958, 1970, 1982, 1994, 2006
Boar	gallant, noble	1959, 1971, 1983, 1995, 2007

Activities

- Read/discuss some Chinese folktales or fairy tales. Compare these to fairy tales popular in our country.

- Discuss the attributes of the different animals of the Chinese zodiac. Have the children choose one or more of these animals to write a fictional story about using personification.

- Prepare for your celebration in the traditional Chinese manner by settling differences, paying off debts (does anyone need to turn in overdue library books or homework assignments?), and cleaning the classroom or students' desks.

- Compare this holiday to other new year's celebrations around the world.

- Use paper lunch bags to create puppets of Buddha, the twelve animals of the zodiac, and other animals and put on a puppet show. To make puppets draw, color, and cut out the character's head (this should be about 6 inches wide and 4 inches tall). Glue to the bottom of an unopened bag, chin pointing toward the opening. Next draw, color, and cut out the character's body. Lift the flap where the bottom of the bag folds up and glue to the bag, feet facing the opening. Let dry then insert hand, curving fingers down over the fold in the bottom of the bag. By flexing and unflexing one's fingers the puppet's head can be moved.

- Have children create their own lion masks, then pair up with a friend to become the lion (the second child, covered with a sheet, is behind the one with the mask and holding onto the first child's waist). Two such "lions" dance around each other to the beat of a drum.

- Do a dragon dance. (See "Kunchi Festival," October 7–9, for instructions.) Incorporate this in a Chinese New Year parade that includes noisemakers, drums, banners, lion dancers, and students dressed to represent the animal of the year.

- Have a Chinese New Year feast and taste some traditional dishes. Try eating with chopsticks! (If real chopsticks are not available, drinking straws can be used as a substitute. The small ones that restaurants place in beverages are stronger and work best in little hands.)

- Listen to the music of traditional Chinese songs.

TET

• • • •

January or February
Vietnam

Background

Tet is the shortening of the Vietnamese phrase "Tet Nguyen-Dan," which translated means "first day." It is a celebration of the new year and of the coming of spring. Many of the traditions and practices connected with this holiday are similar to those associated with Chinese New Year (see above). Preparations are made to assure that the new year begins on a positive note and there are fireworks, feasting, and dancing throughout the seven-day celebration.

CARNIVAL

• • • •

January or February
International

Background

In New Orleans and in France it is called Mardi Gras; in Germany it is Karneval, Fasching, or Fastnacht; and in Brazil, Carnaval; but wherever you celebrate and whatever you call it, this celebration is dedicated to merrymaking and fun! The festivities can last from a day to several weeks. Carnival precedes the 40-day period of Lent and fasting in the Roman Catholic

Church year. It is a time to let go of your inhibitions and release your passions. Parades, dancing, music, and much revelry mark the celebration of Carnival. Elaborate costumes and masks abound and people enjoy many of the activities they will forgo during the Lenten season. Feasting is another big part of the celebration, in fact, "Mardi Gras," literally translated, means "Fat Tuesday." Here the reference is to Shrove Tuesday, the day before Ash Wednesday, the latter being when Lent officially begins. (See also "Mardi Gras," February.)

Activities

- Have children research and write about the variations of this celebration in various countries of the world.

- Form bands using rhythm instruments and have each group perform for the class.

- Make imaginative masks of construction paper or papier-mâché. (See "Yam Festival," September, for instructions for paper masks and "Junkanoo," December 26, for papier-mâché masks.) The children might enjoy working in groups to design the masks or simple costumes to wear as a group when their band performs.

- Have children list all of the favorite foods they would want to eat before they began a fast, then classify the foods into food groups including "junk food" as a group.

- Discuss the importance of balancing work and play and the emotional and psychological value of letting go and having fun.

- Plan your own Carnival celebration. Include a parade (use the costumes and bands created in the activities above) and/or a "Fat Tuesday" feast. Since many people give up sweets for Lent, allow children to bring in their favorite desserts or treats to share. Be sure to reiterate that we usually choose healthy snacks but that on special occasions most people splurge a little with junk foods!

MARTIN LUTHER KING JR. DAY
• • • •
Third Monday in January
United States

Background

Born on January 15, 1929, Martin Luther King Jr. became a minister and the United States' greatest civil rights leader. Basing his actions and his leadership on the teachings of Indian nationalist leader Mohandas Gandhi, he led African Americans in peaceful boycotts, freedom marches, sit-ins, and demonstrations, which did much to effectively eliminate segregation in the country. In 1963 King led hundreds of thousands of blacks and whites in a great march on Washington, D.C., where he gave his famous "I Have a Dream" speech, and in 1964 he was awarded the Nobel Peace Prize. On April 4, 1968, while preparing for a march in protest of inequities of pay between black and white sanitation workers in Memphis, Tennessee, Dr. King was shot and killed by James Earl Ray. Today King's birthday is a national holiday—a time to remember this great leader and the lessons he taught.

Activities

- The poet, Langston Hughes, was a source of inspiration for Martin Luther King Jr. Read and study some of his poems and/or the works of other black authors. *Nathaniel Talking*, by Eloise Greenfield, is a good source of poetry that children can really relate to.

- Have the students write their own "I have a dream ..." speeches and read them to the class.

- Use role-playing to illustrate segregation. Have the students switch roles as you act out several different situations (e.g., buses, restaurants), then discuss their feelings and reactions.

- Research and study the Nobel Peace Prize, including other people to whom it has been awarded.

- One well-remembered line of King's "I Have a Dream" speech states "I have a dream that ... children will one day live in a nation where they will not be judged by the color of their skin." Have children cut out paper doll chains and color them to represent the children of the world.

LANTERN FESTIVAL

• • • •

January or February
China

Background

On the 15th day of the first month of the lunar calendar the Lantern Festival is celebrated in China. This falls on the night of the first full moon of the year, about ten days after the Spring Festival. The Lantern Festival dates back to the first century when Emperor Ming Di of the Han Dynasty, in an effort to promote the learning of Buddhist doctrines, ordered the lighting of lanterns as a symbolic means of paying homage to Buddha.

Modern-day celebrations include fireworks, people walking on stilts, and folk dancing. Lanterns of all shapes and sizes are displayed. In some areas it is popular to hang riddles from the lanterns and give prizes to those who guess the answers. The traditional food of the festival is sweet dumplings, which symbolize reunion.

Activities

- Discuss the symbolism of light in various religions.

- Allow the students to make paper lanterns and to create their own exhibit by displaying them in the room. Use this art project as a way to teach symmetry, measurement, and/or design. (See page 108 for instructions.)

- Read some riddles to children and have them try to solve them. Later have them write their own riddles to hang from their lanterns. *Funny You Should Ask: How to Make Up Jokes and Riddles with Wordplay* by Marvin Terban (New York: Clarion Books, 1992) is a good resource for this activity.

- Make and eat some Dim Sum, the sweet dumplings traditional to this holiday. (See Appendix B for this recipe.)

JANUARY HOLIDAYS WITH FIXED DATES

NEW YEAR'S DAY

• • • •

January 1
International

Background

Although customs vary widely, this holiday is celebrated in countries throughout the world. In some countries children receive gifts on this day. This is the greatest holiday of the year in Japan where everyone celebrates his or her birthday (in Japan you are one year old on the day you are born and turn two on New Year's Day). In Scotland the holiday is known as Hogmanay, which is characterized by the custom of visiting friends and relatives after midnight on New Year's Eve. Traditionally it is believed that the "first-footer," the first person to set foot in one's home on New Year's Day, will foretell the family's future for the following year. In the United States, after staying up late on New Year's Eve to see in the new year, many people sleep late on New Year's Day then spend the remainder of the day attending church services and/or visiting with friends and relatives.

Feasting on traditional New Year's foods is a widespread practice, although the types of food vary widely. In the southern part of the United States people eat black-eyed peas to represent prosperity

(traditionally each bean eaten represented a dollar in income during the upcoming year). Other people eat leafy green vegetables such as cabbage to represent money and prosperity. Others propose toasts as eggnog is served from a wassail bowl ("wassail" comes from an Old English word meaning "good health"). And many people eat a sweet food such as whipped cream to symbolize a wish for a sweet new year. (See also "New Year's Eve," December 31.)

Activities

- On New Year's Day Germans used to use onions to predict the weather for the coming year. You can do this by cutting six onions in half and placing salt on the cut, flat side of each piece. Designate one onion half for each month of the coming year, then sprinkle each with salt. Allow the onions to sit for a while then check to see if the salt has dissolved. If it has, that month will be wet; if not, it will be dry. Write down your predictions and watch to see how accurate they were as the year progresses.

- Have the students write about and compare the New Year's traditions of their families. (This could include anything from eating traditional foods to watching the Rose Bowl parade or football games on TV.)

- Have students discuss what they would wish for in the new year that relates to school then have them come up with a new "tradition" to symbolize this. For example, if they wish for good grades, sharpen all of the pencils in the room so that all the students will be "sharp"; if they hope to make lots of friends, move the desks so that everyone sits by a different person than before and has a chance to get to know someone new.

- Young children can review the names of the months of the year. Older children might research the origins of the names of the months.

- Fill in blank calendars. Discuss number patterns, the names of the days of the week, etc.

- Have the students bring a kind of food that they would choose to serve on New Year's Day then tell what it represents (e.g., luck, money, good health, happiness) and why. After all the children have done their oral sharing they can share the food!

EMANCIPATION DAY

• • • •

January 1
United States

Background

On January 1, 1863, President Abraham Lincoln issued his Emancipation Proclamation legally terminating slavery in the United States. In many localities slaves did not receive news of the proclamation until some time after it was actually delivered, and for this reason various areas of the country hold freedom celebrations on different dates. January 1 is the date on which the most widespread celebrations take place, ranging from Boston to Georgia and encompassing most of the states along the East Coast. (See also "Juneteenth," June 19.)

Activities

- Do an activity such as dusting the room, with some students volunteering to play the role of the slaves and others the slave owners. Discuss personal feelings after completing the activity. If the students want, you can then switch roles and have them do another chore (e.g., arranging bookshelves, cleaning paintbrushes) and discuss again.

- After achieving freedom, the former slaves had many adjustments to make. Brainstorm a list of things that would be different and challenges that they faced.

- Read biographies of historical figures (e.g., Harriet Tubman, Lincoln) who were instrumental in bringing about the abolition of slavery.

- The news of the Emancipation Proclamation did not reach all areas of the country at the same time. Examine methods of communication in the 1800s and compare them to modern technology and communication today.

INDEPENDENCE DAY

• • • •

January 1
Australia

Background

In 1788 a British convict colony was established at Botany Bay in Australia and for 63 years the continent was considered nothing more than a place of exile. This changed in 1851 when gold was discovered causing a flood of immigration into the country. Political control rested with Britain until the Federal Constitution, based in part on the Constitution of the United States, was drawn up in 1900. Australia became an independent commonwealth on January 1, 1901, when the constitution went into effect.

INDEPENDENCE DAY

• • • •

January 1
Cameroon

Background

In 1884 Germany took control of the area now known as Cameroon. Near the beginning of World War I the British invaded the area and in 1916, with the help of French and Belgium forces, ousted the Germans. The colony of Cameroon, under a mandate from the League of Nations, came under French control until 1960 when it became an independent republic. Meanwhile, Southern Cameroon was under British control until 1961 when it was united with the newly formed Republic of Cameroon. English, French, and African languages are spoken in the nation. The major religions are Christian, Muslim, and traditional African religions.

INDEPENDENCE DAY

• • • •

January 1
Haiti

Background

The island of Hispaniola was "discovered" by Christopher Columbus in 1492 and declared a colony of Spain. Over the next 50 years European disease, enforced labor, and famine caused the death of many of the Indians native to the island and African slaves were introduced to meet the demand for a labor force. During the seventeenth century French buccaneers established a base for their piracy operations in the western part of the island, and in 1697 Spain ceded the western third of the island, now called Haiti, to France. When the French denied the blacks in Haiti their rights, revolutions ensued, which brought about the abolition of slavery in 1793. Independence from France came about several years later, in 1804, when Haiti became the first black republic.

INDEPENDENCE DAY

• • • •

January 1
Sudan

Background

The history of the people of Sudan, Africa's largest nation, can be traced back to 750 B.C. when the area was part of the Kingdom of Nubia. In the sixth century A.D. the people embraced Christianity, and in the sixteenth century, Islam. A powerful Muslim state was developed, which endured until the 1920s when Egypt conquered the area, which was then placed under the joint rule of Egypt and Britain. Following World War II the Sudanese yearned for autonomy. Independence was declared on December 19, 1955, and soon recognized by both Egypt and Great Britain.

INDEPENDENCE DAY

• • • •

January 1
Western Samoa

Background

Although Dutch Admiral Jacob Roggeveen was the first European to come in contact with Samoa in 1722, European influence on the islands was relatively minor until the 1830s. At that time the London Missionary Society, along with members of missionary societies from other countries, arrived in Samoa and successfully converted the natives to Christianity. By 1861 Germany, Great Britain, and the United States had all laid claims on the islands. Years of unrest and imperial rivalries followed until 1899 when the United States took possession of the eastern islands, and Germany annexed the four western islands which now constitute Western Samoa. Germany remained in control until 1914 when the islands were taken from the Germans by New Zealand and Australian forces. Under a League of Nations mandate New Zealand administered the government of Western Samoa until January 1, 1962, when it became the first independent Polynesian state.

INDEPENDENCE DAY

• • • •

January 4
Myanmar (Burma)

Background

Formerly a colony of Great Britain, the Union of Burma gained its independence on January 4, 1948. The new republic adopted a policy of isolationism and elected not to remain inside the British Commonwealth. In 1989 Burma, the largest country in mainland Southeast Asia, changed its name from Burma to Myanmar and the name of its capital from Rangoon to Yangon.

EPIPHANY

• • • •

January 6
Christian

Background

January 6, the twelfth night after Christmas, marks the date on which it is believed that the three wise men reached Bethlehem and paid homage to the Christ child. This celebration, commonly known as Twelfth Night or the Feast of the Epiphany, marks not only the end of the Christmas holidays but also the start of the Carnival season, which climaxes with Mardi Gras. It is common in some countries, such as the Czech Republic and Slovakia, for children (mostly boys) to go from house to house on this day dressed up as the three kings. In their roles as the wise men they sing about the birth of the Christ child and pay homage to "the king of kings." They are rewarded with praise and cookies.

Activities

- Listen to the song "The Twelve Days of Christmas." Ask the children to estimate how many gifts in all are mentioned in the song, then add up the numbers $[1+(1+2)+(1+2+3)+(1+2+3+4) ... (1+ ... +12)]$ to find the actual total and see how close their estimates were. It may be best to give them $\frac{1}{2}$-inch graph paper and let them make a chart like the following

GIFT LIST - 12 DAYS OF CHRISTMAS

Day 1	Day 2	Day 3	Day 4	Day 5	Day 6	Day 7	Day 8	Day 9	Day 10	Day 11	Day 12	
1	1	1	1	1	1	1	1	1	1	1	1	12
	2	2	2	2	2	2	2	2	2	2	2	22
		3	3	3	3	3	3	3	3	3	3	30
			4	4	4	4	4	4	4	4	4	36
				5	5	5	5	5	5	5	5	40
					6	6	6	6	6	6	6	42
						7	7	7	7	7	7	42
							8	8	8	8	8	40
								9	9	9	9	36
									10	10	10	30
										11	11	22
											12	12
												TOTAL
1	3	6	10	15	21	28	36	45	55	66	78	364

or have the children assign dollar values to each of the twelve items and figure out how much was spent on gifts during the twelve days.

- According to tradition, Jesus was already twelve days old when the three kings arrived at Bethlehem. Discuss the reasons for this lengthy delay. Compare ancient modes of transportation to modern ones. Have the children compute the distance that the kings walked if they averaged 20 miles a day ... 15 miles a day. Ask them to figure the amount of time it would take to travel the same distance in a car averaging 60 miles per hour ... 45 miles an hour.

DÍA DE LOS REYES MAGOS
(Three Kings Day)

• • • •

January 6
Latin America

Background

Día de los Reyes Magos is the Latin American celebration of Twelfth Night, the night when the wise men reached Bethlehem and the Christ child. The tradition, in this culture, is not of Santa Claus, but of the wise men as the bringers of gifts just as they brought gifts to Jesus at the time of the first Christmas. Customs are similar to those of Christmas Eve. Children write letters to the wise men telling them how good they have been and what gifts they would like to receive. They leave water and greens out for the camels to eat, and wake up early, full of excitement and eager to open their presents.

Activities

- Compare traditions of Día de los Reyes Magos and Christmas Eve. Discuss why the custom of exchanging gifts began.

- Compare camels and reindeer, their habitats, the food they eat, and the ways in which they are used by people. Generate a list of other animals that are used for transportation. Link the animals to different countries/cultures, climates, and/or topographical areas.

- Compare the climate and seasons of Latin America to those of Europe. Discuss how this may influence the way in which people celebrate the winter holidays.

MAKRA SANKRANT
(Winter Festival)

• • • •

January 11–13
India

Background

Makra Sankrant, also known as Pongal, is a three-day festival of South India in celebration of the winter solstice, a celebration of the coming of longer days. It is characterized by bathing in rivers, the giving of alms, and family reunions. Special sweets and cakes are prepared for the celebration and always contain sesame seeds and brown sugar. Small silk bags containing sesame seeds mixed with sugar are offered to friends with the greeting "Eat this sweet sesame and speak sweetly to me," an expression intended to assure that there will be no quarreling throughout the year. This holiday is especially enjoyed by children who delight in all of the sweet food they get to eat!

Activities

- Compare this holiday to other celebrations where sweet foods are offered to sweeten the disposition (e.g., Rosh Hashanah, Chinese New Year, Halloween). Discuss foods and the traditional roles they play in holiday celebrations.

- Discuss why ancient people expressed joy in the lengthening of the days (e.g., the weather would improve and become warmer, they would spend fewer hours in darkness, they could plant their crops, they may have harbored superstitious beliefs).

- Have the children measure, mix, and taste sesame seeds mixed with brown sugar. Have them experiment with the proportions and come up with their own favorite recipe.

ST. KNUT'S DAY

• • • •

January 13
Sweden, Finland

Background

Prior to the calendar reform in the seventeenth century, St. Knut's Day was celebrated on Twelfth Night. The calendar reform moved the date of the celebration ahead a week, so the Swedes and Finns simply extended their holiday period for that length of time. In Finland the straw goat associated with the harvest festival (see "Pikkujoulu," December) was simply transferred to St. Knut's Day, which became an occasion for straw goat pageants, masquerading, and carnivals. St. Knut's Day marks the end of the Christmas season. In Sweden it is often the occasion for a final party, this one especially for children. The Christmas tree is dismantled until only the edible ornaments (gingerbread, candies, etc.) remain. The friends and classmates of the children of the family are invited over to eat cakes and candies and to "plunder" the tree before throwing it outside the house.

Activities

- Discuss how the pagan goat took on human characteristics and changed as the times changed. Examine the way in which authors of children's stories give human characteristics to the animal characters in their books. Read or write fairy tales that show examples of personification.

- Use pipe cleaners to make your own straw goat decorations or to create other animals.

- Eat some cakes, candies, or other sweets.

REPUBLIC DAY

• • • •

January 26
India

Background

After many years of British rule in India, demands for a greater degree of self-government and protests against existing discrimination against Indians in favor of Europeans began as early as the 1880s. Following World War I, Mohandas Gandhi emerged as the leader of the Congress party. Gandhi advocated a policy of nonviolent civil disobedience and self-help. In spite of Gandhi's efforts bitterness grew between Moslem and Hindu factions in the country, and eventually the country was partitioned. The smaller Moslem dominion came to be known as Pakistan. The remainder of the country retained the name of India and was made up of a primarily Hindu population. Jawaharlal Nehru was elected as the first prime minister of the country and India's constitution went into effect on January 26, 1950. Celebrations of this holiday in the state capitals are colorful and often include parades, cultural pageants, and folk dance festivals.

INDEPENDENCE DAY

• • • •

January 31
Nauru

Background

Nauru, one of the Gilbert Islands, was discovered by the British in 1798. It was annexed by Germany in 1888 and, under a mandate of the League of Nations, was held by Australia from 1914 until 1947. Following World War II the island became a United Nations trust territory assigned jointly to Australia, New Zealand, and Britain, which it remained until gaining independence in 1968.

2
FEBRUARY HOLIDAYS

NONFIXED DATES

Hai Ba Trung	Vietnam	
Presidents' Day	United States	Third Monday
Brotherhood Week	United States	Week of Washington's Birthday
Purim	Jewish	February or March
Mardi Gras	International	February or March
Ash Wednesday	Christian	First Day of Lent (February or March)
Green Monday	Cyprus	First Day of Lent (February or March)
Feast of Okambondondo	Angola	February, March, or April
100th Day of School		
Magha Puja	Buddhist	February or March

FIXED DATES

February 1–28/29	Black History Month	United States
February 2	Groundhog Day	United States
February 2	Candlemas	Christian
February 3	Setsubun (Changing of the Seasons)	Japan
February 4	National Day	Sri Lanka
February 6	Waitangi Day	New Zealand
February 11	Founding Day	Japan
February 14	Valentine's Day	International
February 18	Independence Day	Gambia
February 18	Independence Day	Nepal
February 21	Shaheed Dibash (Martyrs' Day)	Bangladesh
February 25	National Day	Kuwait
February 27	Independence Day	Dominican Republic
February 29	Leap Year Day	International

FEBRUARY HOLIDAYS WITH NONFIXED DATES

HAI BA TRUNG

• • • •

Vietnam

Background

This celebration is special to the women of Vietnam. It commemorates the anniversary of the death of the Trung sisters. In A.D. 41 these two sisters led a successful revolt against the ruling Chinese, winning freedom for Vietnam. Today Vietnamese schoolgirls dress in uniforms of earlier days, carry colorful banners, and ride elephants in reenactments of the historical event.

Activities

• Compare this holiday to other celebrations of victory and freedom such as Purim, Passover, Emancipation Day, Veterans Day, or the Fourth of July.

• Read the folktale, *The Blind Men and the Elephant* by Karen Backstein (New York: Scholastic, 1992). Discuss how people's perceptions of an object or event may differ. Relate this to history by explaining that even when people have adequate data and documentation, versions of historic events are always colored by the interpretation of the author as well as by that person's point of view. To illustrate this concept, have students rewrite the story of Hai Ba Trung from the point of view of the Chinese.

• Have students compute how many years ago this event occurred.

• Begin keeping a timeline on which historical events can be marked. Take advantage of the opportunity to introduce the concept of negative numbers when events that occurred in the years B.C. are studied.

PRESIDENTS' DAY

• • • •

Third Monday in February
United States

Background

Presidents' Day is celebrated in memory of two great American presidents, George Washington, first president of the country, and Abraham Lincoln, president during the Civil War and author of the Emancipation Proclamation. Lincoln's birthday is February 12, and Washington's follows ten days later on the 22nd. The date assigned to Presidents' Day always falls between these two dates. The decision to combine the two celebrations into one was motivated by the desire to create a national holiday on which businesses and schools could be closed. By choosing a Monday instead of a given date, legislators assured that employees and students would consistently be able to enjoy a three-day weekend in February.

Activities

• Have children use encyclopedias or other reference books to find the requirements for becoming president of the United States.

• Compare and contrast the backgrounds and boyhoods of the two presidents.

• Washington was a general during the Revolutionary War and Lincoln was commander in chief during the Civil War. Discuss and compare freedom for the United States as a nation and freedom for the slaves as a group in society. Talk about majority and minority rights.

• Read the first line from Lincoln's Gettysburg Address, "Four score and seven years ago ... ." Define the term "score." Have children determine the year in which the address was delivered.

• Have the children write letters to the current president giving their opinion on an issue that affects or will affect them personally (e.g., the environment, the war on drugs, endangered species).

BROTHERHOOD WEEK

• • • •

Week of
Washington's Birthday
United States

Background

At the suggestion of Monsignor Hugh McMenam, the National Conference of Christians and Jews first sponsored the idea of Brotherhood Week. George Washington was chosen as the symbol of the intent of the celebration—freedom from religious and racial discrimination. Each year since 1934 the president of the United States has proclaimed that Brotherhood Week be observed during the week of Washington's birthday. The purpose of Brotherhood Week is to emphasize the common brotherhood of all peoples and to bring about understanding between the different races, cultures, and religions.

Activities

• Discuss the basis of our government and the freedoms it assures. Draw from the Bill of Rights or use amendments to the Constitution as specific examples. Discuss the implications for us as individuals and our responsibilities to one another.

• As a group, brainstorm a list of ways in which people are alike and ways in which they are different. Emphasize that "different" does not mean "wrong." Point out that we have many more commonalities than we have differences. Discuss the importance of accepting the differences of others and our right to expect them to do the same for us.

• Have children work in groups to collect data on the children in the class—age (in years and months), height, number of brothers and sisters, number of rooms in their homes, time it takes them to get to school, etc.—then use the data to compute the mean and create a picture of the typical boy or girl at that grade level. Older children can examine the mode, median, and range of the statistical information gathered. This activity will illustrate to children that sometimes statistics can tell a lot about a group but very little about the individuals within the group. Use this to initiate a discussion about stereotyping, the importance of individuality, etc.

• For fun you might compare the country or the classroom to a produce stand. Have the children choose their favorite fruit or vegetable and make drawings of the fruits and vegetables with arms, legs, eyes, mouth, etc. Now group the students and their drawings around the room as if they were displayed in a produce stand. Next have a group discussion about life in the produce stand. ("This banana and this potato do not have to be best friends, but what would happen to our produce stand if they started a war with each other?" "Do all of the apples have to be friends and agree on everything?" "Which piece of fruit is most important if we want to make a fruit salad?" etc.) Have the students write creative stories from the point of view of the fruits or vegetables they chose.

• Read aloud the book *The Pushcart War* by Jean Merrill (New York: Harper and Row, 1985). As you progress through the story have the students discuss or write about the attitudes and viewpoints of the various characters.

PURIM

• • • •

February or March
Jewish

Background

Purim is the celebration of the victory of Mordecai and Ester over the anti-Semitic Haman in Persia. The scroll of Ester, which recounts that event, is read in the synagogue night and morning. This is a joyous holiday that reveres a triumph over violence and bigotry. Gifts are given to the poor, food is exchanged among friends and neighbors, and a special holiday meal is eaten by the family. Hamentashin (fruit-filled cookies) are eaten and students enjoy dressing in costumes and having masquerade parties. Many towns in Israel host Carnival-like Purim pageants and parades.

Activities

- Discuss bigotry, racism, and prejudice as it applies to other countries and time periods.

- Have students design and make costumes for a class masquerade party or parade. Before the celebration they could write creative stories or riddles about the character they will become and have their classmates try to guess what their costumes are. (If your community is sensitive about the observation of Halloween this may be a good time to allow your students to throw their inhibitions to the wind as they dress up and celebrate.)

- Make Hamentashin cookies (see Appendix B for recipe) or cookies of colored paper. Use these as a basis for study of geometric shapes (roll the dough into a sphere before refrigerating, cut circles, fold into equilateral triangles).

MARDI GRAS

• • • •

February or March
International

Background

Mardi Gras is celebrated in France and in other areas of the world where French influence is felt (such as the French Quarter of New Orleans, Louisiana). It is not generally a legal holiday, but is celebrated widely as a day of revelry, drinking, and feasting before the 40-day penance of Lent. The French term "Mardi Gras" literally means "Fat Tuesday," another name for Shrove Tuesday, the day before the start of Lent. Since Lent is a time of penance and fasting, this is ostensibly the last time for six weeks that people of the Catholic faith can enjoy alcohol and feasting.

In France it is traditional to eat a large meal which usually includes crepes or waffles. The celebration features a grand parade of flower-covered floats and giant cardboard figures. At the close of the day a grotesque effigy (which represents evil) is burned.

In New Orleans all inhibitions are thrown aside as costumed celebrants parade, drink, and party long into the night. Traditional food includes the King Cake in which a pecan or charm is hidden. The person who gets the piece of cake with the charm or nut in it is

dubbed the "king" of that year's Mardi Gras and carries the responsibility of baking or purchasing the King Cake for next year's celebration. (See also "Carnival," January.)

Activities

- Bake a King Cake or prepare some crepes as a special treat (see Appendix B for recipes).

ASH WEDNESDAY

• • • •

First Day of Lent
(February or March)
Christian

Background

In Western Christian Churches Ash Wednesday marks the first day of Lent and the beginning of the Lenten fast. It always falls 40 days before Easter, Sundays excluded. Its name is derived from the custom of marking the foreheads of the faithful with ashes that have been blessed, a sign of penitence and humility.

GREEN MONDAY

• • • •

First Day of Lent
(February or March)
Cyprus

Background

On the island of Cyprus the first day of Lent, known as Green (or Clean) Monday, has special significance. People generally enjoy their major meal of the day in the form of a picnic in the fields. They observe a fast that includes avoidance of meat, eggs, dairy products, and animal or vegetable oils. The meal usually consists of bread, olives, and raw vegetables.

FEAST OF
OKAMBONDONDO

• • • •

February,
March, or April
Angola

Background

Okambondondo is a children's harvest festival celebrated in the villages of Angola. It has no given date but may be celebrated at any time during the harvest season (February to April) and is sometimes celebrated more than once in a given year. For this celebration the children usually divide into groups, six to ten year olds meeting at one house, eleven to fifteen year olds in another, and those sixteen and up having their own feast in yet a third house. Each child brings a contribution to the feast. The boys bring dried fish or meat and the girls bring cornmeal, beans, and corn. The children gather in the evening to play games and tell folk stories. Then the girls go to sleep in the kitchen while the boys sleep in another part of the house. At about one or two o'clock in the morning the girls wake up and begin to cook the feast. When it is ready they run to awaken the boys. They all eat together then leave the house for the village common where there is singing and more games. At the first sign of dawn they gather the remaining food from their feast to carry home for their parents to enjoy while they have a much needed rest.

Activities

• Begin a unit of study on African folktales.

• Discuss the traditional male and female roles illustrated in this celebration (males bring the meat, females stay in the kitchen and cook, etc.). Discuss whether such roles are necessary in simple agricultural societies. Discuss changing roles in modern technological societies.

100TH DAY
OF SCHOOL

• • • •

Background

This day is not recognized as an official holiday by any country or group of people in the world, but students enjoy it and it is a good opportunity to celebrate and learn! Most school systems in the United States still operate on a 180-day school year, and the 100th day generally falls sometime in February. On this day many teachers like to focus lessons on the concept of "100" and to plan special activities around that theme.

Activities

• Have children write creative stories that focus on the theme—"What Life Will Be Like 100 Years from Now," "If I Had $100," etc.

• Visit a nursing home and interview people who are 100 years old or approaching that age. Have children ask about things that have changed over that person's lifetime and then research those changes.

• Watch the newspapers for articles about people who have lived 100 years or more. Read and discuss.

• Have children bring in collections of 100 objects (e.g., bottle caps, pencils, stamps, miniature toy cars). Use these for lessons on counting, grouping, and classifying.

- Have children estimate the distance they will travel if they walk 100 steps, then have them walk it to see how close their guess was.

- Ask children if 100 seconds is a long time or a short time. Next time them while they sit without talking or moving for 100 seconds. Now time them again, this time allowing them 100 seconds to talk, play, or do whatever they choose. Discuss how time can be relative.

- Have children estimate which of three groups of objects has 100 items in it. Make a graph showing the number of children who estimated the group with 100 objects to be group A, group B, group C. Count the objects in the three groups to check and see which group contained 100.

- Group 100 objects by twos, fives, and tens. Skip count to 100. Discuss the concept of multiplication as it relates to the groups of objects.

- Help children to learn the value of a dollar by doing a magic trick. Tape the top of a shirt box onto the bottom then cut a slot wide enough for your hand to fit through in the short end. Reach inside and use a piece of tape to fasten a dollar bill inside the box. (If you tape it to one side on the end with the slot, it is in shadow and very difficult to see when you look in.) Allow several children to look in the slot to "prove" that the box is empty, then have children count as they drop 100 pennies into the box. Now say the magic words, "Abracadabra, Dabra da collar, turn 100 pennies into a dollar!," reach through the slot, and pull out the dollar bill! (Now put the box away quickly being careful not to shake it!)

- Study the works of Grandma Moses.

- Have children draw pictures of how they might look when they are 100 years old.

- Count out 100 peanuts in the shells and tell the students that you will use them to make peanut butter. Have them estimate if this will make too much, too little, or just enough for the class. Shell the peanuts. Most shells will have two peanuts inside (four halves if they come apart). Discuss fractions. Now place the peanuts in a blender and puree them to make peanut butter for a small snack. (You may want to add a little salt and a teaspoon or so of vegetable oil to make the peanut butter creamier.)

- Run in place for 100 seconds, do 100 arm circles, or skip 100 times.

- Place students in small groups. Give each group a kind of food (raisins, peanuts, cereal, tiny marshmallows, candies). Have groups count out 100 pieces of food and then decide how to divide it fairly among the members of the class. When all the students have their share of each of the treats they can stir them together and enjoy eating their "100 Mix."

MAGHA PUJA

• • • •

February or March
Buddhist

Background

According to Pali scriptures, nine months after the Lord Buddha achieved his enlightenment more than 1,200 believers assembled to pay him homage. This event took place at the time of the full moon of the third lunar month and occurred without any prior planning. On the evening of that day Lord Buddha spoke to the assembly, laying down the principles of his teachings. The basic concepts that he outlined were to do good, to abstain from actions that are bad, and to purify the mind. Specifically he stated that one should refrain from destroying life, stealing, engaging in immoral sexual behavior, lying, and taking mind-confusing drugs or alcohol. Each year at the full moon of the third lunar month, Buddhists carrying candles, flowers, or joss sticks pay homage to the effigy of Buddha in their temples to commemorate this event.

Activities

- Do a lesson on drugs and drug abuse. Begin by discussing how some things can be beneficial when used correctly and harmful when used incorrectly. Illustrate this with examples: It is good to play outside in the fresh air and sunshine, but if you stay out too long you can get a sunburn; we need food, but too much food can cause stomachaches or obesity. Now define the terms "drug" and "abuse." Briefly discuss the benefits of modern medicine and drugs then lead into a discussion of the misuse of prescription drugs and other substances.

- Discuss the teachings of Buddha. Point out that Buddhism is a religion that has an estimated 300 million adherents worldwide.

FEBRUARY HOLIDAYS WITH FIXED DATES

BLACK HISTORY MONTH

• • • •

February 1–28/29
United States

Background

The month of February has been designated Black History Month or African-American History Month. It is a time to honor the accomplishments of African Americans and the contributions they have made to society.

Activities

- Although it is important to acknowledge Black History Month, take care not to isolate or limit your study of African Americans solely to the month of February. Tie in other topics that you have studied—Kwanzaa, the emancipation of the slaves, Martin Luther King Jr., etc. Also, continue your inclusion of African Americans and their history beyond February, integrating this study into all areas of the curriculum whenever it is appropriate to do so.

- Have each student choose a famous African American, either historical or contemporary, to research and write about.

- Do a unit of study focused on African-American folktales. African Americans are the only group outside of Native Americans who have made large contributions to the collection of folktales native to the United States. Read some of these (e.g., "Uncle Remus" stories) and compare them to African literature.

- Read and discuss books written by black authors.

- Study the life and work of the famous black scientist, George Washington Carver. When the children are aware that Carver developed over 300 uses for the common peanut give them objects (pipe cleaners, plastic lids, or meat trays work well) and have them work individually or in groups to brainstorm a list of uses for the objects.

- Learn an African dance or game.

- As you study personages and events place them chronologically on a timeline.

- Listen to traditional African music. Move to the beat. Listen to contemporary African-American music and compare the two.

- The xylophone was an African invention and the banjo was an adaptation of an African instrument. Research and discuss other contributions that Africans and African Americans have made in the field of music.

GROUNDHOG DAY

• • • •

February 2
United States

Background

Thousands of years ago, when animalism and nature worship were prevalent, the people in the area of Europe now known as Germany believed that the badger had the power to predict the coming of spring. They therefore watched the badger to know when to plant their crops. By the time the first German immigrants settled in Pennsylvania they were probably sophisticated enough to know that this was not true, but the tradition lived on. Unfortunately, there were precious few badgers in Pennsylvania so the Pennsylvania Dutch found the closest relative to the badger— the groundhog—and watched it instead. Tradition has it that if the groundhog sees his shadow on February 2 he will be frightened by it and will return to his burrow, an indication that there will be six more weeks of winter. If he does not see his shadow, spring is on the way. Although other states have in some cases adopted their own groundhogs, the "official" groundhog, Punxsutawney Phil, lives at Gobbler's Knob near Punxsutawney, Pennsylvania. Each year on the second of February members of the Punxsutawney Groundhog Club, newspeople, and other interested persons meet at Gobbler's Knob to await Phil's appearance and his weather prediction.

Activities

• Do a lesson on shadows.

• Study the winter habits of different animals (animals that stay active, that hibernate, that migrate, etc.).

• Discuss why knowing when to plant their crops was and still is so important to people. Talk about the adverse affects of frost, cold weather, and snow on young plants. Examine modern methods that farmers use to determine when to plant.

• Have the students begin to watch the newspaper for examples of weather conditions that are adversely affecting crops.

• Research and write about other superstitions that are related to animals (e.g., crickets bring good luck, a black cat crossing your path is bad luck, stepping on ants will bring rain) or write about real animal predictors (e.g., dogs barking in warning, cattle getting restless before a storm).

• Use a paper cup, Popsicle® stick, and construction paper to make a simple pop-up groundhog puppet. Cover the paper cup with green paper, fringed at the top to represent grass. Next draw a small groundhog, cut out, and glue onto the end of the stick. Poke the other end of the stick through the bottom of the paper cup and pull the puppet down inside the cup and out of sight. Go outside and make the groundhog puppet pop out of its "burrow" and note whether or not it sees its shadow.

CANDLEMAS

• • • •

February 2
Christian

Background

This Roman Catholic holiday has a trifold purpose. It is the celebration of the purification of the Virgin Mary, the presentation of the child Jesus, and the first entry of Jesus into the temple. Since Jesus is considered by Christians to be the light of the world, it is fitting that candles are blessed on this day and that a candlelit procession precedes the mass. In France it is traditional to eat crepes on the day of Candlemas. Each member of the family prepares and cooks a crepe while holding a coin in hand. This is thought to assure wealth and happiness until the next Candlemas celebration

Activities

- Compare the French custom mentioned above to New Year's customs in which eating special foods are thought to bring happiness or wealth.

- Prepare and eat some crepes (see Appendix B for recipe).

SETSUBUN
(Changing of the Seasons)

• • • •

February 3
Japan

Background

According to the old lunar calendar Setsubun is a spring festival and marks the official end of winter. It is the custom in Japan for people to scatter as many beans throughout their house as they are years old. The purpose of this ritual is to bring good luck and to drive out evil spirits. At large temples, rites that are open to the public feature a celebrity who was born under the zodiac sign of the given year. This celebrity performs the function of throwing the roasted beans to expel the demons and ensure good luck for all those present.

Activities

- The evening before Setsubun put some dry lima beans in water to soak. The next day they will be ready for the children to remove the outer covering, take apart, and examine. Magnifying glasses help in seeing the tiny plant inside but are not necessary. Have the children draw and label pictures of their experiment. (You may also want to have them draw pictures to predict what they think they will find before they open the beans.)

- Grow your own bean sprouts. Put $\frac{1}{4}$ cup of dried peas or lentils in a quart jar. Fill with warm water and cover with nylon netting secured with a rubber band. Allow to soak overnight in a warm, dark place then pour off the water leaving the beans in the jar. For the next three or four days rinse the beans with water twice a day. On the last day place the jar in the sun to turn the sprouts green. Rinse the beans to remove the hulls and they are ready for the children to examine for plant growth or to eat!

- Make Chinese Bean Sprout Salad with some of the bean sprouts you grew. Pour boiling water over the sprouts then rinse with cold water. Make a dressing of 6 parts soy sauce, 1 part peanut oil, and 1 part sugar. Toss, chill, and eat!

NOTE: For all of the above activities legumes should be purchased from a grocery store. Seeds meant for planting should not be used as they are sometimes sprayed with poisonous chemicals and could be harmful.

NATIONAL DAY

• • • •

February 4
Sri Lanka

Background

This small island nation off the southeast tip of India was formerly known as Ceylon. As early as 600 B.C. Aryan raiders invaded the area. They were followed by invaders from India, Portugal, Holland, and most recently, Britain. The Tamils, descendants of the invaders from southern India, gained a strong foothold in the northern part of the island where they still live, speaking their own language and practicing Hinduism. The Sinhalese make up nearly three-quarters of the population; they speak Sinhala and/or English and practice Buddhism. In 1948 Ceylon gained its independence from Great Britain, and in 1974 the country changed its name from Ceylon to Sri Lanka. Civil strife between the Tamil and the Sinhalese continues to be a problem.

WAITANGI DAY

• • • •

February 6
New Zealand

Background

Waitangi Day is New Zealand's national day, celebrated in remembrance of the Treaty of Waitangi, a pact between the British settlers and the native Maori tribes. Under this treaty, signed in 1840, the Maoris conceded the sovereignty of the British government in return for protection. Since that time New Zealand has become a self-governing British dominion (1907) and a founding member of the Commonwealth (1926).

FOUNDING DAY

• • • •

February 11
Japan

Background

According to ancient Japanese records, Jimmu Tenno founded the imperial dynasty and empire of Japan (then called Dai Nihon) on February 11, 660 B.C., when he ascended to the throne at Kashiwabara. Japanese chronology begins with that year so that the Occidental-Christian year of 1993 is, in Japan, the year 2653. The dynasty begun by Jimmu is the longest lineage known to historians.

Activities

- Have children figure the year of their birth, the present year, or other significant dates according to the Japanese calendar.

VALENTINE'S DAY

• • • •

February 14
International

Background

Valentine's Day was probably originally related to the pagan celebration of Lupercalia that focused on Mother Nature's breeding aspect and the fact that many animals begin mating around this time of year. In Roman times it became a ritual celebration of the goddess Juno. St. Valentine himself was a Roman priest who was martyred on February 14, 271. He is regarded as the patron saint of lovers. Legend has it that while incarcerated St. Valentine wrote messages of hope, love, and cheer and used birds to send them to his friends and family. The first valentine cards, fashioned of satin and lace and ornamented with birds, flowers, cupids, and ribbons, appeared in England in the 1880s.

Activities

- Use this opportunity to practice letter-writing formats as the children write valentine letters to friends, family, or classmates.

- Use commercial valentine cards or candy hearts with messages printed on them to introduce a lesson on puns and plays on words.

- Most modern valentines contain verses written in rhyme. Discuss meter and rhyming and have the children write poetry.

- Before children begin writing their own poetry, illustrate the numeric patterns in familiar poems to help them to establish the meter of their own poems. When they have finished they might like to set their poetry to music. Again, math will figure in to the lesson in the form of the values assigned to the notes. With very young children it is best to reverse this process. First discuss a simple, well known song with rhyming lyrics (e.g., "Mary Had a Little Lamb") and then have the children write their own words to that tune and meter.

- Study ways that people have conveyed written messages throughout history, from messengers and homing pigeons to modern-day satellites and fax machines.

- Read and study stories of Roman mythology.
- Do a lesson on the heart.

INDEPENDENCE DAY

• • • •

February 18
Gambia

Background

This African nation has a small coastline on the Atlantic Ocean and extends eastward along the Gambia River to form a long and narrow country. In 1588 Britain purchased trading rights in Gambia from the Portuguese. In 1723 the Royal African Company, mainly concerned with the slave trade, took over administration of the territory. In 1888 Gambia became a separate crown colony and independence was gained on February 18, 1965.

Activities

- This celebration affords an excellent opportunity to tie in Black History Month, slavery, the African roots of the slaves, and the significance of freedom to both the people of Gambia and to the Africans captured and sold into slavery.

INDEPENDENCE DAY

• • • •

February 18
Nepal

Background

Nepal was a collection of small kingdoms until the eighteenth century when the area was conquered by the Gurkhas. There followed 104 years of autocratic rule by the hereditary prime minister. On February 18, 1951, King Tribhuvana deposed the existing prime minister and proclaimed a constitutional monarchy. This date is recognized in Nepal as the most politically significant in modern history. Citizens of Nepal pay tribute to the late King Tribhuvana (1906–55), "Father of the Nation," and celebrate their independence through rallies and processions during the day and illumination at night.

SHAHEED DIBASH
(Martyrs' Day)

• • • •

February 21
Bangladesh

Background

In 1952 a dispute over language raged between West Pakistan and East Pakistan (now Bangladesh). Urdu had been proclaimed the official state language, but at this time the people of East Pakistan demanded that Bengali be instituted as a second state language. When West Pakistan refused, fighting broke out. Shaheed Dibash is a day set aside to commemorate and honor those who died in the fight to retain their native language.

Activities

- Examine the difficulties that people (e.g., immigrants) face when living in a land where their native language is different from the official language used to conduct business.

- Discuss the importance of preserving one's culture, language, etc.

NATIONAL DAY

• • • •

February 25
Kuwait

Background

After 62 years of British rule Kuwait became fully independent in 1961. This Arab nation, comprised of Sunni and Shiite Muslims, celebrates its National Day on February 25 with a public holiday on which schools and businesses are closed.

INDEPENDENCE DAY

• • • •

February 27
Dominican Republic

The Dominican Republic, which occupies the eastern two-thirds of the island of Hispaniola, was "discovered" by Christopher Columbus in 1492 and colonized by the Spaniards the following year. Between 1795 and 1844 control of the territory passed back and forth between Spain and France several times, with brief periods of independence interspersed, until the Dominican Republic gained full and lasting independence on February 27, 1844.

LEAP YEAR DAY

• • • •

February 29
International

Background

On the Gregorian calendar, every year that can be divided evenly by four (except centenary years not divisible by 400) is designated as a leap year and an additional day known as leap day is added to February. This is done to adjust the calendar since a year, the time it takes for Earth to rotate around the sun, is not exactly 365 days but closer to 365 days, 6 hours, and 9 minutes. Customarily this is the one day out of every four-year cycle when women can propose marriage. This custom may have come about as an effort to balance the traditional roles of men and women, just as the leap day balances the calendar.

Activities

- As we approach March and Women's History Month this would be a good time to discuss traditional roles of males and females, equality of the sexes, the Equal Rights Amendment, etc.

- Do a lesson on the rotation of Earth and the resultant seasons.

- Have older children solve math problems comparing the solar year and the 354-day lunar year (e.g., "How many lunar years are there in 100 solar years?"; "How long is the average month on our calendar? On a lunar calendar?").

3

MARCH HOLIDAYS

NONFIXED DATES

Holi	Hindu	Late March or Early April
Palm Sunday	Christian	March or April
Good Friday	Christian	March or April
Easter	Christian	March or April
Dyngus (Easter Monday)	Poland	Day after Easter

FIXED DATES

March 1–31	Women's History Month	United States
March 3–5	Hina-Matsuri (Girls' Day/Doll Festival)	Japan
March 3	National Day	Morocco
March 6	Independence Day	Ghana
March 12	Independence Day	Mauritius
March 17	St. Patrick's Day	Ireland, United States
March 20	National Day	Tunisia
March 21–22	Vernal Equinox	International
March 21–22	No-ruz (New Year)	Iran
March 21–22	Pimia (New Year)	Laos
March 21–22	Shunki Korei	Japan
March 21–22	Higan-E	Buddhist
March 25	Independence Day	Greece
March 26	Independence Day	Bangladesh
March 28	Teachers' Day	Czech Republic and Slovakia
March 29	Youth Day	Taiwan

MARCH HOLIDAYS WITH NONFIXED DATES

HOLI

• • • •

Late March or Early April
Hindu

Background

This lively Hindu festival is a celebration of the victory of truth over falsehood and light over darkness, the end of cold weather, and the coming of spring. Holi lasts for eight days and ends at the time of the full moon. It is a celebration of colors, a time when people douse each other with colored water or toss colorful confetti or powders on one another. Adults as well as children enjoy participating in the color throwing, and greetings and sweets are sometimes exchanged. In Nepal the festival is marked by the placing of a pole decorated with colorful streamers next to the old royal palace at Basantapur. The pole is burned on the night preceding the full moon signaling the end of the festivities.

Activities

• Use this opportunity to study primary and secondary colors. Use water and food coloring to create the three primary colors (red, blue, and yellow) then mix part of the colored water to make the secondary colors (green, orange, and purple). Before mixing, have the children predict what color will be created. Tie in the holiday by putting the colored water in squirt guns or empty spray bottles then going outside and spraying an old sheet or large pieces of white paper.

• Discuss the bleakness of winter and the colors of spring. Have the children write creative stories about how nature sprays its colors in the form of new buds, spring flowers, and returning birds at this time of year.

• Study rainbows or prisms. (Inexpensive prisms can be purchased from the Cuisenaire Co. of America, Inc., 10 Bank Street, P.O. Box 5026, White Plains, NY 10602-5026; phone number (800) 237-0338. Write or call for a catalog.)

• Compare Holi to the celebration of Carnival or to other spring festivals and celebrations. Or compare the decorated pole in Nepal to the Maypole used in May Day celebrations.

PALM SUNDAY

• • • •

March or April
Christian

Background

Palm Sunday commemorates the triumphal entry of Christ into Jerusalem one week before his resurrection. On that day his followers hailed him as king and laid palm leaves in his path, thus the name of this holiday. Since the Middle Ages Western churches have observed the custom of blessing palms and distributing them to the congregation on this day.

GOOD FRIDAY

• • • •

March or April
Christian

Background

The anniversary of Christ's passion, crucifixion, and death is always observed on the Friday preceding Easter. This is a solemn observance during which people fast and pray. Church services are held between the hours of noon and 3:00 P.M. commemorating the three hours during which Christ hung on the cross.

EASTER

• • • •

March or April
Christian

Background

Christians celebrate Easter Sunday as the day of the resurrection of Jesus Christ, but the roots of this holiday, like so many other celebrations, can be traced back to pagan celebrations. Indeed the name Easter comes from Eostara, the German goddess of rebirth. In early times the Feast of Eostara was the celebration of the resurrection and rebirth of Earth. Easter eggs and the Easter Bunny are both fertility symbols, holdovers from the feast of Eostara. Other parallels include the pagan joy in the rising sun of spring, which coincides with Christians' joy in the rising Son of God, and the lighting of candles in churches, which corresponds to the pagan bonfires.

In early days there was much controversy over the proper date for the celebration of Easter. This controversy was settled in 325 when the council of Nicaea ruled that Easter should be celebrated on the first Sunday after the first full moon following the vernal equinox. Eastern Orthodox churches, despite Russia's adoption of the Gregorian calendar in 1923, still figure the date of Easter based on the Julian calendar. Therefore their celebration of Easter rarely coincides with observances of other Christian churches.

Activities

- Compare the celebration of Easter to other spring festivals and celebrations.

- Discuss the death of Jesus and compare it to the martyrdom of others who refused to deny their religious beliefs.

- Compare different calendar systems. Give children limited information about next year's calendar (dates of full moons, when the vernal equinox will occur) and have them work together to figure the date of Easter.

- Study the rebirth that occurs in the spring of the year. Learn about animals that give birth in the spring and those that lay eggs then. Plant some flower seeds.

- Cut around and around a circular piece of heavy paper or poster board moving gradually toward the center to form a coil (or "spring"). Have the children choose different symbols of Easter or spring to draw or make out of construction paper. Attach the pictures to the center of the coil of paper then attach the other end to a bulletin board labeled with the caption "Spring Is ... ." Alternatively you could use the spring as part of a pop-up book or as the inside of a spring greeting card; for either of these ideas, however, you would want a thicker and shorter spring to assure that it would fold back up into the book or card.

DYNGUS
(Easter Monday)

• • • •

Day after Easter
Poland

Background

Dyngus, or Splash Monday, is a riotous water day that arises from an old Polish custom. On this day village children, armed with sprinkling cans and pails of plain or scented water, lie in wait for friends or unsuspecting victims, whom they sometimes give a gentle sprinkling and other times a thorough dousing. The origin of this celebration is uncertain, but one theory is that it originated because of difficulties over individual, and the need for communal, baptisms.

- Compare Dyngus to other festivals that center around water: Pimia (see below), San Khuda (see April), or Holi (see above).

- Fill a sink or water table and allow children to play in it or to practice liquid measurement; or do a lesson on objects that sink or float.

MARCH HOLIDAYS WITH FIXED DATES

WOMEN'S HISTORY MONTH

• • • •

March 1–31
United States

Background

The month of March has been designated Women's History Month in the United States. It is a time to honor the achievements of women and the contributions they have made to society and was originally instituted to balance history texts and curricula geared toward the accomplishments of males.

Activities

- Although it is important to acknowledge and study Women's History Month, take care not to isolate or limit your study solely to the month of March. Integrate this study into all areas of the curriculum whenever it is appropriate to do so.

- Examine roles of women in the past and how they have changed. Have children use primary sources to gather their information about the past—interviews with mothers or grandmothers, videos of old movies or TV shows, and old letters or diaries (you can sometimes find fascinating ones at flea markets)—and personal experiences for present-day information.

- Study women's suffrage.

- Have each child choose a famous woman, either historical or contemporary, to research and write about.

Discuss how history would differ if these women had not existed and/or if the society had no women.

- During this month, choose literature in which a woman is the main character or heroine.

- Study interviewing techniques, then have children interview women who make a difference in their lives. This could include family members, school staff, local businesswomen or politicians, and so on.

HINA-MATSURI
(Girls' Day/Doll Festival)

• • • •

March 3–5
Japan

Background

Celebrated beginning on the third day of the third month, and lasting for three days, Hina-Matsuri is primarily a girls' festival but it has come to be one that the entire family enjoys. On this day a set of ceremonial dolls are elaborately displayed on a stand consisting of numerous shelves covered with red cloth. The display is set out in the best room of the house. A standard set of dolls consists of fifteen figures dressed in ancient costumes made of silk. The dolls represent the emperor and empress, ministers, musicians, court ladies, and dignitaries. Also included in the display are miniature household articles, tiny candle stands, and vases of peach blossoms. During the festival it is the job of the girl or girls in the family to care for the display and to play hostess. Dressed in formal kimonos they greet guests, usher them in to view the doll display, and serve tea and tiny cakes.

Activities

- Compare this festival to Navaratri, the Doll Festival celebrated in South India (see October).

- Beginning with emperor and empress, brainstorm a list of names for heads of state. After the list is developed split the class into pairs or small groups and have them use dictionaries to look up the definitions of the various terms. When they have completed their research bring the group back together to discuss the differences between an emperor, president, prime minister, queen, dictator, chieftain, etc.

- Allow each girl to bring a doll to school for one day. Develop oral language skills by having the students stand before their classmates and tell the history of the dolls. If desired, boys may also be included in the activity, but I prefer to have them wait for Kodomono-hi (see Boys' Day, May 5) for their turn to celebrate.

- To make a kimono, take a 2-foot by 7-foot piece of butcher paper or other long paper. Cut halfway down the middle of the paper lengthwise. At the end of the cut draw a 6-inch circle and cut out. Have the girl put it on, placing her head in the circle with the long cut going down the front. Decorate with crayons, paint, or markers if desired. Tie with a crepe paper sash.

- Have the boys leave the room for a few minutes while the girls arrange a display of their dolls and prepare a snack. When the boys reenter the room the girls can serve them hot or iced tea and small pieces of cake or cookies.

NATIONAL DAY

• • • •

March 3
Morocco

Background

King Hassan II, who claims to be a descendant of the prophet Mohammed, ascended to the throne of Morocco on March 3, 1961. At that time Morocco became a constitutional monarchy free from the influences of the United States, France, Spain, and other European nations who had so long held influence there. The primary religion (99 percent) is Sunni Muslim. Languages spoken in Morocco include Arabic, Berber, and French.

INDEPENDENCE DAY

• • • •

March 6
Ghana

Background

In 1471 the Portuguese reached by sea the area now known as Ghana and named it the Gold Coast. They were later followed by the Danes, Dutch, Germans, and British, all of whom established trading posts along the coast and competed for trade in gold and slaves. During the 1800s Britain increased its influence and on March 6, 1957, the Gold Coast became an independent member of the British Commonwealth and took the new name of Ghana.

INDEPENDENCE DAY

• • • •

March 12
Mauritius

Background

Mauritius, formerly known as Ile de France, is located in the Indian Ocean. This small (2,040-square-mile) coral-ringed island was ruled by the Dutch, the French, and most recently, the British. Independence came on March 12, 1968. The population of Mauritius is dense and is composed of a mixture of Africans, Europeans, Chinese, and Indians; its citizens practice a variety of religions and speak many different languages.

ST. PATRICK'S DAY

• • • •

March 17
Ireland, Unites States

Background

Born in England in A.D. 389, Patrick was captured by pirates at the age of sixteen and taken to Ireland where he was made a slave of the Chieftain of Ulster. After spending six years in slavery he escaped to France where he became a monk. In A.D. 423 he returned to Ireland after seeing a vision revealing that his mission was to bring Christianity to the Irish. He lived another 30 years during which time he started more than 300 Christian churches and baptized more than 120,000 Irish citizens.

Legend has it that St. Patrick drove the snakes from Ireland (and there are no snakes in Ireland today!), but the actual reference is probably to the pagans he drove from the land. The shamrock, symbol of St. Patrick's Day, was made popular by his teachings in which he used the shamrock to represent the trinity of Father, Son, and Holy Spirit. Green is worn on this day because it is the color of Ireland, the "Emerald Isle."

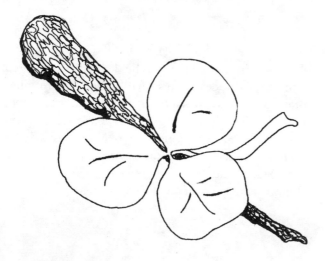

Most of the "real" celebrating of this holiday occurs in the United States and other countries where Irish immigrants have settled. In these places huge parades are staged, traditional foods and beverages are enjoyed, and Irish ballads are sung at songfests. Although Dublin has in recent years held a parade on St. Patrick's Day, most of Ireland regards this as a saint's day and any celebrations are of a solemn nature.

Activities

- Potatoes are a staple in the Irish diet, yet before the colonization of the Americas this vegetable was unknown in Europe. Discuss the connection between the Incas (the potato originated in the Andes), Spanish explorers, and the spread of the acceptance of the potato as a staple in the British Isles.

- The Irish became so dependent on the potato that the potato blight of 1845–46 caused a famine that led to disease, death, and widespread emigration. Learn about Irish immigrants in the United States and other groups who emigrated to this country because of economic or political reasons and the contributions they made.

- Read stories about leprechauns, banshees, or pookas—all of which were believed to exist in pre-Christian times in Ireland.

- After reading a story, have each child cut four pieces of green paper into heart shapes. Glue the four points together to form a lucky shamrock then write the elements of the story on each of the "leaves": (1) characters, (2) setting, (3) main idea or problem, and (4) conclusion or solution. Have the children write in the specific information for the story read.

- Have children plan and write about how they would go about capturing a leprechaun and/or what they would wish for once they had caught one.

- Learn an Irish ballad (an excellent source is *Soodlum's Irish Ballad Book,* London: Oak Publications, 1982).

- Listen to traditional (pennywhistle, harp, etc.) Irish music and compare it to contemporary Irish music (for example, the group U-2).

- Purchase pennywhistles and a beginner's instruction book (both are available through most music stores at very reasonable prices) and teach the children to play some simple tunes.

- Cut potatoes into shamrock, leprechaun hat, pot of gold, or other shapes and use green tempera paint to make potato prints. Add details with felt-tipped markers.

NATIONAL DAY

• • • •

March 20
Tunisia

Background

The area that corresponds to the present-day nation of Tunisia was originally settled by the Phoenicians who established the port city of Carthage in the ninth century B.C. Control of the region changed several times over the centuries; dominant powers included the Romans, Vandals, Arabs, Turks, and French. During World War II Germany awarded the country to the Vichy French government for a short time, but U.S. and British troops regained control and in May 1943 restored Tunisia as a protectorate of the Free French government. Following the war Tunisia experienced a surge of nationalism and in 1956 France recognized the country's full independence.

VERNAL EQUINOX

• • • •

March 21–22
International

Background

Twice each year, around March 21 and September 23, the sun shines directly on the equator and the length of day and night are equal in all parts of the world. These two days are known as the vernal (or spring) equinox and the autumnal equinox. In the Northern Hemisphere the vernal equinox marks the start of spring and has long been celebrated as a time of rebirth. It is an ancient Chinese custom to balance eggs—a symbol of fertility—on this day to bring good luck and prosperity. If you pick the right time of day an egg actually will balance on its wide end for 15 minutes or so before rolling over.

Activities

• Discuss the symbolic use of eggs by different cultures and for different holidays.

• Take a nature walk and look for signs of spring.

• Make a list of animals that hatch from eggs—do not forget the reptiles and amphibians! Research and study some of the animals or study the development of an animal from the time the egg is laid until the young animal hatches.

• Give children a hard-boiled egg and a raw egg. Have them spin the eggs to try to determine which is which. After they have guessed have them explain their hypotheses, then crack the eggs to see if they were right. (The *real* answer is that the hard-boiled egg will spin easily but the raw egg will slosh around inside the shell and the weight of the yolk will make it tip over.)

• Patricia Polacco has written several wonderful children's books that feature eggs. Read and enjoy *Rechenka's Eggs* (New York: Philomel Books, 1988) or *Just Plain Fancy* (New York: Bantam Books, 1990).

• Have the children read and follow a recipe to make deviled eggs. Arrange the finished eggs in circles to form flower shapes and add celery "stems" to make a special springtime snack.

NO-RUZ
(New Year)

• • • •

March 21–22
Iran

Background

The celebration of No-ruz, Iranian New Year, begins on the first day of spring and lasts for twelve days. This observance dates back to pre-Islamic times when the area was known as Persia, thus the celebration is also known as Persian New Year. Preparations begin well in advance and include the purchase of new clothes for all family members and a thorough cleaning of the house. It is also customary to place a piece of cloth in a bowl and sprinkle it with wheat or lentil seeds. By keeping the cloth moist for several days prior to the celebration it will become a lovely mass of greenery and the centerpiece of the No-ruz dinner table.

On the last day of the old year piles of brush are laid out up and down the streets of the neighborhoods and at dusk they are lit. Both young and old run down the line jumping over the small fires and calling for the redness of the fires to take away their paleness and bring them good health in the new year.

The new year begins when the sun crosses the equator. At this time the entire family, dressed in their new clothes, must be gathered around their table, which is decorated with candles (one for each family member), the greenery, and a goldfish in a glass bowl. It is said that at the moment the year begins the goldfish will

turn over in its bowl. The table is also piled high with a variety of special foods for the occasion. During the twelve days of the feast people visit relatives and friends; on these visits the children receive gifts of money and sweets. On the last day of the feast the family leaves the house and picnics near a stream. At the end of the day the bowl of greenery is thrown into the running stream signifying the tossing off of any ills from the old year.

Activities

- Use a historical atlas and a modern-day map to examine how boundaries of the area of Persia have changed over time.

- Compare No-ruz to other new year celebrations and spring festivals.

- Place grass seed or birdseed on a moist piece of cloth or a sponge. Keep damp and have the children write brief daily reports on the growth of the seeds.

PIMIA
(New Year)
• • • •
March 21–22
Laos

Background

Pimia, the Laotian New Year celebration, begins at the vernal equinox and lasts for three days. In ancient times the people believed that at the end of the year the goddess left and that a new goddess came to take her place. Between the leaving of the old goddess and the coming of the new there was thought to be one day when there was no goddess at all.

On the first day of the celebration, which is called "the goddess leaves," people go to the temples and help the monks wash the statues in honor of the new goddess. Afterwards they thoroughly clean their homes or businesses. Following the cleaning everyone brings sand to the temples and makes mounds in the temple courtyards. This sand will later be used to make repairs to the temples, but on this day it is used for play. The mounds are decorated with flowers, tiny flags, toys, and money. It is said that if you build a sand mound with a friend you will remain friends throughout the new year and that if a boy and girl build a mound together they may get married during the coming year. The first day of Pimia is also a water day when both students and adults spray each other with water pistols or douse each other with water thrown from bowls or buckets.

The second day of Pimia, called "the day stops," is the day on which there is thought to be no goddess. Everyone is very careful on this day and avoids doing anything serious or strenuous because there is no goddess to protect them.

On the third day the new goddess arrives. Laotians take food and flowers to the temple to welcome her and say special prayers for the new year. Students make promises to their parents that they will be obedient and well behaved all year, much as people make New Year's resolutions in Western societies. The day includes more water throwing and much feasting. According to legend, the happier you are on Pimia, the happier you will be throughout the new year, so there is much laughter and fun.

Activities

- Allow children to work in pairs with a friend to write plans for and design a sand mound.

- Compare Pimia to other new year's celebrations or spring festivals. Discuss other celebrations that include water throwing (see "Holi" and "Dyngus," both above).

SHUNKI KOREI

• • • •

March 21–22

Japan

Background

All school and businesses in Japan are closed for the day of Shunki Korei, the feast of the vernal equinox. This is a time for the Japanese to worship their imperial ancestors and welcome spring.

HIGAN-E

• • • •

March 21–22

Buddhist

Background

Higan-E is celebrated twice a year, at the time of the autumnal equinox around September 23, and then again at the vernal equinox around March 21. During these two days of the year there is a balance of light and darkness with day and night being of equal length.

The balance enjoyed on these days symbolizes harmony, peace, and equality, important elements of the teachings of Buddha.

Activities

- Discuss Asian art through an examination of pictures of statues of the Buddha.

- Do a lesson on weights and measures using a balance scale.

- Discuss the importance of equality to all people and the battles that have taken place in our country (e.g., women's suffrage, civil rights movement, Equal Rights Amendment) to ensure equality for all.

- Discuss words that are opposites and then have the children think of a word that represents a balance of the two (e.g., hot/cold—warm, black/white—gray, infant/adult—child).

INDEPENDENCE DAY

• • • •

March 25

Greece

Background

The history of Greece goes back nearly 4,000 years to when the island of Crete was inhabited by the people of the Minoan civilization. The people of the mainland, called Hellenes or Greeks, were influenced by the Minoans and further developed the Minoan civilization. During the classical period (fifth century B.C.) Greece was made up of city-states, the largest of these being Athens, Sparta, and Thebes. It was during this time that democracy was first conceived. The Greeks were fiercely independent and strove to uphold their democratic ideals. Alexander the Great, during the fourth century B.C., led the Greeks in conquering and Hellenizing most of the then-known world. In 146 B.C. Greece fell to the Romans, and in A.D. 330 the emperor Constantine moved the capital of the Roman Empire to Constantinople. This laid the foundation for the Byzantine Empire, a civilization that spread and influenced most of Western Europe. In 1453 the Byzantine Empire fell to the Turks and Greece remained under the yoke of the Ottomans for nearly 400 years. The Greeks revolted against their oppressors on March 25, 1821, and declared their independence, which was won in 1830.

Activities

- Have children look up "democracy" in encyclopedias and discuss the Greek roots of the word (literally translated it means "rule by the people"). Compare democracy to other forms of government.

- Begin a unit on Greek mythology, or a comparative study of Greek and Roman gods and myths.

- Sample some Greek food (see Appendix B for recipes). Listen to traditional Greek music.

INDEPENDENCE DAY

• • • •

March 26
Bangladesh

Background

At midnight of March 25, 1971, the nation of Bangladesh declared its independence and the Liberation War for separation from Pakistan (then known as West Pakistan) began. Independence Day, known in Bangladesh as Swadhinata Dibash, is a national holiday and is celebrated widely.

TEACHERS' DAY

• • • •

March 28
Czech Republic and Slovakia

Background

Education is held in high esteem as a profession in Slovakia and the Czech Republic, and on this day teachers are honored.

Activities

- Have the children write letters to former teachers telling what they learned in that teacher's class, why that teacher was special to them, and/or how that teacher made a difference in their lives. If possible, deliver the letters to the teachers.

- Examine the profession of educator.

- During a group discussion have students try to think of an adult job they could hold if they lacked a basic education.

YOUTH DAY

• • • •

March 29
Taiwan

Background

Following the Communist takeover of mainland China in 1949 more than two million Chinese Nationalists moved to the island province of Taiwan. These people revered freedom and saw the youth of the nation as the hope of the future. March 29 is set aside as a day to honor the young.

Activities

- Examine reasons for a country to honor its youth. What contributions do the young make to a family or society? What would happen to a civilization that had no students?

4

APRIL HOLIDAYS

NONFIXED DATES

Baswant	India, Pakistan
Feast of Nganja	Angola
Lich'un	China
Passover (Pesach)	Jewish
Sakura (Cherry Blossom Festival)	Japan
San Khuda (New Year)	Sierra Leone
Tulip Festival	Netherlands
Matatirtha Aunsi (Mother's Day)	Nepal

FIXED DATES

April 1	April Fools' Day	International
April 4	National Day	Senegal
April 6	Chakri Day	Thailand
April 8	Hanamatsun	Buddhist
April 13	Songkran (Buddhist New Year)	Thailand
April 13 or 14	Nava Varsha (New Year)	Nepal
April 14	Pan American Day	North America, Central America, South America
April 17	Independence Day	Syria
April 18	Independence Day	Zimbabwe
April 19	Independence Day	Venezuela
April 21–May 2	Ridvan	Baha'i
April 22	Earth Day	International
April 25	Anzac Day	Australia, New Zealand
April 26	Union Day	Tanzania
April 27	Independence Day	Sierra Leone
April 27	Independence Day	Togo
April 30	Walpurgis Eve (Feast of Valborg)	Norway, Sweden

APRIL HOLIDAYS WITH NONFIXED DATES

BASWANT

• • • •

India, Pakistan

Background

The spring festival of Baswant (or Baswanta) is celebrated in northern India and Pakistan. During the festival everyone wears yellow, the sacred color of India and the color of spring. In fact, in Sanskrit "Baswant" means yellow. In the morning the family makes an offering of food and white flowers to Saraswati, the goddess of learning, while they observe a fast. At noon the fast is broken and everyone goes outdoors to enjoy a picnic lunch. During the afternoon the boys and men enjoy flying gaily colored kites made of bamboo and tissue paper. As in many Asian countries, the first hundred feet or so of the kite string is covered with glue holding ground glass. The purpose of this is to enable one to cut the string of other kites when the strings are crossed. Exciting kite battles end in a chase by the boys to retrieve and "capture" kites as they fall to the ground.

Activities

• Compare this festival to China's Kite Festival (see September 9) and/or to other spring festivals.

• Discuss the significance and symbolism of colors in art.

• At lunchtime, enjoy a picnic outdoors. Allow the children to make kites of tissue paper or bring kites from home to fly during the celebration. (See "Kite Festival," September 9, for more information on making kites.)

FEAST OF NGANJA

• • • •

Angola

Background

Every year at the time of the corn harvest in Angola the children plan and enjoy a day of celebration called the feast of Nganja. On the mutually decided day each child goes out to the family's field and gathers some fresh, ripe corn. The children, who range in age from about eight to twelve, then congregate in small groups in a prearranged location. Here they light fires and roast their corn. While they are cooking and eating the corn the children need to be very vigilant lest someone from one of the other groups comes to rob them of their corn. This is the real fun of the day, the attempts of the children to trick, plunder, and steal corn from the other groups of their friends. The fun continues until sunset when the full and happy children return home to the village.

Activities

• Have children find Angola on a map or globe. Discuss why the harvesttime in this country varies from that in our own country.

• Discuss the pattern of kernels growing on an ear of corn. Cut other vegetables or fruits, such as apples, carrots, or oranges, in half and examine the patterns and/or symmetry. If desired these can then be used with tempera paint to make fruit and vegetable prints.

• The kernels of corn that we eat are actually the seeds of the plant. Brainstorm a list of other seeds we use as food.

LICH'UN

• • • •

China

Background

This Chinese festival is linked to the agricultural cycle and spring. The major feature of the celebration is a procession of musicians and dancers led by a papier-mâché ox and ox driver. These are constructed and painted only after a careful examination of the almanac under official direction. Five colors of paint are used—red, black, white, green, and yellow—which

represent metal, wood, fire, water, and earth, five of the elements of nature. The use of these colors and the appearance of the ox and driver are highly symbolic. If, for example, the head of the ox is painted red, drought is predicted for the spring. Yellow indicates heat; green, sickness; white, high winds; and black, much rain. The appearance of the ox driver is also of significance. If he is wearing a hat and shoes, there will be rain; if he is barefooted, drought. Many clothes indicate cold weather; few clothes indicate heat. A red belt warns of sickness while a white one predicts good health. On this day people erect bamboo poles with feathers attached in front of their homes. As the spring breezes blow off the feathers everyone celebrates the fact that spring has actually arrived.

Activities

- Examine methods of predicting weather from ancient beliefs through modern use of satellites, computers, etc. Discuss the reasons why foreknowledge of the weather is important.

- Have children work in small groups to consult an almanac, analyze the information regarding weather conditions, and use their predictions to create their

own ox and ox driver. They could paint a picture, make the figures of papier-mâché, and paint them with appropriate colors, or make figures of colored clay.

PASSOVER
(Pesach)

• • • •

Jewish

Background

Passover is a weeklong celebration of the "passing over" to freedom from the slavery and bondage the Jews suffered under the Egyptian Pharaoh. When the Jews made their exodus from Egypt they left so hurriedly that they had no time to allow their bread dough to rise and were forced to bake unleavened cakes. These cakes, called matzo, are eaten today as a remembrance of the exodus. Matzo is eaten at the evening meal, which is called the seder. A bitter herb is also eaten as a reminder of the bitterness of slavery, and a sprig of greens is eaten as a reminder that Moses freed the Jews during the spring of the year. During the seder there is singing, prayers, and a reading of the events of the exodus (Haggadah). Following the meal the children play a game where they try to find a piece of matzo that has been hidden and for which the parents give prizes. On the second day of the celebration Jews attend the synagogue where the sermon, prayers, and music remind them of the importance of freedom. Their prayers include a wish for peace, freedom, and justice for all the people of the world.

Activities

- Compare the struggles of the Jews with other people of the world who have lived under slavery. Discuss the meaning of the words in our Pledge of Allegiance, "liberty and justice for all."

- Taste some matzo. Compare it to breads of other countries or cultures. Compare it to leavened bread.

- Do a science lesson on the action of yeast and/or other leavening agents. In film canisters or other small containers place powdered yeast, baking soda, baking powder, salt, unscented talcum powder, and cornstarch. Mark the containers with numbers and note what is in each, but do not tell the children. Give these containers to the children along with measuring spoons, a supply of flour, warm water, and small ovenproof bowls for mixing. Have them mix $\frac{1}{4}$ cup flour, 2 tablespoons water, and $\frac{1}{2}$ teaspoon of one of the "mystery powders" in each bowl. Observe every 15 minutes or so and note any changes over a 2-hour period. (The yeast mixture will rise visibly. Poke the other mixtures with a finger and listen carefully to hear which ones have bubbles that pop.) Next put the mixtures in a microwave for 3 minutes or in an oven set at 350° F for 30 minutes. After the mixtures are "baked" cut in half and examine (yeast, baking powder, and baking soda will all have tiny bubbles in the dough). Have the children conclude which of the powders are leavening agents.

- Design a math game where children have to solve eight problems. The answers should be 1, 6, 9, 11, 15, 13, 5, and 14, and should appear in the order given. Now have them assign a letter of the alphabet to each number (A=1, B=2, C=3, etc.) to find the piece of hidden matzo. (The name for the hidden matzo is Afikomen.) Give a sticker or other "prize" to everyone who finds the Afikomen!

SAKURA
(Cherry Blossom Festival)

• • • •

Japan

Background

The cherry blossom is the national flower of Japan and a very tangible sign of the coming of spring for the people. Although Sakura is not a legal holiday, many families arrange their schedules so that they will have some time to visit the country or a nearby park to enjoy the beauty and fragrance of the cherry trees in bloom.

Activities

- Use this opportunity to study the purpose of flowers and blossoms and their function in the cycle of a plant's growth.

- Do a unit of study on the sense of smell or begin with smell and study all five senses. A good way to demonstrate the power of smell is to blindfold the children and place a fruit-flavored lifesaver in their mouths without allowing them to smell it first. Have the children try to guess the flavors, then have them smell the lifesavers and try again. (It is very difficult to guess the flavor by taste alone.)

- Many countries and states have official flowers or plants. Research some of these and try to determine the significance of the choices made.

SAN KHUDA
(New Year)

• • • •

Sierra Leone

Background

San Khuda is a traditional festival celebrated by Sierra Leone's Mandingo tribe. It falls at the full moon in late April or early May, the time when the dry season is ending and the rainy season is just beginning. For centuries the Mandingos have believed that water is the source of all life and that through use water loses its power. They equate the dry season with an act of God—the taking away of the old, worn-out water—and believe that new water is provided at the start of the new year. On New Year's Eve houses and yards are cleaned and receptacles are prepared to receive the new water. Everyone gathers in the center of the town or village. Women and children begin singing to the accompaniment of drums and flutes as their neighbors arrive carrying buckets. At the signal of the leader everyone goes to the river or spring. They then return home carrying containers of water balanced on their heads and palm fronds in their hands. The palm branches are dipped in the water and used to sprinkle everything and everyone in the village they wish to bless in the new year. Gift-giving and feasting are sometimes a part of the celebration, but the central focus is always on the water.

Activities

- Compare San Khuda to other water festivals and/ or spring celebrations.

- The Mandingos believe that water is the source of all life. Illustrate the truth in this by having children brainstorm a list of essential uses for water without which there could be no life on our planet.

- Older children can investigate the uses of water in rituals, religious ceremonies, and celebrations.

- Consider the old adage "April showers bring May flowers" and discuss how that compares to the Mandingo belief that "new" water gives new life.

TULIP FESTIVAL

• • • •

Netherlands

Background

The Netherlands is one of the world's largest exporters of flowers and bulbs, and is renowned for its tu-lips. This holiday was created as an opportunity to showcase their product for the tourists. The festival usually occurs during the last week of April and the first of May when the flowers are at their peak. The biggest day of the festival is the Sunday between the two weeks, known as "Bulb Sunday." On this day everyone is outdoors purchasing flowers, viewing the flower mosaic contests, or participating in the auto race or other activities that have come to be a part of the festivities.

Activities

- Examine and study bulbs and tubers.

- Study the parts of a flower by cutting a tulip flower in half vertically.

- Study the Netherlands and the land reclamation that has taken place there.

- List other holidays that have been "invented" because someone saw a need or a commercial use for such a holiday (Kwanzaa, Mother's Day, Grandparent's Day, etc.).

- The flower mosaics of the Tulip Festival are reminiscent of the flower bedecked floats of our Rose Bowl parade. Have the children make tissue paper flowers and work together to tape them to a wall or chalkboard to form their own picture or design.

MATATIRTHA AUNSI
(Mother's Day)

• • • •

Nepal

Background

Matatirtha Aunsi is an official holiday in Nepal with schools and businesses closed. It is a day on which individuals perform acts that show their filial devotion and respect for their mothers. Those whose mothers are still living present them with sweets or other gifts and receive blessings from their mothers. Those whose mothers are dead show their respect by going to bathe and offer ablutions to their mothers.

APRIL HOLIDAYS WITH FIXED DATES

APRIL FOOLS' DAY

• • • •

April 1
International

Background

Celebrated on April 1, April Fools' Day, also known as All Fools' Day, is a day for mischief and playing pranks on people. It probably arose in France at the time of the adoption of the Gregorian calendar. Prior to that time, under the Julian calendar, it was the custom to celebrate the new year and to exchange gifts on April 1. Following the calendar change, people continued to send mock gifts and to visit one another on this day. The tradition grew and spread to other countries and currently is unofficially celebrated in a number of countries around the world.

Activities

- Do a lesson on the importance of following directions. Prepare what looks like a complicated and time-consuming test with a wordy set of directions to the students ending with the instruction to write their name on the paper and turn it in without making any other marks on the test. Distribute the test, telling them that the test will be timed to see how well they can do in two minutes. Remind them to read the directions first. Invariably students will either get a score of 100 percent or 0 percent. After a discussion about what is "fair" and about following directions you can tear up the tests and say "April Fool!" Hopefully the students will have learned a valuable lesson!

- Have children write stories about All Fools' Day tricks, real or imaginary, with the child either the doer of the trick or on the receiving end.

- Discuss the names of the months of the year and relate them to historical figures and ancient Roman gods. The following list will give children a starting point for researching:

- January: from the Latin *Januarius*, named for the Roman god Janus

- February: from the Latin *Februarius*, named for Februa, the festival of purification held on February 15

- March: from the Latin *Mars*, named for the Roman god Mars

- April: from the Latin *Aprillis* (month of Venus) or the Greek *Aphro* (for Aphrodite)

- May: from the Latin *Maius*, named for Maia, goddess of fertility

- June: from the Latin *Junius*, named for the goddess Juno

- July: from the Latin *Julius*, named for Julius Caesar

- August: from the Latin *Augustus*, named for Augustus Caesar

- September: from the Latin *septem* (seven); on the Roman calendar, which preceded the Gregorian calendar, September was the seventh month

- October: from the Latin *octo* (eight); October was the eighth month of the Roman calendar

- November: from the Latin *novem* (nine); November was the ninth month of the Roman calendar

- December: from the Latin *decem* (ten); December was the tenth month of the Roman calendar

NATIONAL DAY

• • • •

April 4
Senegal

Background

On April 4, 1960, Senegal was granted its freedom after three centuries of French domination. Senegal is located on the west coast of Africa and surrounds the much smaller country of Gambia. It is now a democracy in which Sunni Muslim is the major religion. Both French and African languages are spoken in the country.

CHAKRI DAY

• • • •

April 6
Thailand

Background

On April 6, 1782, a great warrior named Somdet Chao Phya Maha Kasat Suek entered the gates of the capital of Thailand and took over the reins of the government. By common consent of the people this hero was proclaimed king and came to be known as King Rama I, establishing the Chakri Dynasty, which still rules the country. The present and ninth king is the great-great-grandson of King Rama I. On this day, the anniversary of the founding of the Chakri Dynasty, people show their reverence and respect for their past and present rulers by worshipping with lighted joss sticks and candles at the Chapel Royal and by visiting the Royal Pantheon and the statue of King Rama I.

HANAMATSUN

• • • •

April 8
Buddhist

Background

Siddhartha, the founder of Buddhism, was born in India in 563 B.C. He is thought to have lived and taught there for 80 years, until his death in 483 B.C. He came to be called the Buddha, which, in Sanskrit means "the enlightened one." Hanamatsun, the celebration of the birth of the Buddha, is the most important of all Buddhist holidays. Tradition has it that it rained flowers at the time of Siddhartha's birth. For that reason contemporary celebrations center around the image of the baby Buddha, which is housed in a special shrine the roof of which is covered with flowers. The statue of the baby Buddha is often placed in a tub of licorice tea. Members of the congregation use ladles to pour tea over the figure of the Buddha, symbolic of bathing him. They then drink licorice tea to signify the cleansing of their souls and their wish to become as the Buddha.

In Thailand the celebration of the birth of Buddha differs somewhat and is held on a different date (see "Visakha Puja Day," June).

Activities

- Compare this holiday to Christmas or to other celebrations that honor the birth of religious leaders.

- Discuss the symbolic cleansing ceremony and compare it to practices in other religions.

- Smell some flowers. Eat some licorice. Or enjoy a cup of licorice tea by placing $\frac{1}{2}$ teaspoon anise extract in hot water and adding sugar to taste.

SONGKRAN
(Buddhist New Year)

• • • •

April 13
Thailand

Background

Songkran, the traditional New Year celebration and rite of spring of the Thai people, is a true folk festival embodying both religious ceremonies and popular entertainment. Formerly determined by the lunar calendar, Songkran is now celebrated on April 13. The more serious aspects of the festival include visiting the monasteries and making offerings of food to the Buddhist monks and priests as well as visiting the *chedis* (pagodas) where the ashes of one's ancestors are entombed. Following this, the Thais return home where they pour scented water into the palms of the elders and offer them gifts in exchange for their blessings. Parades, music, and dancing have become an added part of the festival, existing alongside the traditional activities of water throwing and releasing fish into the waterways. Both of these latter activities are symbolic—the water throwing symbolizes adequate rainfall during the rice planting season, while the freeing of the fish indicates a wish that the fish will multiply and be plentiful in the rice paddies during the monsoon season when the villages are isolated from one another by the flooding. In Thailand, Songkran is also a public health day and is so declared by the government. Prior to the holiday people work together to thoroughly clean their homes and communities and on the eve of Songkran all of the refuse is burned. The neighboring Buddhist country of Myanmar enjoys a similar water festival at this time of year to welcome the new year.

Activities

• Compare Songkran to other festivals of spring, new year celebrations, or water festivals around the world.

• Study the teachings of Buddha and compare Buddhism to other world religions or philosophies.

• Do a lesson or unit on fish. Tie this in with the Easter or spring activity of studying animals that hatch from eggs.

• Examine the methods of planting, growing, and harvesting rice and compare to the methods used for other grains or crops.

• Study weather patterns, monsoons, or types of storms.

NAVA VARSHA
(New Year)

• • • •

April 13 or 14
Nepal

Background

Nava Varsha, Nepalese New Year Day, is exceptional in that it is the only holiday in Nepal that does not follow the religious lunar calendar. By contrast it always falls in mid-April on the first day of Baisakh, the first month of the Nepalese solar calendar year. Nava Varsha is a national holiday. On this day many people travel to Bhaktapur City to celebrate. Here the festival is known as Bisket Jatra (the festival after the death of the serpent). The festivities last for a week during which time images of Bhairav, Bhadrakali, and other goddesses are pulled through the town in chariots. The most important and exciting event of the festival is the erection of the *lingo*, a ceremonial pole made of a thick tree trunk approaching 80 feet in length. Neighboring Bangladesh also holds a New Year celebration at about this time of year (usually on April 15) known as Bangla or Bengali New Year.

PAN AMERICAN DAY

• • • •

April 14
North America, Central America, South America

Background

In 1930 the Pan American Union adopted a resolution establishing Pan American Day as a day to express the solidarity and friendship shared by the member nations of the Organization of American States (OAS). President Herbert Hoover issued a proclamation designating April 14, 1931, as the first Pan American Day in the United States, and the other countries belonging to the OAS proclaimed similar celebrations. Although not a legal holiday, this is a time to examine and enjoy the cultural and social life in the countries of South, Central, and North America.

Activities

- Discuss the importance of getting along with one's neighbors whether they be individuals or countries. Draw parallels between the two.

- Have the children plan a trip to a country of their choice in Central or South America. Have them estimate costs, calculate distances, and learn to exchange dollars to other forms of currency. After researching the country they might make up travel brochures or posters and try to "sell" their trip to their classmates.

- Relate this holiday to Hispanic Heritage Month (see September–October 15). Use some of the activities listed under that celebration to enhance the children's understanding of cultures in Latin America.

INDEPENDENCE DAY

• • • •

April 17
Syria

Background

Historical records of the area now known as Syria date back as far as 2500 B.C. In A.D. 1516 the Ottomans overtook the area and for four centuries the Syrians, reduced to the status of serfs, remained a part of the Ottoman Empire. In 1920 the country came under French mandate, with independence gained on April 17, 1946. In 1958 Syria merged with Egypt and for five years the area was known as the United Arab Republic. Both Arabic and Kurdish are spoken in this predominantly Muslim nation.

INDEPENDENCE DAY

• • • •

April 18
Zimbabwe

Background

Zimbabwe is a landlocked African nation bounded by Mozambique, South Africa, Botswana, and Zambia. In 1888 the British colonialist, Cecil Rhodes, and his British South Africa Company obtained a mining concession and by 1890 the first British settlers had arrived in the area (which came to be known as Rhodesia). In 1923 Rhodesia gained colonial status and in 1965 was unilaterally declared independent by the white minority government. Guerrilla warfare against the illegal regime, along with international sanctions, led to legitimate independence in 1980. At that time the name Zimbabwe was adopted, a reference to the Great Zimbabwe, a medieval trading center of the native Shona tribe. English, Shona, and Ndebele are spoken in Zimbabwe and both Christianity and traditional religions are practiced.

INDEPENDENCE DAY

• • • •

April 19
Venezuela

Background

The first European to sight the coast of Venezuela was Christopher Columbus on his third voyage in 1498, and the first permanent European settlement on South America was established in 1521 at Cumana in Venezuela. During the seventeenth century the area became part of the Spanish-ruled New Granada. The following century saw several unsuccessful revolts against the Spanish viceroy by the Indians. In 1797 a new effort to gain independence began that resulted in the formation of the Republic of Great Colombia in 1819. Great Colombia included the present-day countries of Venezuela, Colombia, and Ecuador. The war of independence lasted until 1821 when, under the leadership of Simon Bolívar and José Antonio Paez, the Spanish were decisively defeated. On April 19, 1830, Venezuela seceded from Great Columbia and Paez became the country's first president.

RIDVAN

• • • •

April 21–May 2
Baha'i

Background

In 1844 the Babi Faith was founded in Persia (now Iran) by Mizra 'Ali Muhammad, also known as the Bab ("Gate"), who announced that he was the herald of a messenger from God who would usher in an age of peace. On April 21, 1863, Baha'Allah declared publicly that he was the prophet of whom the Bab had spoken. Ridvan, the most joyous of all Baha'i feasts, lasts for twelve days, from April 21 to May 2.

EARTH DAY

• • • •

April 22
International

Background

Earth Day was first organized in 1970 in an effort to promote ecology and respect for life on the planet as well as to encourage awareness of the growing problems of air, water, and soil pollution. It is currently observed in more than 140 countries around the world. In many areas the day is celebrated with outdoor performances or fairs. Individuals or groups perform acts of service to Earth. Television stations frequently air programs dealing with environmental issues.

Activities

- Invite a representative of a local conservation or environmental group to come and speak to your class.

- Brainstorm a list of ways in which children can help Earth—conserving water, paper, electricity, etc.; not purchasing articles made of fur, exotic woods, or ivory; recycling; writing letters to legislators outlining their concerns; and so on. Have children make promises to Earth.

- Study rain forests or other areas of the world that are imperiled.

- Study the effects of pollution on plants, animals, and humans.

- Have children research and report on endangered species.

- Plant a tree, some grass, or flowers.

- Begin a classroom or schoolwide recycling project.
- Go outdoors and hold your own Earth Day celebration!
- Read and discuss the speech of Chief Seattle. Discuss lessons that modern people can learn from the Native Americans with regard to conservation and caring for Earth.

ANZAC DAY

• • • •

April 25
Australia, New Zealand

Background

Anzac Day is a national holiday set aside to honor those who fought in wars. It is the equivalent of our Veterans Day. The acronym "ANZAC" stands for "Australia/New Zealand Army Corps."

UNION DAY

• • • •

April 26
Tanzania

Background

Originally two independent and separate countries, Tanganyika and Zanzibar signed an act of union on April 26, 1964, thereby forming the nation of Tanzania.

INDEPENDENCE DAY

• • • •

April 27
Sierra Leone

Background

In 1462 the Portuguese explorer, Pedro de Cintra, named this area of the east African coast Sierra Leone ("lion mountain"). Trade stations were established, and by the 1700s Sierra Leone had become an important source of supply for British slave traders. By the end of the next century concerns on the part of English reformers led to the establishment of colonies in Sierra Leone for freed and runaway slaves. Following 1807, when Great Britain declared slave trading illegal, blacks rescued from slave ships by the British Navy were brought to Sierra Leone, although slavery within the colony continued. In 1895 a British protectorate over Sierra Leone was established and the following year the British outlawed slave raiding and trading within the protectorate. Domestic slavery continued until 1927 when Sierra Leone's supreme court outlawed the practice. On April 27, 1961, Sierra Leone was granted independence and membership in the British Commonwealth. Traditional religions and Muslim are practiced in the country. The primary language is English, but many traditional African languages are also spoken.

INDEPENDENCE DAY

• • • •

April 27
Togo

Background

During the eighteenth century, while under Danish authority, the coast of Togo saw much slave trading. European control of the coastal trading posts changed hands several times during the nineteenth century until 1884 when a treaty was signed putting Togoland (Togo and part of what is now Ghana) under German protection. After German forces capitulated to end World War I, Togo came under the direct control of the French colonial department. Following World War II the French mandate was changed to a United Nation trusteeship, and independence was achieved on April 27, 1960.

WALPURGIS EVE
(Feast of Valborg)

• • • •

April 30
Norway, Sweden

Background

Walpurgis was an English nun, born in the 1700s, who served as a missionary in Germany. Her day coincides with Beltain, an ancient Celtic spring festival of witches and fertility. It is still believed by some that on this day witches and devils meet and dance on the mountaintops, and Walpurgis is believed to be a protector against their black magic. The majority of the people, however, think little of the witches and basically consider Walpurgis Eve a celebration of spring.

It has become traditional to "sing in the spring" around large community bonfires. There are also many parties held in the evening, and the celebration frequently continues into the following day, May Day.

Activities

• Make a list of common superstitions and research their origins. If the origins cannot be found, make up your own and use them to write creative stories.

• Provide the children with books on magic tricks. Have them demonstrate tricks and explain scientifically how they work.

• Make a list of holidays in which singing or other music plays an important part.

5

MAY HOLIDAYS

NONFIXED DATES

Victoria Day	Canada	Monday before May 24
Mother's Day	United States	Second Sunday
Mother's Day	France, Sweden	Last Sunday
Memorial Day	United States	Last Monday
Bun Hill Day	Hong Kong	
Dragon Boat Festival	China	
Bird Week	Japan	
Shavuot	Jewish	
Yom Ha'atzmaut (Independence Day)	Israel	
Kadazan Harvest Festival	Malaysia	Weekend in Mid-May
Pentecost (Whitsunday)	Christian	Seventh Sunday after Easter
Trinity Sunday	Christian	First Sunday after Pentecost
Corpus Christi	Christian	First Thursday after Trinity Sunday
Ploughing Ceremony	Thailand	

FIXED DATES

May 1–31	Flores de Mayo	Philippines (Christian)
May 1–31	Asian-Pacific Month	United States
May 1	May Day (International Labor Day)	International
May 4	Yom Ha-sho'ah (Martyrs' and Heroes' Remembrance Day)	Jewish
May 4 and 5	Remembrance Days	Netherlands
May 5	Cinco de Mayo	Mexico
May 5	Kodomono-hi (Boys' Day)	Japan
May 5	Urini Nal (Children's Day)	Korea
May 8	Parents' Day	Korea
May 8	Liberation Day (V-E Day)	United States
May 11	National Day	Laos
May 12	Constitution Day	Cambodia
May 14	Independence Day	Paraguay
May 14	Constitution Day	Philippines
May 15	Pista Ng Anihan (Harvest Festival)	Philippines
May 17	Constitution Day	Norway
May 22	National Day	Yemen
May 25	Independence Day	Jordan
May 25	National Day	Argentina
May 25	African Liberation Day	International
May 26	Independence Day	Guyana
May 31	Republic Day	South Africa
May 31	National Day	Brunei

MAY HOLIDAYS WITH NONFIXED DATES

VICTORIA DAY

• • • •

Monday before May 24
Canada

Background

Queen Victoria was born on May 24, 1819, and the present queen of Great Britain, Elizabeth II, was born on April 21, 1926. The birthdays of both queens are commemorated on this date. Formerly known as Empire Day, this occasion is also a time when Canadians celebrate the continuing association of their country with Great Britain.

Activities

- Compare Victorian England with present-day England. Have students work cooperatively to research different aspects of the two periods—economic, political, social, etc.

- Study the historical ties of Canada and Great Britain. Compare to the association of the United States with Great Britain both before and after the Revolutionary War.

- Create a timeline outlining important events between the rule of Victoria and that of Elizabeth.

- Using a conversion chart and ads from the newspaper have children convert the prices of different items from American dollars to Canadian dollars and/or British pounds. (For younger children you may want to simplify the charts.)

- Have children investigate how royal birthdays are celebrated and then plan a "royal" party of their own with various students acting as the guest of honor and other guests.

MOTHER'S DAY

• • • •

Second Sunday in May
United States

Background

The idea of setting aside a special day to honor mothers was first conceived in 1907 by Ann M. Jarvis, a resident of Philadelphia, Pennsylvania. The celebration was observed nationwide by 1911 and was originally highlighted by a special church service. In 1912 a Mother's Day International Association was founded to promote the holiday in other countries. On this day children give cards and presents to their mothers and adult children try to return home for a visit or at least phone their mothers.

Activities

- Have the children write biographical sketches of their mothers. As an alternative they could write letters or poems to their mothers telling why they love them.

- The children might draw portraits of their mothers, make handmade cards, or create gifts for their mothers. One unique and easy-to-make gift is individual hand soap. Mix a mild soap powder (such as Ivory) with enough water to make it stick together; add some drops from a small bottle of food coloring. It is more fun if you divide the soap powder into smaller batches and make several colors. Taking one heaping tablespoonful at a time, press the soap mixture firmly between your palms and roll into balls. Allow four to five days drying time, turning the soap balls about once a day so they dry evenly. When dry, place the pastel soap balls in small plastic bags and tie with a colorful ribbon.

- It has become a tradition to serve mother breakfast in bed on Mother's Day. Write "secret" notes home to the fathers asking their help in arranging this. The fathers can send in dry cereal in individual boxes, instant coffee, tea bags, breakfast rolls, bananas, paper cups, bowls, napkins, plates, and plastic spoons. Ask a local restaurant to donate individual packets of sugar and creamer, and collect enough soda can "flats" from a local grocery store so that each child has one to decorate as a tray.

- Discuss the mothers of the students in your class, their roles, and their contributions to the family. This will no doubt differ from family to family and you will want to point out that there is no one "right" answer.

MOTHER'S DAY

• • • •

Last Sunday in May
France, Sweden

Background

The observance of this holiday was adopted from the United States (see above).

MEMORIAL DAY

• • • •

Last Monday in May
United States

Background

The origins of this holiday are indistinct and it is most probable that its inception lies in ancient traditions. Memorial Day, or Decoration Day as it was formerly known, is a secular holiday set aside to honor those who died in war, with people visiting and placing flowers on the graves of loved ones and ancestors. Memorial Day has become a time for family gatherings and picnics and serves as the unofficial start of the summer season.

Activities

- Read and learn more about Memorial Day and the places where ceremonies to honor the war dead are held. Three excellent nonfiction books for children are *Memorial Day* by Geoffrey Scott (Minneapolis: Carolrhoda Books, 1983); *Arlington National Cemetery* by Catherine Reef (New York: Dillon Press, 1991); and *A Wall of Names: The Story of the Vietnam Veterans Memorial* by Judy Donnelly (New York: Random House, 1991).

- Make American flags (see "Flag Day," June 14, for instructions).

- Have children write poems to honor those men and women who fought and fell for our country. If desired, students could choose different wars to write about, from the Revolution to Vietnam.

- Have your own Memorial Day ceremony. Sing "The Star Spangled Banner" or other patriotic songs, recite the Pledge of Allegiance, and have children read the poems they have written for the occasion.

BUN HILL DAY

• • • •

Hong Kong

Background

The Bun Hills Festival is celebrated in the city of Cheung Chau, which is located on one of the small islands of Hong Kong. The festival lasts for four days and includes musical performances, religious ceremonies, and parades featuring people dressed in costumes from the past. The grandest celebration takes place on the third day, Bun Hill Day. Huge mounds of buns are stacked and everyone gathers to watch the men of the community climb the hills of buns gathering as many of the buns as they can. These sacred buns are thought to assure good fortune for the coming year, and it is believed that the higher up on the hill the bun is located the more good luck it will bring.

Activities

- Discuss the reasons behind symbolizing good fortune with bread or buns. Brainstorm a list of foods that fall under the category of bread and grains.

- Discuss the history of Hong Kong. Have students speculate on the changes that will occur in 1997 when the British return Hong Kong to the Chinese.

- Bake bread (see recipe under United States in Appendix B). Use math skills to measure ingredients, determine the temperature at which the oven will need to be set, and/or to double or halve the recipe. While the bread is rising examine it from time to time and do a science lesson on the action of the yeast. Before eating the bread examine it to find the tiny holes (pockets of gas) made by the yeast. Compare your yeast bread to unleavened bread (see "Passover," April, for more information).

DRAGON BOAT FESTIVAL

• • • •

China

Background

The Dragon Boat Festival is celebrated in China on the fifth day of the fifth moon or month of the lunar calendar and for this reason is sometimes called Double Five Day. The celebration is held in honor of a former scholar and official, Ch'u Yuan, who lived in the third century B.C. According to legend Ch'u Yuan tried to advise his king wisely but the king did not want to hear what he was saying so he banished Ch'u Yuan to an isolated village, where he lived for seven years writing scholarly books. When, on the fifth day of the fifth month of the seventh year, he heard that his predictions had all come true he drowned himself in the river in an act of despair. Some fishermen who had seen him leap into the river took out their boats and tried to save him while their wives wrapped cooked rice in banana leaves and threw the rice balls into the river hoping that the fish would eat them instead of Ch'u Yuan's body. On this day the Chinese still eat special rice balls called *tsungs*, throw some of the rice balls into the river as an offering to the spirit of Ch'u

Yuan, and hold dragon boat races to the beat of drums as they re-create the search for the body of Ch'u Yuan.

Activities

- Begin by showing a picture of a dragon boat and brainstorm a list of methods of water transportation. Extend this to include land and air travel if desired.

- Discuss what life in China might have been like in 300 B.C.

- Eat some rice cakes or fried rice. Study rice and other grains and the food group they represent.

BIRD WEEK

• • • •

Japan

Background

During World War II many trees in Japan were cut down and used to fuel munitions factories. As a result numerous bird nests were destroyed and countless birds died. Consequently, Japanese farm crops suffered because the birds were no longer available to eat the many insects that damage crops. Japan's Education Ministry instituted the celebration of Bird Week as a way to encourage people to respect and care for birds and to provide the birds with places to nest. Throughout the country prizes are given to individuals, schools, and other groups who render services to the birds.

Activities

- Generate a list of other effects the cutting down of forests has on animals and the environment. Draw parallels between what happened in Japan and what is happening today with the world's rain forests.

- Do a unit on birds, food chains, and/or the balance of nature.

SHAVUOT

• • • •

Jewish

Background

Like the other two Jewish pilgrimage festivals (Passover and Sukkoth), Shavuot marks both a season of the agricultural calendar and an event in the history of Israel. Shavuot commemorates the encounter on Mount Sinai during which God revealed himself to Moses and the Jewish people, and gave to Moses the two tablets upon which were inscribed the Ten Commandments. It is a time to honor God's covenant with Israel. It is also a celebration of the wheat harvest and was originally the festival of the first fruits. In Hebrew the word "Shavuot" means "weeks," the name stemming from the celebration's occurrence seven weeks after Passover.

YOM HA'ATZMAUT
(Independence Day)

• • • •

Israel

Background

Yom Ha'atzmaut is the celebration of the establishment of the State of Israel in 1948 following World War II. During its brief history Israel has been torn by four Arab-Israeli wars. Over a million Arabs have fled to neighboring countries, but a constant influx of Jewish immigrants has swollen the population of this socialist country. Nevertheless, Israel today remains a country of two distinct cultures. The main religions are Judaism and Islam and both Hebrew and Arabic are spoken in the country.

KADAZAN HARVEST FESTIVAL

• • • •

Weekend in Mid-May
Malaysia

Background

This festival is celebrated in Sabah, the region of Malaysia that occupies the northern part of the island of Borneo. The Kadazans of this area believe that Kinoingan Minamangun (the God/Creator) and his wife, Suminundu, had one daughter, Huminodun, and that, when the god was preparing for the creation of the Kadazans, he sacrificed his daughter by planting seeds in the various parts of her body. From these seeds sprang the plants that provided food for the Kadazans including *padi* (rice). The *padi* is thought to embody Bambaazon, the spirit-life of Minamangun, and is therefore sacred to the Kadazans. Much ceremony surrounds the ripening and harvesting of the grain including the offerings of food to the Bambaazon. After the priestess and her attendants have performed their ceremonies and all of the prayers have been said, the people enjoy feasting, buffalo races, arm and finger wrestling, gong beating, dancing, and *tapai* (rice wine) drinking competitions.

Activities

- Compare the Kadazan Harvest Festival to other festivals of thanksgiving.

- Compare Suminundu to the Native American concept of Mother Earth. Read the picture book *Mother Earth* by Nancy Luenn (see Appendix A, "Earth/Environment") and then have the children write their own stories about the gifts we get from the earth (or the gods).

- Study the importance of having rice and/or other grains in our diet and the vitamins and minerals that they provide. Discuss how a lack of these would have affected the "spirit-life" of the people.

PENTECOST (WHITSUNDAY)

• • • •

Seventh Sunday after Easter
(May or June)
Christian

Background

Pentecost, or Whitsunday, is a Christian holy day commemorating the descent of the Holy Ghost upon the disciples. That this miracle occurred on the Jewish Shavuot heightened its impact to the point that, following its occurrence, thousands of people came to the disciples ready to be baptized and to accept Christianity. Consequently it has become a traditional day for baptisms to take place. Pentecost is also linked to pagan spring rites and many people still enjoy family gatherings, picnics, or outings to the country on this holiday.

TRINITY SUNDAY

• • • •

First Sunday after Pentecost
(May or June)
Christian

Background

This holy day, instituted in 828 by Pope Gregory IX, is dedicated to the Christian belief in the Trinity—Father, Son, and Holy Spirit—and falls on the Sunday following Pentecost. In pre revolutionary Russia Trinity was a grand celebration. Churches and homes were decorated with wreaths, fresh flowers and grasses, and saplings. It was a time of weddings, and young unwed women would sometimes toss fresh wreaths into streams to foretell whether they would marry during the next year; if a wreath floated the woman was destined to marry; if it sank, she would remain unwed. With the coming of communism came the belief that holidays were a way of exploiting the masses and preventing productivity, and the Soviets forbade the celebration of most holidays and religious rituals. This particular holiday was turned into an arbor day.

CORPUS CHRISTI

• • • •

First Thursday after Trinity
Sunday (May, June, or July)
Christian

Background

This Christian festival, which falls on the first Thursday after Trinity Sunday, is a celebration of the Eucharist. Commonly known as communion, the Eucharist is a sacrament commemorating the Last Supper of Christ, and consists of bread and wine that have been consecrated. In Poland and some other areas of the world, churches sponsor festive processions on this day and church altars are beautifully decorated. In Mexico the holiday is also a celebration of the first fruits of the harvest. Parades, in which the children carry rattles, clay miniatures, and other good-luck charms, as well as music and colorful masks, are all a part of the Mexican festivities. In some remote areas Mexicans also enjoy watching the Valadores (Dance of the Flying Men) in which a musician stands on a small platform erected on top of a tall pole. Four other men, with ropes tied around their waists, leap from the platform; as the musician sings and dances they circle the pole thirteen times while suspended upside down.

Activities

- Discuss this and other holidays (or holy days) that contain both solemn and festive aspects.

- Have children bring good-luck charms from home and write or tell about their personal good-luck tokens.

- Make miniature animals or good-luck charms of clay.

- Provide yogurt containers, small plastic bottles, dried beans or pebbles, glue, tape, and paints and have the children "invent" rattles. Play some traditional Mexican music and have them join in with their musical instruments.

PLOUGHING CEREMONY

• • • •

Thailand

Background

Thailand's annual Ploughing Ceremony takes place on a date, usually in May, fixed by the royal astronomer. The ceremony for fertility of the crops is performed prior to this date to ensure a bountiful harvest. The Ploughing Ceremony itself is the official opening of the new agricultural season and the beginning of the time for plowing the fields.

On this day the Lord of the Harvest (a role formerly filled by the king, but in more recent years executed by the undersecretary of state for agriculture and cooperatives) performs a number of rituals. He predicts the amount of rainfall by choosing from one of three pieces of cloth offered to him. All look identical, but when unfolded are of differing lengths. If the Lord of the Harvest chooses the shortest piece of cloth the rain will be heavy, if he chooses the longest; light. Following this the Lord of the Harvest, accompanied by Brahmans blowing conch shells, and four Celestial Maidens, plows the earth using a sacred red and gold plow drawn by sacred oxen. The Celestial Maidens scatter rice seeds into the freshly plowed earth. When this ritual is concluded the oxen are offered seven different kinds of food. The bowl they choose to eat from first determines the best crop for that year. Although this may seem a rather risky way of determining one's crops, it has been documented that the predictions made during the ancient ceremony are rarely wrong! Following the ceremony people from the crowd scramble to retrieve the consecrated seeds sown by the Lord of the Harvest as these are thought to bring the possessor good luck and wealth.

Activities

- Compare this holiday to Groundhog Day (see February 2), the Chinese festival of Lich'un (see April), or other celebrations in which determining the weather, crops, and/or growing conditions are a part of the ceremony.

- The Ploughing Ceremony has become a time for leading agriculturists and farmers to meet and for private companies to display the latest in agricultural machinery and techniques. Discuss and study the evolution of farming techniques, inventions that played an important role, and/or modern technology.

MAY HOLIDAYS WITH FIXED DATES

FLORES DE MAYO

• • • •

May 1–31
Philippines
(Christian)

Background

Celebrated throughout the Philippines, Flores de Mayo (Flowers of May) is a tribute to the Blessed Virgin Mary. Every afternoon during the month little girls dressed in white make offerings of flowers at the altar of the Blessed Virgin Mary. On the final day of the month processions of young girls carrying flowers and wearing white dresses ornamented with flowers move through the towns.

Activities

• Use Flores de Mayo to kick off your study of Asian-Pacific Month. Prepare a floral bulletin board. On construction paper "stems" write questions that will be answered through the month's studies. Have the children make large paper flowers to attach to the stems. Cut a flower shape with five or six petals of brightly colored construction paper. Roll each petal around a pencil to curl the paper and give the bulletin board a 3-D effect. Have yellow circles of paper prepared in advance. As the questions are answered have children write the answers on the circles and add them to the bulletin board as the centers of the flowers.

ASIAN-PACIFIC MONTH

• • • •

May 1–31
United States

Background

The month of May has been set aside as a time to study and honor the civilizations, cultures, countries, and contributions of the people of Asia and the Pacific. As with Black History Month or Women's History Month these studies should be integrated into the curriculum throughout the year, but a focus during the month of May is appropriate.

Activities

• Asian-Pacific studies cover a wide geographic area and diverse cultures. Prepare a data retrieval chart (such as the one below) for the children's use in-

ASIAN-PACIFIC COUNTRIES

	Size	Climate	Religion	Language(s)	Population	Crops
Malaysia						
Japan						
Thailand						
Korea						
China						
Vietnam						

cluding countries that you plan to study and other information that you wish for them to learn. As the children discover facts in their reading and studies they can fill in the chart and use it to compare and contrast the different countries.

- Read and discuss folktales or fairy tales from Asian-Pacific countries. Compare them to European tales. Discuss the lessons learned from each story and why such stories are important to children's development and understanding of the "real" world.

MAY DAY
(International Labor Day)

• • • •

May 1
International

Background

Originally a celebration of spring and the rebirth taking place in nature, May Day dates back to pagan cults that worshipped trees and other symbols of nature. Traditionally, May Day is characterized by the gathering of flowers and the fertility rite of dancing around the maypole. As recently as a generation or two ago it was a common custom in the United States to surprise family and neighbors with May baskets. Children would make simple paper baskets and fill them with wildflowers. They would then place them on the doorstep of the person they wished to surprise, ring the doorbell, and hide, waiting to see the expression on the recipient's face. In recent years, particularly in socialist and Communist countries, May Day has become a labor festival honoring the military and industrial might of the country.

Activities

- Compare May Day to other spring celebrations. Compare the traditional maypole to the lingo erected in Nepal during the celebration of Nava Varsha (see April 13 or 14).

- Discuss the evolution of this holiday and the effects of politics on this and other nonpolitical celebrations.

- May Day is one of the few holidays that is widely celebrated in Russia and other countries that were once a part of the USSR. Discuss the reasons these countries have few nationally celebrated holidays. (Religious holidays were discouraged under the Communist regime and the political holidays observed in the USSR are no longer celebrated.)

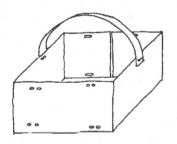

- Revive the tradition of giving May baskets. Have the children fill paper baskets with flowers and deliver them to family or neighbors. To make the baskets, begin with a 9-inch square of construction paper. Fold twice in each direction to divide the paper into sixteen equal sections as shown. Make four cuts as indicated by the dark lines on the illustration. Fold up the four sides of the basket, then fold in the tabs created by the cuts made earlier and glue or staple in place to the two short sides. Staple on a paper handle to complete the basket.

YOM HA-SHO'AH
(Martyrs' and Heroes' Remembrance Day)
• • • •
May 4
Jewish

Background

This relatively new holiday is a time to memorialize the six million European Jews who died in the Nazi Holocaust. It is felt that it is important that this tragic historic event be remembered in order that another genocide not occur. On this day schoolchildren in Israel are told of the disaster that befell the Jews and memorial services are held throughout the country as well as at the Yad Vashem Memorial in Jerusalem. The observance, which emphasizes respect for human dignity, is not limited to Jews.

Activities

• Discuss the Holocaust at a level appropriate for the students in your class. (See Jewish listing in Appendix A for suggested trade books.)

• Cut poster board in the shape of a large wreath or Star of David. Have the students brainstorm to make a list of ways in which we show our respect for other people. Then have students write their favorite idea on a piece of paper and attach it to a flower made of construction paper or tissue paper. Finally, affix the flowers onto the frame with a stapler. This can become your classroom memorial to the past and words to live by for the future.

REMEMBRANCE DAYS
• • • •
May 4 and 5
Netherlands

Background

In the Netherlands May 4 is set aside as a day to remember those who fell during World War II. This day is known as Dodenherdenking. The following day, May 5, is Bevrijdingsdag, or Liberation Day, a celebration of the end of World War II.

CINCO DE MAYO
• • • •
May 5
Mexico

Background

Prior to the Spanish conquest of the area now known as Mexico, in the early sixteenth century this area was a center of advanced civilizations, most notably the civilizations of the Mayans and Toltecs. Ruled by the Spanish for nearly three centuries, Mexico gained independence in 1821. In 1845 the country lost some of its territory when the United States annexed Texas, but it remained independent. In 1861 Spain, England, and France sent expeditionary forces to Mexico to collect debts owed them. Spain and England withdrew after receiving satisfaction from the Mexican government, but French troops remained because the French emperor Napoleon III had become interested in conquering Mexico and placing Maximilian on the throne of Mexico. On the fifth of May (Cinco de Mayo), 1862, the Mexicans defeated the French troops. The day has become a symbol of the bravery, determination, and desire for independence and democracy of the Mexican people. Its celebration much resembles our Fourth of July.

Activities

• Examine the ancient civilizations of the Mayans and/or Toltecs. Compare to other ancient civilizations.

• Discuss the concepts of freedom, independence, and democracy. Compare the struggles of the Mexicans to those of other countries or cultures within a country. Discuss the meanings of these ideas at a personal level.

• Cinco de Mayo is celebrated in many areas of the American Southwest. Through discussion lead the students to form conclusions as to why this is so. Discuss other groups who have moved to the United States yet have retained celebrations from their homelands.

- Examine Mexican art. Focus on the study of symmetry, or on the use of natural, readily available materials.

- Check the foreign exchange rates in the local newspaper, then have students use advertisements from local businesses to convert prices from cents to pesos.

- Learn the numbers to ten and/or the months of the year in Spanish. Try doing some simple oral addition and subtraction problems using the Spanish names for the numbers. Compare the names of the months to their English names.

- Eat some Mexican food. Listen to Mexican music.

KODOMONO-HI
(Boys' Day)

• • • •

May 5
Japan

Background

On the fifth day of the fifth month the Japanese celebrate Kodomono-hi, a special day for boys. On that day all families with sons erect bamboo poles in front of their homes. To the pole they attach colorful fish-shaped banners, one for each boy in the family. The fish vary in size according to the ages of the sons. The banner of the eldest son may be as long as 15 feet and hangs at the top of the pole. Younger sons get smaller fish, which are hung lower on the pole down to a very small size at the bottom if the family has a baby boy. The fish have round open mouths so that when the wind blows the fish fills with air and "floats" as it would in water. The fish represent carp, an animal that is considered strong and brave because it swims upstream and is even able to leap up waterfalls. This is symbolic of the wish that the boys will grow up to have courage, strength, and determination. Inside the house specially constructed platforms are set up to display collections of warrior dolls, miniature suits of armor, or other such paraphernalia. The postures of the dolls illustrate proper manners and good conduct. Another custom of this day is bathing the boys in water with iris leaves or petals in it. This, too,

is supposed to give the boys strength. Kodomono-hi, Boys' Day, has been designated as a national holiday since World War II.

Activities

- Tape a paper strip to represent a bamboo pole outside of your doorway. Have each boy paint or draw a fish banner to attach to the pole. Make a graph representing the boys' ages. Hang the fish on the pole placing the oldest boy's at the top and working down.

- Do a lesson on fish. Learn why carp or salmon swim upstream. Or have each student research a different fish or sea creature and tell the class five interesting facts about their animal.

- Do physical activities that center on strength or endurance. Who can do the most push-ups? Run the most laps around the playground? Throw a ball the farthest?

- Have the boys plan a party and invite the girls to be their guests. Snack on goldfish crackers and have the boys bring dolls to school. (Whether they like to acknowledge them as dolls or not, young boys almost all own "action figures" that they enjoy playing with.) During the celebration each boy should be given a chance to read a story he has written about his doll or to make an oral presentation to the group.

- Compare this celebration to the celebration of Hina-Matsuri (Girls' Day, see March 3–5).

URINI NAL
(Children's Day)

• • • •

May 5
Korea

Background

May 5 is set aside by South Koreans as a special day to honor their children. It was first proposed in 1919 by Chung Hwan Bang who felt that children deserved a day of recognition for the respect and obedience they are expected to give adults throughout the year. It is a day of family outings and is characterized by a variety of programs and activities designed to amuse and delight the young. The Children's Park in Seoul offers free admission as do many movie theaters. There are exhibitions of tae kwon do, wrestling, and dancing; plays; and puppet shows. Children receive prizes for the best painting and creative writing in specially arranged contests. Another contest, frequently popular in rural areas, involves swinging high enough to kick a bell that has been suspended between two poles in front of the swing. Sweets and special foods are offered by vendors and bakeries and prepared by parents.

Activities

• Have a swinging contest on your own. Straighten out a coat hanger. Tape to a yardstick leaving about 8 inches of the hook end of the hanger protruding beyond the end of the stick. Bend down the hanger to form a right angle with the yardstick and hang a bell from the hook. Stand to one side of the swing holding the yardstick and allow children to take turns swinging and trying to kick the bell. The child who kicks it in the fewest swings is the winner.

• Have a contest in which children write poetry, prose, or nonfiction works with Children's Day themes. They may choose to write about martial arts, Korea, responsibilities of children to their elders, a visit to an amusement park, or any other topic that ties in.

• Look at examples of Korean or other Asian art. Check with a local museum or cultural center to try and find a local artist or expert on Asia who could teach a lesson on art forms used in Korea and other Asian countries. Have students attempt to copy the style in their own paintings.

• Eat rice cakes or traditional Korean dishes. Listen to Korean music in the background as children paint or write.

PARENTS' DAY

• • • •

May 8
Korea

Background

On this day Korean children honor their parents. Grown children return home to visit their fathers and mothers. Gifts are given to the parents as tokens of respect and love.

Activities

• Have children create gifts that show the respect and love they have for their parents. One simple-to-make but creative and individual gift is a coupon book. Have children brainstorm a list of things they could do to make their parents happy. Then give the children a supply of 3" x 5" cards or slips of paper and colored pencils or fine-line markers and have them create their own coupons for use by their parents. Use another 3" x 5" card to make a cover and staple together into a coupon booklet.

Examples of coupons include: "I will clean my room," "Good for one hug!," "Free car wash, good any Saturday."

munist republic is Lao. The primary religion of the four million inhabitants is Buddhism.

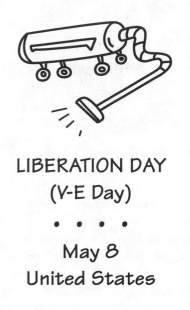

LIBERATION DAY
(V-E Day)

• • • •

May 8
United States

Background

Liberation Day, celebrated on May 8, is the legal holiday commemorating the end of World War II. The end of the war came with the collapse of Germany after the meeting of German and Allied armies at Torgau in Saxony and the suicide of Adolf Hitler amid the ruins of a Berlin falling to the Russians. Germany's unconditional surrender was signed at Reims on May 7, 1945, and ratified in Berlin the next day. On Liberation Day, known as V-E Day—Victory in Europe—in the United States, wreaths are placed on the Tombs of the Unknowns and time is taken to remember those who died for the cause of liberty.

NATIONAL DAY

• • • •

May 11
Laos

Background

Following 54 years of colonial rule by France, Laos, a landlocked country in Indochina, gained its independence on May 11, 1953. The language of this Com-

CONSTITUTION DAY

• • • •

May 12
Cambodia

Background

Cambodia is the remnant of the former Khmer Republic, which once included nearly all of Indochina. In 1863 Cambodia became a protectorate of France. Independence was gained on May 12, 1953. The language of the country is Khmer, and Buddhism is the religion of nearly all Cambodians.

INDEPENDENCE DAY

• • • •

May 14
Paraguay

Background

In 1527 Sebastian Cabot, an Italian navigator in the service of Spain, was the first European to visit Paraguay. Spanish interest had been aroused by reports of silver mines and by the belief that there might be a water route through Paraguay leading to the mineral mines in the Andes. By 1537 Spanish rule was established over the Guaranis, the native tribe of the area. This rule continued until 1810 when the Paraguayans joined in the insurrections against Spain. Independence was declared on May 14, 1811.

CONSTITUTION DAY

• • • •

May 14
Philippines

Background

The first European known to have visited the Philippines was Ferdinand Magellan who reached the islands in 1521. Spanish conquest of the islands, which had been named in honor of Philip II of Spain, began in 1565. The Filipinos were quickly converted to Christianity and to a considerable degree the Roman Catholic Church dominated affairs in the Philippines for the remainder of Spanish rule. In 1898, following the Spanish-American War, the islands were ceded to the United States. The Filipinos, however, were eager to gain independence and resistance to U.S. rule led to the attainment of commonwealth status in 1935 and full independence as the Republic of the Philippines in 1946.

Activities

• Have children research the route Magellan took on this and other voyages. Give children blank world maps and have them draw the routes. If desired, this activity can be expanded to include other explorers—Hernando Cortés, Vasco Balboa, Hernando de Soto, Vasco da Gama, Ponce de León, Sebastian Cabot, and so on. Children may also be interested in listing the explorers' major "discoveries" or accomplishments.

PISTA NG ANIHAN
(Harvest Festival)

• • • •

May 15
Philippines

Background

Pista Ng Anihan, the annual Philippine harvest festival, takes place on May 15, the feast day of Saint Isidro, a twelfth-century farmer who became the patron saint of the harvest. Well in advance of the festival, homes are adorned with decorations made of fresh fruits and vegetables, and anoks, a kind of scarecrow, are displayed. At noon on May 14 church bells ring out and the festivities begin with firecrackers and bands playing. Parades feature large bamboo arches decorated with paper streamers, fruit, and candy (the children strip the arches of their treats at the close of the festival). On Pista Eve there is a dance in the plaza of the town, which is ruled over by the Pista queen and her court. On the morning of the 15th people go to church and then participate in contests, which include climbing greased poles, trying to catch greased pigs, *sips* (a form of badminton), and softball, volleyball, or basketball games with neighboring towns competing. Some small towns include ceremonies in which they honor their *carabao* (water buffalo), without which there would be no harvest, by bedecking them in ribbons and flowers and taking them to the churchyard to be blessed. In the afternoon friends and relatives gather for a feast. The festival ends that evening with a great candlelit procession, led by a statue of Saint Isidro, with the people singing and praying.

Activities

• Play one of the games that are enjoyed at the Pista Ng Anihan festival—badminton, softball, basketball, or softball.

• Talk about water buffalo and other beasts of burden and/or discuss the machinery that has replaced these animals on modern farms.

• Discuss ways in which the people of the Philippines appear to combine the celebrations of their harvest festival (May 15) and the newer holiday,

Constitution Day (May 14). Discuss why both types of holidays are such festive occasions in any culture.

- Have the children work in small groups to create arches for a parade. Give each group a hula hoop, crepe-paper streamers, construction paper, small candies wrapped in cellophane or paper, tape, and string. Have them decorate about two-thirds of the hoop leaving the bottom third bare (they can use this part to carry their "arch").

- Parade to another class. Designate children to be the queen and her court, have other students form a rhythm band, and have the remaining children carry the decorated arches. Have the queen give a short speech about the holiday then invite the other class to join yours in a game of basketball or softball. At the end of the game allow the children to strip the arches and share the candy and decorations.

CONSTITUTION DAY

• • • •

May 17
Norway

Background

Although we most closely associate the Vikings with Norse history, it is known that Norway has been inhabited since the Stone Age. Norway remained fiercely independent until 1350 when the Black Death killed between one-third and one-half of the population. Agriculture in the region took nearly two centuries to recover. In 1380 Norway entered into a union with Denmark and by the end of the sixteenth century was little more than a province of Denmark. In the following years dramatic differences of opinion and political interests arose between the two kingdoms and Norway invoked the right of self-determination. On May 17, 1814, a permanent Norwegian constitution was signed.

NATIONAL DAY

• • • •

May 22
Yemen

Background

Yemen, which is situated on the southwestern tip of what was once Arabia, was in ancient times an important trade route from Africa and Asia to the Mediterranean. For years much of the territory was dominated by the Turks while the British controlled the southern port of Aden and surrounding areas. In 1904 a boundary was established between the two regions, which then became known as North Yemen and South Yemen (Aden). The two countries merged in 1990 to become the Republic of Yemen. Both Shiite and Sunni Muslims live in Yemen and the language spoken is Arabic.

INDEPENDENCE DAY

• • • •

May 25
Jordan

Background

In 1923, following World War I and the dissolution of the Ottoman Empire, Jordan was included in the British mandate of Palestine. At that time the British recognized the independent state of Trans-Jordan, under the rule of King Abdullah ibn-Hussein, to be superintended by Great Britain. Complete independence came in 1946, following World War II, at which time the country became officially known as the Hashemite Kingdom of Jordan.

NATIONAL DAY

• • • •

May 25
Argentina

Background

The first Spaniard to explore the area, now known as Argentina was Juan Diaz de Solis in 1516. The Spanish influence spread steadily in this area, which was originally administered as part of the viceroyalty of Peru. By 1776 the importance of the area was recognized and Buenos Aires became the major city of the new and separate viceroyalty of the Rio de la Plata under which Argentina remained a colony of Spain. In May 1810, following the overthrow of the Spanish king by Napoleon, a revolution began. Although originally in the name of the Spanish king, the revolt in the La Plata colony soon became a genuine movement for independence. Independence was officially declared in 1816.

AFRICAN LIBERATION DAY

• • • •

May 25
International

Background

In 1958, delegates at the Conference of Independent African States passed a resolution declaring April 25 African Freedom Day. The intention was to create a holiday that would focus on the goal of liberation for all African nations. Unlike most holidays, this day would not center on past historical events but rather on the progress of the liberation movement as more and more African nations freed themselves from colonialism and foreign exploitation. On May 25, 1963, the Organization of African Unity (OAU) was formed. On this date delegates from the 31 independent African countries voted to change the name of African Freedom Day to African Liberation Day (ALD) and the date of its observance from April 25 to May 25. Rallies, marches, and parades typify ALD celebrations throughout Africa as well as in Russia, the United States, Canada, and Brazil.

Activities

• Compare this holiday to other celebrations of liberation or freedom. While most African nations have gained their political freedom from colonial powers, in some instances those imperialist powers still hold much influence and economic control. Compare the situation of Africans living in these countries to African Americans in the United States following emancipation.

• Have students compare current maps of Africa to older maps noting any boundary or name changes of the countries.

• Using current world maps or maps of Africa have students work in pairs or groups to list the names of the countries of Africa. Make a contest of this activity by having the groups compete to see who can find all of the countries. (There are 54 countries including the island nations.) Groups could then compete again to try to be the first to arrange the names of the countries in alphabetical order.

INDEPENDENCE DAY

• • • •

May 26
Guyana

Background

Guyana was first visited by Spanish navigators in 1498. During the sixteenth and seventeenth centuries Dutch, English, French, Portuguese, and Spanish explorers all searched the area for the legendary city of El Dorado. While the Dutch controlled the neighboring area of Suriname, the British gained control of Guyana and in 1831 a colonial administration was formed. Full independence was achieved in 1966.

REPUBLIC DAY

• • • •

May 31
South Africa

Background

South Africa became a republic on May 31, 1961, but its government remained in the hands of the white minority, which consisted of the Boers (Afrikaners) who are descendants of the Dutch and the English. Their political system of apartheid segregated blacks and forced them to live in crowded townships and "homelands." In 1989, spurred by domestic protests and international economic pressures, the government began to make reforms. By mid-1991 all apartheid legislation had been revoked.

NATIONAL DAY

• • • •

May 31
Brunei

Background

The sultanate of Brunei, a small country on the northern edge of the island of Borneo, was a powerful state that held control of all of Borneo and the adjacent islands from the sixteenth to nineteenth centuries. Decline came about as a result of internal instability and growing British influence and in 1888 a treaty was drawn up that placed Brunei under the protection of Great Britain. In 1963 it was expected that Brunei would become part of the Federation of Malaysia but the sultan decided against the move and the country remained under the protection of Great Britain. This Muslim sultanate won its independence in 1984.

6
JUNE HOLIDAYS

NONFIXED DATES

Father's Day	United States	Third Sunday
Labour Day	Bahamas	First Friday
Midsummer Festival	Scandinavia	Weekend Closest to June 24
Visakha Puja Day	Thailand, Buddhist	
Sun Dance Ceremony	Native American	June or July

FIXED DATES

June 1	Gawai Dayak	Malaysia
	(Iban New Year and Harvest Festival)	
June 2	Republic Day	Italy
June 6	National Day	Sweden
June 7	Vestalia	Ancient Rome
June 10	National Day	Portugal
June 12	National Day	Philippines
June 13	Feast of Epona	Celtic
June 14	Birth of the Muses	Ancient Greece
June 14	Flag Day	United States
June 17	National Day	Iceland
June 19	National Day	Algeria
June 19	Juneteenth	African-American
June 23	National Day	Luxombourg
June 24	St. John's Eve	International
June 26	Independence Day	Madagascar
June 26	Independence Day	Somalia
June 30	Independence Day	Zaire

JUNE HOLIDAYS WITH NONFIXED DATES

FATHER'S DAY

• • • •

Third Sunday in June
United States

Background

The first Father's Day was celebrated in 1910 in Spokane, Washington. The idea for the holiday was inspired by Mrs. John Bruce Dodd who wanted to honor her own father who, upon the death of his wife, had successfully reared, as a single parent, Mrs. Dodd and her siblings. The popularity of the holiday spread to other states but it was not until 1934 that the national custom of celebrating on the third Sunday in June was established. On this day children give cards and presents to their fathers, and adult children try to return home for a visit or at least phone their fathers. France has also adopted this holiday and the date of its celebration.

Activities

• Have the children write biographical sketches of their fathers or other males who are key figures in their lives.

• The children might make handmade cards or simple gifts for their fathers. One idea would be to have children make simple stick puppets representing the characters of a familiar story. Wrap the puppets along with a bag of popcorn and two tickets in a box. When dad chooses to cash in his tickets the child should set up a puppet theater by getting behind a chair or sofa. Two seats facing the "stage" will accommodate dad and the friend with whom he chooses to share his popcorn and theater tickets. Coupon books are another good idea for a gift (see "Parents' Day," May 8, for instructions).

• Discuss the fathers of the students in your class, their roles, and their contributions to the family. This will no doubt differ from family to family and you will want to point out that there is no one "right" answer.

• Discuss traditional two-parent families and the roles of each parent, then discuss single-parent families and the changes in the role that the single parent plays in the family. Talk about the effect on the children and the roles they play. Be sure to stress the positive as well as the negative aspects of being a part of a single-parent family. You may want to start with a hypothetical discussion of Mrs. Dodd and her childhood.

LABOUR DAY

• • • •

First Friday in June
Bahamas

Background

In the Commonwealth of the Bahamas the first Friday in June is set aside as a day to honor the labor force of the country. During the morning workers from the various trade unions march in a parade that includes floats and junkanoo bands. Following the parade a rally is held that includes speakers from political parties and from the unions. The afternoon is spent picnicking and relaxing with family and friends.

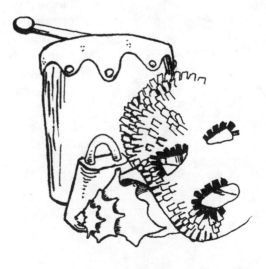

Activities

• Have your own "rally" during which the students present informational speeches about their "trade" (e.g., babysitter, newspaper carrier, lawn care, student).

- Tourism is of primary importance to the Bahamas. Have the children research the attractions of the islands and design tourist brochures.

- Celebrate by making and eating a tropical fruit salad. Include bananas, pineapple, citrus fruits, and any other fresh tropical fruits that are available.

- For other activities see "Labor Day," September.

MIDSUMMER FESTIVAL

• • • •

Weekend Closest to June 24
Scandinavia

Background

In Scandinavian countries the Midsummer Festival, most festive of the summer celebrations, actually takes place at the start, not in the middle, of summer. The festival occurs at the time when summer days are at their longest; in the north it is the time of the midnight sun. Midsummer's Eve and Midsummer's Day have been celebrated since pagan times. Although the Midsummer celebration remained a festive time, with the advent of Christianity many of the pagan customs had to be incorporated into the new religion. The celebration continued, but was now observed on June 24, St. John's Day, in honor of St. John the Baptist instead of the pagan gods. In Sweden the two celebrations have been separated, St. John's Day maintaining its June 24 date and Midsummer's Day being celebrated on the Saturday closest to St. John's Day.

The Midsummer Festival is a celebration of summer and of the fertility of Mother Earth. In Sweden and parts of Finland people erect and dance around maypoles. Bonfires are lit and homes are decorated with flower garlands, greenery, and tree branches. It is not uncommon for people to stay up all night dancing, visiting with family and friends, eating specially prepared foods, and performing some of the ancient rites (today done mostly for fun!) to assure prosperity or fertility of livestock and fields, or to determine one's future spouse. Ancient tradition included the belief that dew gathered on Midsummer's Night had special curative properties and that this was the one night of the year when ferns would blossom. Foods for the occasion include pickled herring, new potatoes boiled with fresh dill, dairy products, and fresh strawberries. When they finally tumble into bed, many young women (and men) sleep with a bouquet of nine different wildflowers, a copper coin, or a four-leaf clover under their pillows in hopes that they will dream about their future mate. (See also "St. John's Eve," June 24.)

Activities

- Give each child a penny to sleep on for "homework." The following day have them write about their dreams as a creative writing assignment. (Those who do not remember their dreams may be given a few minutes to daydream before starting to write.)

- Study the rotation of Earth with an emphasis on why some countries have daylight 24 hours a day during part of the summer and no sunlight at all for part of the winter.

- Do a lesson on wildflowers. Discuss the definitions of "flowers" and "weeds" (desired and unwanted plants).

- Study ferns and other plants that never bloom.

VISAKHA PUJA DAY

• • • •

Thailand, Buddhist

Background

Visakha Puja Day is a triple anniversary of events that took place in the life of Lord Buddha. It is believed that Buddha was born on the fifteenth day of the waxing moon in the sixth lunar month (which usually falls in our month of June). He is believed to have attained his enlightenment exactly 35 years later on the same date, and to have died, also on the same date, at the age of 80. Buddha founded a way of life based on *Metta*, loving kindness. Through *Metta* it is believed that one can overcome anger through love, evil through good, and untruth through truth. On this official and sacred holiday Thais extend the spirit of *Metta* to all the peoples of the world, wishing peace and abundance to all. Religious ceremonies are held and in the evening throngs of people can be seen circling the temples of the Buddhist monasteries carrying flowers and lighted candles or joss sticks. (See also "Hanamatsun," April 8.)

Activities

- Briefly discuss the teachings of Buddha. Have the children work in groups to describe instances when anger can be overcome by love, evil by good, or lies by truth. Have them share and discuss their examples with the whole group. Compare Buddha to other leaders who taught peace, for example Mohandas Gandhi or Martin Luther King Jr.

- Review the phases of the moon and introduce "waxing" (growing larger) and "waning" (growing smaller) into the children's vocabularies.

- While discussing this holiday, burn some incense to simulate the smell of joss sticks.

SUN DANCE CEREMONY

• • • •

June or July
Native American

Background

The timing of the Sun Dance Ceremony is determined in different ways by different tribes, but it is always held during the summer, frequently around the time of the full moon in June or July. It honors the sun, the most notable manifestation of the Great Mystery, bearer of light and life. This ceremony, performed primarily by Plains Indians, is probably the best known and least understood of all Native American rites because of the voluntary suffering of some of the participants.

This aspect of the ceremony is performed because of the belief that the Great Mystery gave us all things and that when one wants to give thanks or ask for help the only offering that a human has to give is his or her own body and blood. The candidates who participate in the Sun Dance do so to avert disaster, to help an ailing relative or friend, to gain spiritual power, or because of a pledge made during a time of adversity. These candidates go without food or water for days, and sometimes make offerings of small pieces of their own skin or flesh cut from their arms or shoulders. In some cases even more severe physical ordeals are undertaken.

The Sun Dance Ceremony can last from eight to fifteen days. During the first days of the ceremony the candidates are given instruction while other participants feast and dance. Whistles made of eagle wing bones—representative of the voice of the Thunderbird and spotted eagle, who flew closer to the kingdom of the Great Mystery than any other creature—are blown to call in the spirits. A sacred tree is cut down, stripped of its branches and bark, and erected in the center of the ceremonial area. A sweat lodge is erected for the purification rites of the candidates. Warriors, wearing special costumes and with bodies painted, dance while a special Sun Dance pipe is smoked. Drumming and many different dances, including the Sun Dance which lasts a full 24 hours, from one dawn to the next, are significant parts of the ceremony.

Activities

- Study Native Americans from both a historical and current point of view.

- Study the sun as a source of energy. Discuss how it relates to all sources of energy (oil, coal, wood, etc.) on Earth.

- Read and discuss tales from Native American folklore. Have the children select their own animal fetishes and write stories about them.

- Native Americans consider dreams and visions to be sacred messages. Have the children tell or write about their dreams and discuss whether or not they think their dreams contained any symbolism.

JUNE HOLIDAYS WITH FIXED DATES

GAWAI DAYAK
(Iban New Year and Harvest Festival)
• • • •
June 1
Malaysia

Background

Gawai Dayak (or Dyak) is the most important holiday celebrated in the state of Sarawak in the Republic of Malaysia. Its significance is threefold—it marks the gathering of the rice harvest, proclaims the beginning of the new planting season and hence the new year, and is also religious in nature. It is believed that during this time spirits of evil and ill omen are present and must be appeased to ensure a good harvest for the coming year. Ceremonies are held at midnight on the eve of Gawai Dayak to ask the gods for their blessings. The day itself is marked with family reunions, singing and dancing, feasting, games, and public entertainment.

Activities

- Harvest festivals in different countries occur year-round. Make a timeline for one year and mark different festivals on it along with the name of the country in which each is celebrated.

- To honor the rice harvest, have the children draw with ink on rice paper. Rice paper, pens, ink, and books on beginning calligraphy are all available through art supply stores.

REPUBLIC DAY
• • • •
June 2
Italy

Background

In the eighteenth century, control of much of Italy lay with Austria, France, and Spain. Unification of the peninsula came about with the fall of the French empire in 1870. This Roman Catholic nation was declared a republic on June 2, 1946.

NATIONAL DAY
• • • •
June 6
Sweden

Background

In the early sixteenth century Sweden's independence was threatened by the king of Denmark, Christian II. With his troops he occupied Stockholm in 1520 and beheaded 80 Swedish noblemen in what came to be known as the "Stockholm Blood Bath." Gustavus (Gustav) Eriksson Vasa, whose father had been among those executed by the Danes, led a revolt that drove the Danes out of Sweden and put an end to the union of the two countries. On June 6, 1523, Gustav Vasa was formally elected king of Sweden, and to this day June 6 remains the national holiday of the country.

VESTALIA
• • • •
June 7
Ancient Rome

Background

No longer celebrated, this holiday was once held in honor of the Roman fire goddess, Vesta. Prior to the day of the celebration, old branches were cleared from the altars, and the vestal virgins cleaned and beautified the temple in preparation. (At that time the term virgin meant "one within," hence the vestal virgins were the priestesses within the temple.) During the festival the innermost sacred spaces of the temples were open to all priestesses who would pray and perform rituals. No men were ever permitted to participate. The priestesses would also travel to rivers to throw small images of people into the water as a sacrifice to the gods. The first fruits of the grain harvest were prepared by the priestesses and offered in the temples, and bakers and millers were honored.

Activities

• Compare this holiday to the Native American Green Corn Ceremony (see August).

• Most of the Roman gods and goddesses were based on or had counterparts in Greek deities. Vesta, goddess of the hearth and keeper of the fire on Mt. Olympus, for example, was known to the Greeks as Hestia. Have children research Greek gods or goddesses in order to be able to tell who they were and what they were called by the Romans. The following list gives names of Greek gods and goddesses followed by the Roman names:

Zeus/Jupiter (king of the gods)
Hera/Juno (queen of heaven, wife and sister of Zeus)
Poseidon/Neptune (god of the sea)
Hades or Pluto/Orcus (god of the underworld)
Hestia/Vesta (goddess of the hearth fire)
Demeter/Ceres (goddess of the harvest)
Artemis/Diana (goddess of the hunt)
Apollo/Apollo (god of light, healing, music, and poetry)
Athena/Minerva (goddess of wisdom)
Aphrodite/Venus (goddess of love and beauty)
Eros/Cupid (god of erotic love)
Hephaestus/Vulcan (god of fire, metalworking, and handicrafts)
Ares/Mars (god of war)
Dionysus/Bacchus (god of wine)
Hermes/Mercury (messenger of the gods)

If you wish to go one step further, examine the relationships of the gods and goddesses—most were related to Zeus in one way or another.

• Make some bread or rolls. Have the students figure how many loaves or rolls will be needed for the whole class; halve, double, or triple the recipe as needed and measure the ingredients. (See Appendix B, "United States," for recipe.)

• Honor the goddess Vesta by showing your respect for fire. Review fire safety rules, emergency phone numbers, and/or fire drill procedures.

• Read and discuss stories from Roman or Greek mythology. (See Appendix A, "Greek Mythology," for books written at a level children can enjoy.)

• Study the production of a loaf of bread from the

farm to the grocery store. If desired, children may choose another product and research where it comes from and the people involved.

• Take a field trip to a commercial bakery or to a grist mill.

NATIONAL DAY

• • • •

June 10
Portugal

Background

The area now known as Portugal was once called Lusitania, named after the Lusitanians, a Celtic people who settled there sometime prior to 1000 B.C. The Portuguese language is derived from Latin, a result of the Roman conquest by Julius and Augustus Caesar. During the fifth century the entire Iberian Peninsula was overrun by the German Visigoths who in turn were defeated in 711 by the Moors. The Moors were driven out during the Christian reconquest in the eleventh and twelfth centuries, and the independent nation of Portugal, with Alfonso I as its first king, was established. Portugal's independence was recognized by Spain in 1143 and by the pope in 1179.

NATIONAL DAY

• • • •

June 12
Philippines

Background

In 1521 Ferdinand Magellan first landed in the Philippines, and in 1565 it became a colony of Spain. Spanish rule lasted for 333 years until June 12, 1898, when General Emilio Aguinaldo declared independence. For the next 48 years the Philippines was a colony of the United States; during World War II the Filipinos fought side by side with Americans against the Japanese invaders. On July 4, 1946, at the close of the war, the United States granted independence to the Philippines. As a part of this celebration there is a wreath-laying ceremony at the monument of the nation's hero, José P. Rizal, a martyr to the cause of freedom. In addition there is a large parade with the president in attendance, and during the afternoon the music of local entertainers fills the air at free public concerts.

FEAST OF EPONA

• • • •

June 13
Celtic

Background

The Celts worshipped Epona, the horse goddess, from the time of the Iron Age. In ancient Hungary and other parts of central Europe she was portrayed as a magical white horse who would appear on Earth to transport her shamans to the spirit world. Whether depicted as a woman with a horse's head or in her animal form of the horse, Epona represented agriculture, the tool of the warrior, and transportation.

Activities

- Discuss the importance of the horse in ancient civilizations and the things that have replaced horses in modern times in the areas of agriculture, transportation, and warfare.

- Research and read about mythological creatures that were part human and part animal. Have the children make up their own mythological creatures and write about them.

BIRTH OF THE MUSES

• • • •

June 14
Ancient Greece

Background

The ancient Greeks believed that on this date the goddess Mnemosyne (memory) gave birth to nine daughters, the Muses. They were Calliope (epic song), Euterpe (lyric song), Polyhymnia (sacred song), Thalia (comedy), Melpomene (tragedy), Terpsichore (dance), Erato (poetry), Clio (history), and Urania (astronomy). The Muses brought creativity, inspiration, and an appreciation of the arts into the world as well as a basis for social and scientific studies.

Activities

- Have the students work in groups to organize and create a project of their choosing. They should first choose one of the Muses and then, depending on which Muse they chose, write songs, poetry, or plays; choreograph a dance; or do a presentation on a part of history or astronomy. When everyone's project is complete the groups can participate in a class talent show. (If desired you may limit the scope of the projects to fit in with your current unit of study.)

FLAG DAY

• • • •

June 14
United States

Background

Flag Day marks the anniversary of the adoption of the flag by the Continental Congress of the United States on June 14, 1777. It is celebrated with ceremonies and through the display of the flag and is a legal holiday in some states.

Activities

• Read and discuss a biography of Betsy Ross.

• Examine a replica of the original flag with its thirteen stars and study the changes that occurred as new states joined the union. Have the children research to determine whether your state was one of the original colonies or, if not, when it joined the union.

• What will happen if Washington, D.C., or Puerto Rico achieves statehood? Have the students design a new canton for the flag containing 51 stars in a symmetrical pattern.

• Children can learn about fractions and patterns while making a flag to display at home. Give each child a sheet of red paper and a half sheet (cut the long way) of white paper. Fold the white sheets the long way in half then in thirds. When you open up the paper it forms six parts. Cut into strips along the fold lines, position on red paper, and glue in place to form red and white stripes of the American flag. Next give each child a grid on white paper (about one-fourth the size of the sheet of red paper) marked off in eleven squares by ten squares. Have them draw stars in alternating squares (six on the first line of eleven, five on the second line, then

six, then five, etc.). Color around the stars with a blue crayon and glue this "field" onto the top left corner of the striped paper to form a flag.

NATIONAL DAY

• • • •

June 17
Iceland

Background

Although Irish monks, arriving before the ninth century, were the first known visitors to what is now known as Iceland, they abandoned the island when Norse settlers arrived. Iceland became a feudal state that eventually came under the rule of Norway. In 1380 Iceland, along with Norway, passed under the rule of

the Danish crown. During the time in which the Danes ruled, Lutheranism, which remains the principal religion of the country, was imposed on the Icelanders by force. In 1918 Iceland became a sovereign state in personal union to Denmark. The union was terminated 26 years later by overwhelming popular vote and Iceland was proclaimed an independent republic on June 17, 1944.

NATIONAL DAY

• • • •

June 19
Algeria

Background

Algeria, situated on the northern coast of Africa, was first settled by Phoenicians, then by the Romans. During the seventh and eighth centuries Muslim Arabs conquered the country and ousted the Romans. In the late fifteenth century Spain captured the coastal cities and expelled the Muslims. At this point the Algerians appealed to Turkish pirates for help and with the aid of the Ottoman Empire ended Spanish rule. Privateering became rampant along the coast until France imposed a naval blockade and, in 1830, invaded the country. In 1848 Algeria was declared a French territory. The French disenfranchised the indigenous Muslim people and administered control of Algeria under civil departments in Paris. In 1954 Algeria rebelled. A million lives were lost and a million French colonists left the country before independence was declared on June 19, 1962.

JUNETEENTH

• • • •

June 19
African American

Background

Because President Lincoln's Emancipation Proclamation of January 1, 1863, only outlawed slavery in the eleven states that had seceded from the Union, Congress passed the Thirteenth Amendment, which abolished slavery throughout all of the United States and territories subject to its jurisdiction, on January 31, 1865. The Civil War ended in April of that year, but it was not until June 19, 1865, that word of their freedom reached African-American slaves in Texas. The word "Juneteenth" is derived from this June 19 date. While many people believe that this should be a national holiday in celebration of freedom, that is not currently the case and emancipation or freedom celebrations are observed on a wide variety of dates throughout the country based mainly on the date when news of emancipation reached the particular area. (For more information and a list of activities see "Emancipation Day," January 1.)

NATIONAL DAY

• • • •

June 23
Luxembourg

Background

Once part of the Holy Roman Empire, Luxembourg has also been, at various times, under the control of Spain, Austria, and France. The 1814–15 Congress of Vienna made Luxembourg a grand duchy in union with the Netherlands. In 1830 when Belgium rebelled against William I of the Netherlands, Luxembourg joined in the revolt. Independence was gained on June 23, 1839.

ST. JOHN'S EVE

• • • •

June 24
International

Background

Like other celebrations St. John's Eve, also known as Midsummer's Eve, combines both pagan and Christian aspects. While it commemorates the date of the death of St. John the Baptist it also is a celebration of the summer solstice, the longest day of the year. In different countries the celebration takes on varied characteristics. In Haiti it has traditionally been a celebration of the voodoo cult. In Poland people used to light bonfires in the shape of the cross, but this tradition has given way to setting small wreaths topped with candles afloat in the Vistula River. Following this ritual there is usually a parade of decorated boats, feasting and dancing, and a fireworks display. In Brazil, St. John's Day is the foundation of the Festas Junina (June parties). The Festas Junina are highlighted by games and dances with prizes, rural costumes, food booths, hot air balloons, and a mock shotgun wedding. The festivals are often sponsored by schools, churches, or community groups to raise money for charity.

In the Nordic countries of Denmark, Sweden, and Norway, bonfires, symbolic of the power of the sun, are lit on hilltops and sometimes livestock are driven between two such fires in a cleansing ritual designed to ensure the good health of the animals. Circle dances, singing, and joyous celebration also characterize this holiday. It is a day for lovers, as well as a day when fairies and ghosts walk the face of the earth.

Activities

- Learn a circle dance. A simple dance that even young children can participate in, and which works well with almost any kind of music, is the Spiral Dance. Participants stand in a circle holding hands. As the music starts the circle begins to move with the dancers swaying, bouncing, or skipping to the beat. Once everyone is moving together the leader lets go of the hand of the person in front of him and walks past that person on the inside leading the line around and around in a spiral until he reaches the center of the circle. The leader then turns and starts back out of the spiral, walking between the two rows of people who are moving inward. If everyone continues to hold hands throughout the dance you will end up back in a circle, but this time facing outward! (It is best to have an adult lead the dance, because children tend to go too fast, people have difficulty holding hands, and there can be a "whip" effect at the end of the line.)

- Do a lesson on gases. Study what causes helium and/or hot air balloons to rise.

- It is now illegal to release helium-filled balloons during the Festas Junina in Brazil. Discuss the ecological reasons for this decision.

- Plan and carry out a fair or festival to celebrate summer and to raise money for a school project or favorite charity.

INDEPENDENCE DAY

• • • •

June 26
Madagascar

Background

It is estimated that the island of Madagascar broke off from the continent of Africa 165 million years ago. The first settlers of the island were from Africa and Indonesia. Diego Dias, a Portuguese navigator, was probably the first European to see the island in the year 1500. Shortly after this both Portugal and France sent missionaries to Madagascar and established footholds on the island. Years later, in 1883, the French attacked the Malagasy people for the first time and, in 1885, established a French protectorate on the island. By 1904 the French had full control. After several major uprisings against the French, Madagascar gained full independence on June 26, 1960.

INDEPENDENCE DAY

• • • •

June 26
Somalia

Background

Immigrant Muslim Persians and Arabs set up trading posts in the area now known as Somalia between the seventh and tenth centuries. British and Italian imperialism played an active role during the 1800s, with a part of this area becoming a British protectorate while another section became a colony of Italy. During World War II Britain overtook Italian Somaliland and ruled until 1950 when the entire area, renamed Somalia, was made a United Nations trust territory. Independence was awarded on June 26, 1960. Somali is the official language of this Sunni Muslim nation but Arabic, Italian, and English are also in use.

INDEPENDENCE DAY

• • • •

June 30
Zaire

Background

The indigenous people of Zaire are believed to have been the pygmies, but as early as the first century members of the Bantu tribe began moving into the area and by the year 1000 had settled most of the area and significantly reduced the area inhabited by the pygmies. The Bantu had a complex system of government, which was organized into a number of states. The first European to visit the area was a Portuguese explorer who, in 1482, discovered the mouth of the Congo River and sailed up the river for several miles. During the late 1870s King Leopold II of Belgium colonized the area and established the Congo Free State with himself as the head. The Africans were treated poorly and in 1908 the parliament of Belgium voted to annex the area and renamed it the Belgian Congo. Conditions improved slightly but by the 1930s nationalism had begun to grow. This culminated in rioting in 1959 during which Belgium lost control of events in the area. On June 30, 1960, the Belgian Congo became independent. The name of the country was changed to Zaire in 1971.

Activities

• Madagascar, Somalia, and Zaire all gained their independence in late June of 1960. Assign children two African nations each (there are more than 50) and have them research to find the year in which independence was gained and the country that ruled the land prior to independence. Graph the results. Discuss colonialism as it related to Africa.

7

JULY HOLIDAYS

NONFIXED DATES

Alp Feast	Switzerland
Asalaha Puja Day/Buddhist Lent	Buddhist

FIXED DATES

July 1	Dominion Day	Canada
July 1–First Monday in August	Crop Over Festival	Barbados
July 4	Independence Day (Fourth of July)	United States
July 7	Tanabata Matsuri (Star Festival)	Japan, Korea
July 9	Youth Day	Morocco
July 10	Independence Day	Bahamas
July 12	Orangemen's Day	Northern Ireland
July 13	Celebration of Our Lady of Fátima	Portugal
July 13–15	Bon Festival	Japan, Buddhist
July 14	Bastille Day	France
July 17	Festival of Amaterasu-o-Mi-Kami	Japan
July 20	Independence Day	Colombia
July 21	National Day	Belgium
July 23	Birth of Haile Selassie I	Rastafarian
July 24	Pioneer Day	Mormon
July 25	St. Christopher's Day	Roman Catholic
July 25	Constitution Day	Puerto Rico
July 26	Independence Day	Liberia
July 28	Independence Day	Peru

JULY HOLIDAYS WITH NONFIXED DATES

ALP FEAST

• • • •

Switzerland

Background

The Alp Feast, also known as the Feast of St. Jacob (Christian saint of herdsmen and the harvest), is celebrated in midsummer throughout the Swiss Alps with music, dancing, religious services, feasting, and unique athletic competitions. Participants, many wearing traditional costumes, enjoy listening to the yodeling and blowing of the ancient alphorn. Entertainment includes wrestling matches called *Schwingen* held in alpine arenas covered with sawdust, and contests to see who can throw heavy stones the farthest. The celebration of the Alp Feast is an opportunity for city dwellers and country folk to mingle and get to know and appreciate one another.

Activities

• Do a unit on horns beginning with the alphorn and other ancient instruments such as the conch shell and ram's horn.

• Listen to traditional Swiss music, alphorns, and/or yodeling.

• The *Schwingen* matches and stone-throwing contests are probably a bit strenuous for children, but why not modify them? Try arm wrestling or finger wres-

tling and throwing playground balls for distance instead.

• Compare city and country life and discuss their interdependence.

• For additional activities related to Switzerland see "Federal Thanksgiving Day," "National Day," August 1 and September 20.

ASALAHA PUJA DAY/ BUDDHIST LENT

• • • •

Buddhist

Background

Asalaha Puja Day is the celebration of the date in 528 B.C. when Siddhartha Gautama, a wandering monk who later came to be known as the Buddha (the Enlightened One), first attained enlightenment. Also on this day, which falls on the full moon of the month of Asalaha (the eighth lunar month), Lord Buddha preached the sermon that outlined his teachings and ordained the first of his disciples. Because all three things—the Buddha, his teachings, and his disciples—came into existence on the same day this day is also known as the Day of the Triple Gem. On this day all Buddhists perform acts of merit. Many go to monasteries to offer money and/or food to the monks and to listen to the sermon.

The day following Asalaha Puja Day begins the three-monthlong Buddhist Lent, which, in Southeast Asia, lasts throughout the rainy season. Special Lenten candles are lit and religious services are held. During Lent monks are confined closely to their monasteries, and the gifts of food and money offered on Asalaha Puja Day are used to help them through this period. The Lenten time has become a period of special study and instruction for those who have chosen to enter the priesthood. Lent ends with the Kathin Ceremony, usually sometime in our month of September (see September for more information).

Activities

• Learn about monsoons and the rainy season in Southeast Asia. Discuss why, during the Buddha's time, staying in one place during this time of the year was safer and healthier for the monks.

- Using the Buddhist's Lenten candles as a starting place, discuss the symbolism of light over darkness in religion, literature, and/or art. Have children find examples of such symbolism and write about them.

- Discuss the importance and uses of candles before the invention of electricity and the reasons we use candles today. Make candles (materials and instructions are available at most craft stores).

- Burn incense. Bring in some lotus flowers. Both have strong religious links with Buddhism and both are symbols of tranquility and inner peace.

JULY HOLIDAYS WITH FIXED DATES

DOMINION DAY

• • • •

July 1
Canada

Background

In 1497 John Cabot, an English explorer, became the first European to reach the coast of Canada. In 1535 Jacques Cartier led an expedition up the St. Lawrence River for France, and by the seventeenth century both countries were established in the area and benefiting from the lucrative fur trade. During the eighteenth century the two countries fought a series of wars end-ing with the English winning all of Canada at the conclusion of the Seven Years' War in 1763. Nevertheless, the French settlers of Quebec were allowed to retain their language, customs, and religion; Canada thus became a bicultural country. On July 1, 1867, the British Parliament passed a bill allowing Canada to govern itself, whereupon the Dominion of Canada—then consisting of Quebec, Ontario, New Brunswick, and Nova Scotia—came into existence. Since that time six more provinces—Saskatchewan, Alberta, Manitoba, British Columbia, Prince Edward Island, and Newfoundland—as well as the Yukon Territory and the Northwest Territory have joined the Dominion. Celebrations of Dominion Day are much like our Fourth of July celebrations: They feature fireworks, concerts, and outdoor contests and activities.

Activities

- Recently there was a successful movement in Canada to make English the official language of the entire country. Have the students stage a debate with one side in favor of this move and the other side expressing the desire of the French Canadians to maintain their language.

- Like the rest of the Americas, Canada was inhabited before the period of colonization. Study the Native American tribes indigenous to Canada and compare their lifestyles to those of the Native Americans in the United States.

- Canada is our neighbor to the north and it is very likely that some of the students in your class will visit the country at some point. Find the exchange rate for U.S. and Canadian dollars and have the students convert prices of different articles from one country to the other.

CROP OVER FESTIVAL

• • • •

July 1
Barbados

Background

This harvest festival was revived in 1974 and is currently celebrated on a grand scale. Crop Over originated during the time when the sugar industry dominated life in Barbados. During those years, when the growing, cutting, and transporting of the sugarcane to the mills was completed (the "crop" was "over") the enslaved workers were given time off to dress up, adorn with garlands the animals who had helped them in their labors, and enjoy dancing and music. Today Crop Over consists of a full month of celebrations. Street fairs abound and there is music, dancing, and feasting. Special events include sugarcane cutting contests and calypso competition. The winners of the calypso competition are crowned king and queen. Children also participate in a calypso competition and there, too, a king and queen are chosen. On the final day of the festival there is a grand parade with prizes given for the best costumes, the finest steel band, and other honors (see "Kadooment Day," August).

Activities

• Instead of setting up a "class store" this year to practice working with money, why not try a street fair? Students can work cooperatively in groups to invent and create games, letter signs, and write out game rules, advertisements, and prices to post on their booths. On the day of the fair give each child a set amount of real or fake money. The children will have to make decisions about budgeting their money, making change, etc. Students might take turns participating and running the booths. If possible, have steel drum music or calypso tunes playing in the background.

• If you want to get elaborate set up a food booth as well. The day before the fair children can practice their reading and measurement skills as they follow recipes to prepare the food.

• Steel drums are endemic to Barbados and nearby islands. Study drums from different parts of the world, what they are made of, and how they are alike or different. Use desktops to tap out different drumbeats.

• Make your own mini steel drums. Have the cafeteria or a local restaurant save you the large cans that vegetables and sauces come in. Tape around the opened end with duct tape to cover any rough edges and avoid injuries. Tap on the bottom of the can with a ball peen hammer to make dents. Cut the handle off an old broom and hold it inside the can with the rounded end touching the bottom of the can. Tap with a hammer to make dents from this side. These dents will change not only the contour of the can's bottom but its tone as well. Experiment with different cans and on different areas of the same can. Turn cans over and tap out rhythms with drumsticks or dowel rods.

INDEPENDENCE DAY
(Fourth of July)

• • • •

July 4
United States

Background

The first settlement in what would become the United States was founded at Jamestown, Virginia, in 1607. The population of the New World grew steadily and by the mid-seventeenth century there were thirteen colonies of England established along the East Coast. England did not really interfere with its American colonies until the 1760s when it decided to impose taxes on such goods as tea, paper, and glass. The colonists were deeply resentful of this, and their resentment culminated in the Boston Tea Party of December 1773.

The British retaliated by sending troops to Boston and further impinging on the rights of the citizenry. In September 1774 the First Continental Congress met in Philadelphia, Pennsylvania. Although the Congress was upset with British policies, they still considered themselves subjects of England and, in an attempt to get the English Parliament to change its policies, they drew up a declaration of rights. The British were unmoved by this action and conditions worsened. By the time the Second Continental Congress met in 1776 the colonists wanted independence and a committee was appointed to draft a declaration of independence. This document, written primarily by Thomas Jefferson, was approved and signed at the State House (later renamed Independence Hall) in Philadelphia on July 4, 1776. The Philadelphians, upon hearing that the Congress had voted in favor of independence, went wild. The Liberty Bell rang out the news, and as word spread throughout the colonies, bonfires were lit and celebration broke out everywhere. Americans have celebrated with fireworks, picnics, and parades every year since that date.

Activities

- Read the first two paragraphs of the Declaration of Independence. Discuss or have the children restate the meaning. Discuss why independence is important to people and when and why they are ready to fight for it.

- Have children research and write about the people and events leading up to the signing of the Declaration of Independence from a newscaster's point of view. Videotape their newscasts or print their reports in the form of a newspaper.

- Discuss the essence of the Declaration of Independence from the children's viewpoint. What does "life, liberty, and the pursuit of happiness" mean to An eight year old? An eighteen year old? Balance the discussion by talking about the responsibilities that go along with their growing individual liberty and independence. After students have had time to formulate their ideas invite a local newscaster or newspaper reporter to come and interview the children or, if this is not feasible, have the children interview each other.

- Cover a portion of the room with newspaper and let the students go wild as they create pictures of fireworks displays by dripping or spattering paint on their papers.

- Considering that horses were the main form of transportation then, have the children estimate how long it would have taken the news of the signing of the Declaration of Independence to reach people in Boston, Williamsburg, or the city where you live.

TANABATA MATSURI
(Star Festival)

• • • •

July 7
Japan, Korea

Background

This festival originated from an old Chinese belief that the star Vega, the weaver girl, is separated from her lover, Aquila, the shepherd boy, by the Milky Way and that they only meet once a year, on the seventh day of the seventh month. This is a night for wishing on stars. In Japan and Korea the people, especially the children, hang colorful cut paper decorations and long strips of white paper inscribed with written poems or wishes on bamboo poles, trees, and bushes. The colorful decorations represent prayers for advanced learning, particularly in the arts of calligraphy, weaving, and dressmaking. This is also a night for lovers, and some people write the names of their lovers on the strips of paper or parchment for the stars to see.

Activities

- Have the children brainstorm a list of superstitions (wishing on stars, throwing spilled salt over one's shoulder, avoiding black cats, etc.). Each child may then choose one and write an original "myth" about how the superstition originated.

- Relate the legend of Vega to the lore of other cultures regarding stars and constellations, such as the stories from Greek mythology of Orion, Cassiopeia, and Gemini and the Native American tales of "Oot-Kwah-Tah, the Seven Star Dancers" and "How Grizzly Bear Climbed the Mountain." The Greek stories can be found in *The Macmillan Book of Greek Gods and Heroes* and the Native American stories in *Keepers of the Night*. (See Appendix A for more information on these books.)

- Try some simple calligraphy or make cut paper decorations.

- Study the constellations and find out how they got their names.

YOUTH DAY

• • • •

July 9
Morocco

Background

July 9 is the day for Morocco's national holiday of Youth Day. Work is suspended and people take time to enjoy, celebrate, and honor youth. Children get many forms of special treatment and a festive atmosphere characterizes the day.

Activities

- Have the children imagine that they are going to take a trip to Morocco for the Youth Day celebration. After doing some research on the country they might make travel posters, plan an itinerary, and/or compute the cost of the trip.

- Have the children consider the question of why society would honor its youth. Discuss the contributions of the young and the responsibilities they must take on to prepare themselves for adulthood. Bring the discussion to a personal level by having children talk about contributions they make to their family, community, or school.

INDEPENDENCE DAY

• • • •

July 10
Bahamas

Background

In 1492 Columbus first landed in the New World at San Salvador in the Bahamas and claimed the islands for Spain, but they were not colonized until the English arrived in the mid-seventeenth century. The islands exchanged hands and governments several times and on July 10, 1973, the Bahamas finally became a sovereign state within the British Commonwealth of Nations.

ORANGEMEN'S DAY

• • • •

July 12
Northern Ireland

Background

Orangemen are members of the Loyal Orange Institution, a Protestant Irish organization founded in 1795 to preserve the Protestant domination of Ireland. The Institution was named after King William III of England (William of Orange) who defeated the Catholic King James II at the Battle of the Boyne near Drogheda, Ireland, in 1690. The anniversary of King William's victory, July 12, is celebrated yearly by Protestants in Northern Ireland with the wearing of orange sashes and boutonnieres and by marching in boisterous parades.

Activities

- Have the children count off by twos to divide them into two arbitrary groups. Have one group represent the Catholics, the other the Protestants. Have the students close their eyes while you describe a rowdy Orangemen's Day parade marching through a Bogside (Catholic) community. Let each side tell how they felt about the celebration, then let each side choose representatives to meet, discuss, and try to solve the Irish "troubles."

- One of the unique elements of the Orangemen's Day parade is the huge lambeg drum upon which the participants beat. Beat on a drum and discuss the feelings that it arouses. Then listen to recordings of other instruments and examine the emotions that they call forth. Have the children choose stories they have written and then select the type of music they would like to have as background if they were making the story into a movie. If desired, the children can read their stories while you play music. Older children could record their stories while playing musical selections in the background for their friends to listen to at a later time.

- Research the role drums have played in war and in peacetime military ceremonies.

CELEBRATION OF OUR LADY OF FÁTIMA

• • • •

July 13
Portugal

Background

Between May 13 and October 13, 1917, the Virgin Mary is reported to have appeared on six different occasions to three shepherd children in the small village of Fátima, Portugal. During these visitations she is said to have given them instructions for building a shrine in her honor for the healing of the sick. Following this, Fátima became a great center of pilgrimage for Roman Catholics from around the world. In 1944 a grand basilica was built in Fátima.

Activities

- Do a unit on architecture using ancient and modern temples, mosques, and cathedrals.

- Research and study pilgrimages made by different groups from ancient to current times and the reasons for the pilgrimages.

- Discuss traditional medicine, alternative medicine, and faith healing and the pros and cons of each. Allow for and accept differences of opinion.

BON FESTIVAL

• • • •

July 13–15
Japan, Buddhist

Background

This festival, known as the Feast of the Dead, All Souls' Day, and the Feast of the Lanterns, as well as the more common Bon Festival, has been celebrated by Buddhists in Japan for 1,400 years. It is a time to honor and remember one's ancestors and the deeds they performed during their lifetimes. Gravesides are visited, incense burned, and lanterns lit to lead the spirits of the dead "home." Upon arrival back at the house the spirits are met with welcoming fires, altars set up in their memory, and dishes of the foods that were their favorites when they were alive. Homes remain lit all night long and members of the family speak with the spirits as if they were actually present in the flesh. This is a solemn but happy holiday that ends with a dance, the Bon Odori, on the night of July 15.

Activities

- Have the children choose a historical personage whom they admire, and write, in dialogue form, a

conversation they would like to have with that person.

- Compare this holiday to El Dia de los Muertos in Mexico (see November 1–2).

- Involve parents in helping students to learn stories of their own ancestors and personal heritage. Discuss the oral tradition and have students retell their stories to the class.

- Have children trace their family's heritage and draw their own family "gardens." This is less limiting than a family tree and works better in today's society where many children have been adopted, have parents who have remarried, or live with an extended family. It also allows for greater creativity. In the garden different family members can be represented by trees, bushes, or flowers. Various sizes or colors of plants and flowers can be used, and flowers or plants can be clustered to show relationships.

BASTILLE DAY

• • • •

July 14
France

Background

Some of the oldest archaeological finds in the world have been discovered in France, yet little is known about the area prior to the first century B.C. when the Roman conquest took place. The history of France as a separate nation began in 987 with the ascendance of Hugh Capet, first of the Capetian kings. France remained a monarchy for more than 800 years. By the late eighteenth century a strong feeling of independence was developing in the country. France had aided the United States in its war for independence against England and the French people were eager for a government similar to what the Americans had attained. Many of the concepts behind the French Revolution were outlined in a document called the Declaration of the Rights of Man and Citizen, which was quite similar to the American Declaration of Independence and Bill of Rights.

On July 14, 1789, an angry mob attacked the Bastille, a huge fortress and state prison in Paris, which had become a symbol of absolutism and the monarchy. The governor was killed and seven inmates set free. The storming of the Bastille marked the beginning of the French Revolution. Although the French people had to wait for nearly a century to secure a stable democratic government, Bastille Day is still considered to be the day on which the first strike for freedom was made and is celebrated yearly with fireworks, parades, music, and dancing in the streets.

Activities

- In actuality the Bastille was used primarily for prisoners of influence and the treatment of political inmates was not especially harsh; but symbolically, to the French people, it was a place of horror. Research and discuss the Bastille in fact and symbolically.

- Study the economic and political issues that led up to the French Revolution.

- Compare the Declaration of Independence to the Rights of Man and Citizen.

- Learn to count in French or examine some French words or phrases that have been adopted into the English language. Some that might be used include: c'est la vie (that's life); bon mot (witty saying; literally "good word"); coup d'état; comme ci, comme ça (so-so; literally "like this, like that"); nom de plume (pen name); né or née (born; used when giving someone's maiden name); hors d'oeuvre (appetizer).

- Sample some French pastry. Listen to French music or learn simple songs in French.

FESTIVAL OF AMATERASU-O-MI-KAMI

• • • •

July 17
Japan

Background

According to Japanese legend, there was a time long ago when Amaterasu, the Sun Goddess, became distressed over the insensitivity of her brother and in her sorrow hid herself in a cave. With the Sun Goddess gone darkness and great disaster fell upon Earth. The other gods, knowing that they must entice Amaterasu to return, staged a great party to lure her out of the cave. The plan worked and Amaterasu, curious to find out what the laughter and merrymaking were about, peeked out of her cave. Just as she reached the cave's entrance, the other gods reflected her image in a mirror. This fascinated Amaterasu and drew her back into the world where she has remained to this day. The party of the gods is reenacted on this day with parades, celebration, and the rising sun of the Japanese flag flying!

Activities

- Discuss the symbolism of the rising sun on the Japanese flag, both from the perspective of this folktale and from the perspective of the location of the country of Japan. Have children draw flags of other countries and research the symbolism of the flags, the markings on the flags, and the colors used.

- Discuss what would happen if we did indeed have to live without the sun even for a brief period.

- Learn about solar eclipses.

- Learn about mirrors and mirror images. Use mirrors to create reverse images and/or symmetrical patterns (i.e., draw half of a face or pattern and complete the picture by placing a mirror at its edge).

- Research superstitions surrounding eclipses.

- Give a brief background on the beginning of Mark Twain's novel, *A Connecticut Yankee in King Arthur's Court* (the Connecticut Yankee has been mysteriously transported back to King Arthur's court, sentenced to die, and, having convinced everyone that he is a magician, has threatened to blot out the sun). Then read and discuss chapter 7, "The Eclipse."

INDEPENDENCE DAY

• • • •

July 20
Colombia

Background

As early as 1499 Colombia was visited by Spanish explorers and by the middle of the sixteenth century the area was firmly in the control of the Spaniards. In the late 1700s popular uprisings occurred and the movement toward independence began. New Granada (as the area that now constitutes Colombia, Ecuador, Panama, and Venezuela was then known) revolted and declared its independence on July 20, 1810. Within a few years Ecuador and Venezuela had seceded and, following a dispute over the building of the Panama Canal, Panama also seceded in 1903, leaving the Republic of Colombia.

NATIONAL DAY

• • • •

July 21
Belgium

Background

Once a part of Charlemagne's empire, Belgium later became a feudal state after which it was subjected to a period of foreign domination. By 1797 the French occupied Belgium, but following Napoleon's defeat at

Waterloo the Congress of Vienna of 1815 gave Belgium to the newly formed country of the Netherlands. The Belgians resented the Dutch rule and the discrimination they were made to face, especially in the areas of religion and language. In 1830 a rebellion broke out in Brussels and Belgian independence was declared. The European powers signed a Dutch-Belgian separation treaty at the London Conference in 1839.

BIRTH OF HAILE SELASSIE I

• • • •

July 23
Rastafarian

Background

One of the leaders of the Black Nationalist Movement of the 1920s and 1930s was Marcus Garvey. He returned to Jamaica from the United States in 1927 to revive the United Negro Improvement Association. That same year, in Kingston, Jamaica, he proclaimed that people should "Look to Africa, where a black king shall be crowned, for the day of deliverance is here." Three years later, Ras Tafari Makonnen, who took the name Haile Selassie ("Power of the Holy Trinity"), was crowned king of Ethiopia. In Jamaica, followers of Garvey saw Haile Selassie as the fulfillment of Garvey's prophesy and began to worship him as a living god, adopting his former name, Ras Tafari, as the name for their religious-cultural movement.

Activities

• Rastafarians refer to themselves as "dreads" (God-fearers) and their traditional hairstyle has come to be known as dreadlocks. Discuss other hair or clothing styles associated with a particular religion (e.g., the shaved heads of Buddhist priests, the uncut and covered hair of male Sikhs, the simplicity of dress of the Amish, the wearing of yarmulkes by Orthodox Jews).

• When Haile Selassie was crowned, Garvey had strong reservations about the worship of him as Jesus Christ reborn because, for one thing, slavery was still in practice in Ethiopia at the time. Yet Selassie did much to suppress slavery and to bring about other reforms. Study the life of Haile Selassie and the contributions he made to the black freedom movement.

• Listen to reggae music, which is heavily influenced by Rastafarianism.

PIONEER DAY

• • • •

July 24
Mormon

Background

In 1844 the Mormons, under the leadership of Brigham Young, left their settlement in Illinois and began their move westward. According to Mormon tradition, on July 24, 1847, Young is said to have risen from his sickbed as his party of followers entered the Salt Lake Valley in Utah and said "This is the place." Within a year more than 4,000 Mormons had followed Young to Utah and the Mormon settlement. The day is joyously celebrated each year in Salt Lake City and in other Mormon congregations with parades, church services, and feasting.

Activities

• Do a lesson on the Great Salt Lake. Although the salt content decreases as the water level of the lake increases, the salt content can be as high as 10 percent. Tie this in with an activity involving sinking and floating in which the students experiment to determine the effect of different amounts of salt in the water on different objects

- Tie this holiday in with a unit of study on the westward movement in the United States. Generate a list of reasons people moved west (e.g., religion, gold, land, to avoid trouble with the law).

ST. CHRISTOPHER'S DAY

• • • •

July 25
Roman Catholic

Background

Christopher was a giant who converted to Christianity and performed many acts of charity. Legend has it that one of these acts was the carrying of a child across a river. As Christopher walked through the river his load began to feel heavier and heavier—apparently the child he was carrying was the Christ child and the weight Christopher felt was the weight of the world upon his shoulders. Originally revered by ferrymen, he remains popular as the saint of travelers, but because little about his life can be authenticated, the Catholic Church has dropped St. Christopher from the canon.

CONSTITUTION DAY

• • • •

July 25
Puerto Rico

Background

The citizens of Puerto Rico are descendants of the Spaniards who first settled on the island, of the Africans who were brought there as slaves, and of Native Americans. Puerto Rico became a territory of the United States in 1898 when, following the Spanish-American War, the island was ceded to the United States under the provisions of the Treaty of Paris. On July 25, 1952, the Commonwealth of Puerto Rico was proclaimed. In 1967, when Puerto Ricans were given the opportunity to vote between statehood, independence, and maintaining the status quo, an overwhelming majority voted to maintain the commonwealth relationship with the United States. There is, however, a recently renewed interest in statehood and the status of the island could change.

Activities

- If Puerto Rico were to become a state our flag would need to be redesigned. See "Flag Day," June 14, for an activity that gets kids thinking about the possibilities of a new arrangement of the stars.

INDEPENDENCE DAY

• • • •

July 26
Liberia

Background

Around 1820 freed American slaves, under the auspices of the American Colonization Society, began settling on the coast of West Africa. Initially there were many problems to be faced—disease, hostile tribes, and European colonial powers—but the staying power and the desire for freedom was great and these difficulties were overcome. Liberia adopted a constitution modeled on that of the United States and became Africa's first independent republic in 1847. African languages as well as English are spoken in the country, and the population includes Muslims, Christians, and believers in traditional religions.

INDEDENDENCE DAY
• • • •
July 28
Peru

Background

Peru has been inhabited since at least 9000 B.C. and was home to several advanced cultures, the last, and best known, of these being the Incas who settled near Cuzco during the twelfth century A.D. In 1532 the Spaniard, Francisco Pizarro, landed on the coast of Peru and by the end of the following year he and his men, having the advantages of horses and guns, had captured Cuzco and the Incan empire had disintegrated. Large Spanish settlements grew over the next three centuries and the native people were treated poorly. The Spanish continued to rule the area until July 28, 1821, when, largely through the efforts of outsiders José de San Martín and Simón Bolívar, independence was proclaimed.

8

AUGUST HOLIDAYS

Nonfixed Dates

Kadooment Day	Barbados	First Monday
Emancipation Day and Fox Hill Day	Bahamas	First Monday and Tuesday
Gokarne Aunsi (Father's Day)	Nepal	August or September
Green Corn Ceremony	Native American	August or September

Fixed Dates

August 1	National Day	Switzerland
August 1	Lammas (Festival of the New Bread)	Celtic
August 5	Independence Day	Jamaica
August 6	National Day	Bolivia
August 14	V-J Day	United States
August 14	Independence Day	India
August 14	Independence Day	Pakistan
August 15	Assumption Day	Christian
August 15	Birth of Isis	Egypt
August 15	Independence Day	South Korea
August 15	Independence Day	Congo
August 17	Independence Day	Indonesia
August 19	Independence Day	Afghanistan
August 22	Be an Angel Day	United States
August 31	Independence Day	Trinidad and Tobago
August 31–September 6	New Year	Ethiopia

AUGUST HOLIDAYS WITH NONFIXED DATES

KADOOMENT DAY

• • • •

First Monday in August
Barbados

Background

Also known as Emancipation Day, Kadooment Day is a public holiday when all Barbadians gather to celebrate the end of the sugarcane harvest. The festivities begin early in the morning when costumed bands assemble and prepare to parade before the judges. Prizes given include best band, best costumes, and "Tune of the Crop," the most popular song of the day. Food stalls abound and following the parade the revelry continues with feasting, music, and dancing in the streets. When darkness begins to fall a fireworks display signals the end of Kadooment Day and the Crop Over Festival. (See also "Emancipation Day," below.)

Activities

• Listen to steel drum or calypso music.

• Have the children work cooperatively or in groups to write and perform simple songs. Give prizes for the songs with the best lyrics, best tune, snappiest rhythm, etc.

• Have the children create costumes for Kadooment Day that are somehow representative of the holiday, the country, the climate, or the crop. Prizes may be given for the most elaborate, most creative, most colorful, etc.

• Ask the children to bring in individual servings of fruit juice and mix them together to make a tropical punch. Before mixing, place all of the individual containers on a table where the children can see them. Have them estimate how many quarts of punch the juice will make, then add up the ounces in each and divide to get an accurate amount and to see whose estimate was closest. List the kinds of juices under two categories, tropical and nontropical. Have children draw conclusions about why different kinds of fruits grow in different areas.

• In some areas it is possible to order sugar cane through your local supermarket. Check with the produce manager. If possible touch, taste, and smell some raw sugar cane. Discuss the labor involved in cutting the cane and/or the process of refining it into sugar.

• Taste some sugar candy. Or have the children vote on their favorite food that contains sugar. Have the winner for a snack. Make a graph to show how many children voted for each food suggested.

EMANCIPATION DAY AND FOX HILL DAY

• • • •

First Monday and
Tuesday in August
Bahamas

Background

The abolition of slavery in the Bahamas came in 1834. It is commemorated each year on the first Monday in August with church services, family gatherings, and celebrations. The following day, Fox Hill Day, is not a national holiday, but it is equally festive. The Fox Hill area was once a slave community, and Fox Hill Day is really a continuation of the Emancipation Day celebration. Activities that distinguish Fox Hill Day include cookouts, greased pole-climbing contests, dancing around a pole similar to a maypole, outdoor theatrical performances, and a junkanoo parade. (See "Kadooment Day," above, and "Junkanoo," December 26, for more information and activities.)

Activities

- Use ribbons or crepe-paper streamers on a telephone pole or basketball hoop support to plait a "maypole."

- Have pole-climbing contests.

- Have the children work together to prepare skits that center around the theme of emancipation from slavery and have them performed outdoors.

- Have a cookout. Include citrus fruits, pineapple, coconut, and other foods that would be available in the Bahamas. If possible provide a whole pineapple and coconut for the children to examine and then eat!

GOKARNE AUNSI
(Father's Day)

• • • •

August or September
Nepal

Background

In Nepal, Gokarne Aunsi is a time for showing filial piety. Government offices are closed and people perform acts in honor of their fathers. Those whose fathers are already dead bathe and perform special ceremonies in their honor. Those with living fathers visit them with gifts of sweets, favorite foods, and beverages. In turn the fathers bestow blessings upon their children

GREEN CORN CEREMONY

• • • •

August or September
Native American

Background

The Green Corn Ceremony is probably most closely associated with the Creek Indians, but variations of the celebration are found among many Native American tribes. The Busk, as it is sometimes called, is a celebration of the first corn harvest of the season and is frequently held at the time of the full moon, usually in August.

The Green Corn Ceremony is a time of purification and thanksgiving, and many of the rituals are actually connected to the beginning of the new year. This is a time of new beginning when old wrongs are forgiven, and ill feelings are patched up. Homes are thoroughly cleaned and renovated, the family provides itself with new belongings, and old clothing and household items are thrown on a communal pile and burned. A holy man kindles a sacred fire that symbolizes renewed life, health, and spiritual power. The ceremony lasts for several days. During the first few days the people fast, cleanse their bodies, and drink concoctions of medicinal herbs in ritual purification. There is much dancing during the Busk with the women and men performing different dances and sometimes dancing together. The Busk ends with a feast of traditional foods including corn in a variety of forms.

Activities

- Compare the Green Corn Ceremony to other harvest festivals or new year celebrations.

- Learn to do a simple Native American dance.

- Eat some popcorn, cornbread, or Indian fry bread. Listen to Native American music.

  (For additional activities see "American Indian Day," September.)

AUGUST HOLIDAYS WITH FIXED DATES

NATIONAL DAY

• • • •

August 1
Switzerland

Background

Although August 1, Switzerland's National Day, was not decreed a holiday by the Federal Council until 1891, its origins go back to 1291 when the three cantons (states) of Uri, Unterwalden, and Schwyz first united to form an alliance. Also known as Confederation Day, the day is now celebrated with the singing of the national anthem, traditional music and dancing, yodeling, speeches, and torchlit parades in which the children carry paper lanterns and the participants wear traditional costumes. Buildings are decorated with Swiss flags and strings of red and white lights (the colors of the flag). Fireworks are set off and bonfires lit high in the Alps, a reminder of when fires were used as a means to send messages between the isolated mountain villages.

Activities

• Do a lesson on communication. Begin with early forms of nonverbal communication such as bonfires, drumming, and smoke signals. Discuss individual forms of nonverbal communication—hand signals, facial expressions, etc., or study a historical progression of communication up through today's modern technology. Use *The Handmade Alphabet* by Laura Rankin (New York: Dial Books, 1991) as an introduction to signing as a means of communication.

• Swiss banks are world renowned. Research to find out what makes them unique, or do a lesson on banking, interest rates, or international currency and the exchange rates of the same.

• Find a hill in the neighborhood and go "mountain climbing" or do other climbing activities.

• View a travel video on Switzerland or a video on mountain climbing.

• Compare this holiday to our Fourth of July celebration and/or other countries' national holidays.

• For additional activities related to Switzerland see "Alp Feast," July, and "Federal Thanksgiving Day," September 20.

LAMMAS
(Festival of the New Bread)

• • • •

August 1
Celtic

Background

In Old English the word "Lammas" literally means "Loaf Mass." In ancient times this holiday was a time to honor the women who planted the first seeds—the inventors of agriculture. Even today Lammas is a celebration of the gifts of the earth. In Hungary glasses of wine and bread baked from newly harvested wheat are placed on public tables set up at crossroads. Although not a widely celebrated holiday in its original form, the spirit of Lammas continues in county and state fairs where farmers compete and exhibit their produce.

Activities

- Study the basic food pyramid, types of foods included, and suggested daily servings of each. Have the children brainstorm lists of foods that fall under each group. A good introduction for young children is Loreen Leedy's *The Edible Pyramid: Good Eating Every Day* (New York: Holiday House, 1994).

- Read the story *The Little Red Hen*, then have children put the steps required to make a loaf of bread in chronological order and list the people involved at each step.

- Bake bread. (See Appendix B, United States, for recipe.)

- Visit a grist mill or a bakery.

- Discuss how human life changed with the beginning of agriculture and why women were probably the first to plant seeds and grow food.

INDEPENDENCE DAY

• • • •

August 5
Jamaica

Background

Jamaica, third largest island in the Caribbean, is located south of Cuba and west of Haiti. The population is primarily of African descent and while English is the official language, most people also speak a Creole English. Jamaica was sighted by Christopher Columbus in 1494 and conquered and settled by the Spanish in 1509. The island remained under Spanish rule until it was formally ceded to England in the middle of the seventeenth century. In 1958 Jamaica became a key member of the British-sponsored West Indies Federation. In 1961 the Jamaican people decided by popular referendum to withdraw from the federation, and the following year were awarded complete independence from Great Britain.

NATIONAL DAY

• • • •

August 6
Bolivia

Background

Little is known of the early history of Bolivia although remains have been found of the Incan civilization as well as that of a civilization that predates the Incas. Written records go back only as far as the invasion by the Spanish Conquistadors in the 1530s when the Conquistadors, attracted by reports of silver and other precious metals, moved south from Peru into Bolivia. Thousands of the Indians native to the area died as a result of forced labor and diseases brought by the Spaniards, yet the native Indians did not easily accept serfdom. Indian and mestizo uprisings and rebellions were common but, until 1824, futile. In 1824 a decisive battle was won. Fighting continued until the following year when, on August 6, independence was declared.

V-J DAY

• • • •

August 14
United States

Background

Until late 1941 the United States tried to remain neutral with regard to World War II, giving only moral support and financial aid in the form of the Lend-Lease program initiated to help Great Britain. The bombing of Pearl Harbor by the Japanese on December 7, 1941, ended that neutrality and the following day the United

States declared war on Japan. Although the Japanese initially had the advantage, the battle of Midway Island in 1942 began to turn the tide in favor of the Americans. In the summer of 1945 the Allies made an appeal to the Japanese to surrender, but they refused. The United States dropped the first atomic bomb on Hiroshima on August 6, 1945, and the second on Nagasaki three days later. Following the devastation of these two cities Japan announced its surrender on August 14, which has come to be known as V-J Day for "Victory over Japan." The surrender was formally signed aboard the U.S. battleship *Missouri* on September 2, 1945.

Activities

- Study World War II or naval warfare.

- Learn about the effects of the atomic bomb. Debate the issue of whether or not a country should maintain nuclear weapons, or study other uses of nuclear power.

INDEPENDENCE DAY

• • • •

August 14
India

Background

One of the world's most ancient civilizations, the Indus Valley Civilization, existed in India as early as 2500 B.C. Due to centuries of immigration the country is now extremely diverse. Although Hindi and English are the official languages of the country, more than 1,500 different languages and dialects are spoken in India. In 1498 Vasco da Gama became the first Euro-

pean to sail to India. The French, Dutch, British, and Portuguese were all eager to establish trading centers in the country, but by the end of the seventeenth century the British, with their East India Company, had become dominant. The English ruled until 1948 when the Congress of India reluctantly agreed to give up the predominantly Muslim areas of the country. From these areas the country of Pakistan was established (the eastern section later became Bangladesh) and both Pakistan and India gained their freedom from Great Britain. The division of the subcontinent arose primarily from the religious differences of the people living in the two areas. While India's population is 80 percent Hindu, that of Pakistan is predominantly Muslim.

INDEPENDENCE DAY

• • • •

August 14
Pakistan

Background

The northwestern part of the subcontinent of India changed hands many times before it became a part of Imperial British India in 1857. The Muslims who inhabited the area were never absorbed into the Hindu society of India and were displeased with the treatment they received. The idea of a Muslim nation, distinct and apart from Hindu India, arose in the 1930s. Supporters began to use the name Pakistan (which in Urdu means "land of the pure"). On August 14, 1947, as a part of the Indian Independence Act, the country of Pakistan was created.

ASSUMPTION DAY

• • • •

August 15
Christian

Background

The Feast of the Assumption is the celebration of the day on which the Virgin Mary ascended into Heaven following her death. It is the principal feast day of the Virgin Mother. This holiday, which has been celebrated since the fourth century, is actually a Christianization of an earlier harvest festival and, in much of Europe, is known as the Feast of Our Lady of the Harvest. In Italy remnants of the ancient celebration include nighttime bonfires and public illuminations, both probably symbolic of the sun. In years past, some Italian plazas were flooded. Citizens would ride through the temporary "lakes" in carriages and it was common for people to carry bowls of rose-scented water, which they sprinkled on themselves—possibly a carryover from a pagan ritual in which the gods were petitioned to provide adequate rainfall for the crops, or as a tribute to the pagan goddess Isis of the Sea. The idea of prosperity was also evident in the throwing of coins from windows down to street urchins. Assumption Day is also an important holiday in France where the Virgin Mary has been the patron saint since 1638. (See also "Birth of Isis," below.)

Activities

• Discuss symbolic objects or activities related to different holidays—fireworks on the Fourth of July, wearing green on St. Patrick's Day, putting candles in the windows at Christmas, bonfires, water, and so on.

BIRTH OF ISIS

• • • •

August 15
Egypt

Background

The goddess Isis of the Sea is said to have been born on this day. For centuries celebrations were held in her honor. The festival is also known as the Festival of Lights or the Blessing of the Boats. In Egypt many candles were lit in the temples of Isis to honor and mirror her life-giving forces. With the coming of Christianity church leaders decided that the easiest way to handle this pagan ritual was to simply change it into a Christian holiday, hence Assumption Day (see above).

Activities

• Study the sea, animals that live in water, or different types of vessels that transport people over water.

• Delve into the mystery of the pyramids. Children are fascinated by the pyramids of Egypt and would probably enjoy the book *Pyramid* by David Macauley (New York: Houghton Mifflin, 1974). From the study of the pyramids, initiate study of levers, pulleys, and other simple machines.

• Egypt is basically an arid land. Discuss why Isis may have been an important goddess to ancient Egyptians.

• Do a unit of study on ancient Egypt.

INDEPENDENCE DAY

• • • •

August 15
South Korea

Background

The Korean people are descendants of the Tungusic tribe and are a distinct racial and cultural group. Nevertheless, both Chinese and Japanese influences have been strong throughout Korean history. In 1910 Japan formally annexed the country. During their 35-year rule the Japanese instituted vast economic reforms and did much to modernize industry and transportation, but their treatment of the Korean people was harsh and exploitative. At the Cairo Conference, held in 1943 during World War II, the United States, China, and Great Britain promised Korean independence, and Korea officially achieved independence on August 15, 1948.

Activities

• Following the liberation of Korea from Japanese colonial rule the country was arbitrarily divided into two zones, each anxious to unite the country under its own government. This led, in 1950, to the Korean War. Study the Korean War and/or the conflicts that exist between North and South Korea today.

INDEPENDENCE DAY

• • • •

August 15
Congo

Background

The first inhabitants of the Congo were probably pygmies who had immigrated from Zaire. Other early inhabitants included the Bateke, Bakonga, and Sanga. The first European to visit the area was a Portuguese explorer who, in 1482, discovered the mouth of the Congo River and sailed up the river for several miles.

For a time the Portuguese dominated trade in the area, but the French, Dutch, and English also held interests. In 1880 a French protectorate over the north bank of the Congo was established and for the next 21 years the area was administered by French companies who held the rights to the rubber and ivory trade. Scandals broke out in 1905 and 1906 over the decimation of the African population through forced labor, and in 1928 the Africans revolted over these conditions. In 1946 the Congo gained representation in the French parliament and full independence was awarded on August 15, 1960.

INDEPENDENCE DAY

• • • •

August 17
Indonesia

Background

Indonesia, which consists of more than 13,000 islands, is located between the Indian and Pacific Oceans. The capital of the republic is Jakarta, on the island of Java. Early in its history Indonesia came under the influence of traders from India; both Hindu and Buddhism were prominent religions. By the sixteenth century, however, Islam had replaced these as the dominant religion. The Portuguese were the first to establish trading posts in Indonesia, but the Dutch ousted them and were in control from 1610 to 1949. The movement for independence in Indochina increased during World War II when Japan took over the area. Independence was declared on August 17, 1945, and, after four years of conflict, an agreement with the Dutch was finally reached in November 1949.

INDEPENDENCE DAY

• • • •

August 19
Afghanistan

Background

For centuries the mountains of Afghanistan aided the hill tribes in maintaining their independence, but during the nineteenth century both Russia and Great Britain strove to achieve dominance in central Asia, and twice Afghanistan was torn by war. The Anglo-Russian agreement of 1907 allowed for the independence of Afghanistan with the British having authority over foreign affairs. The third Afghan War, in 1919, in which the Afghanis invaded India, ended with the Treaty of Rawalpindi, which gave Afghanistan total independence including full control over its foreign relations.

BE AN ANGEL DAY

• • • •

August 22
United States

Background

This relatively new American holiday was first organized and initiated by the Angelic Alliance of Upperco, Maryland, in 1993. Already it has been declared a holiday in the state of Maryland as well as in the cities of Santa Fe, New Mexico, and Boulder, Colorado. The purpose of the day is to bring out the best in people and to encourage them to be of service to those in need. The motto for the day is: "Be an angel. Do one small act of service for someone. Be a blessing in someone's life."

Activities

- Study angels in art and their symbolism. If desired, this lesson may be expanded to include other common symbols found in art.

- Discuss what it means to be an angel. Brainstorm to make a list of other nouns that we use to describe people and how they are used (e.g., monster, saint, devil, goddess, imp, weasel, butterfly).

- As a group project have children write stories or make get-well cards for later delivery to the children's ward of a local hospital or to a retirement home.

- Discuss service-oriented careers and the meaning of the word "service."

- Encourage the children to be "angels" today, to work cooperatively and to help one another. Give small pieces of angel food cake as a reward to children who show kindness and helpfulness.

INDEPENDENCE DAY

• • • •

August 31
Trinidad and Tobago

Background

The islands of Trinidad and Tobago are situated to the north of Venezuela's Orinoco River delta. Trinidad was first visited by Christopher Columbus in 1498, but the Spaniards never colonized the island. Tobago was first settled by the British in 1616, but the indigenous Caribs drove them out. Both islands were later raided by the Dutch, French, and English. The British formally acquired Trinidad in 1802 and Tobago in 1803. In 1888 the two islands were joined politically and remained in the hands of the English until joining the West Indies Federation in 1958. The federation lasted only four years. In 1962 Trinidad and Tobago became independent, gaining full status as a republic in 1976.

Activities

- The chief export of Trinidad and Tobago is petroleum. Discuss how empty oil drums have been used to create steel drums. Listen to some steel drum music and/or create your own steel drums using different sizes of cans.

NEW YEAR

• • • •

August 31–September 6
Ethiopia

Background

In Ethiopia the new year is ushered in during the first six days of September. The celebration begins on New Year's Eve, the evening of August 31. Children dress in white and gather flowers and arrange them in tiny bouquets. Then, in groups, the children go from house to house. They knock on the door and when invited to enter sing a song and offer the woman of the household one of their small bouquets. In return they are given gifts of money, sweets, cookies, or sometimes a fruit or vegetable. As they take their leave they say thanks with the words "Wakiyo si fakenee" ("God also give to you").

Activities

- Compare Ethiopian New Year's traditions to the Western traditions of caroling at Christmas, trick-or-treating at Halloween, and giving May baskets on May Day.

- Have the children write and perform their own songs about New Year's Day, flowers, or Ethiopia.

- Make up addition, division, or multiplication problems for the children to solve in which they determine how many children visited a home, how many flowers the homeowner received, or how the children divided the flowers into bouquets of equal size. *The Doorbell* Rang by Pat Hutchins (New York: Greenwillow Books, 1986) is a great starting point for this activity. It tells the story of two children who start out with a dozen cookies and have to keep dividing and sharing them in different ways as more and more friends drop in.

9
SEPTEMBER HOLIDAYS

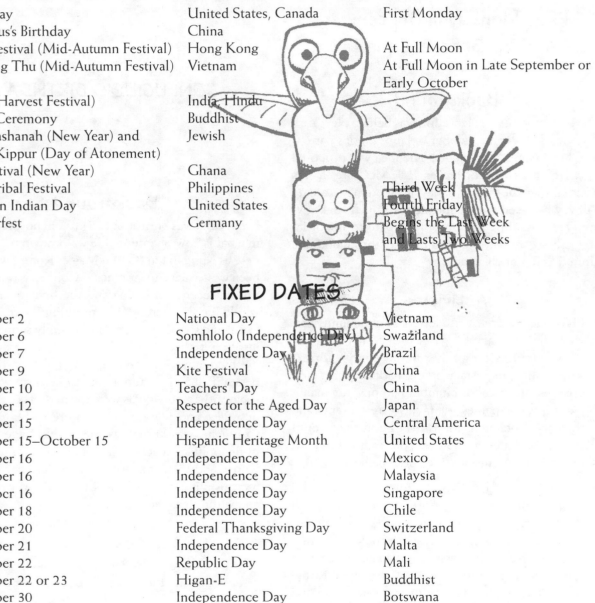

NONFIXED DATES

Labor Day	United States, Canada	First Monday
Confucius's Birthday	China	
Moon Festival (Mid-Autumn Festival)	Hong Kong	At Full Moon
Tet Trung Thu (Mid-Autumn Festival)	Vietnam	At Full Moon in Late September or Early October
Onam (Harvest Festival)	India, Hindu	
Kathin Ceremony	Buddhist	
Rosh Hashanah (New Year) and Yom Kippur (Day of Atonement)	Jewish	
Yam Festival (New Year)	Ghana	
T'Boli Tribal Festival	Philippines	Third Week
American Indian Day	United States	Fourth Friday
Oktoberfest	Germany	Begins the Last Week and Lasts Two Weeks

FIXED DATES

September 2	National Day	Vietnam
September 6	Somhlolo (Independence Day)	Swaziland
September 7	Independence Day	Brazil
September 9	Kite Festival	China
September 10	Teachers' Day	China
September 12	Respect for the Aged Day	Japan
September 15	Independence Day	Central America
September 15–October 15	Hispanic Heritage Month	United States
September 16	Independence Day	Mexico
September 16	Independence Day	Malaysia
September 16	Independence Day	Singapore
September 18	Independence Day	Chile
September 20	Federal Thanksgiving Day	Switzerland
September 21	Independence Day	Malta
September 22	Republic Day	Mali
September 22 or 23	Higan-E	Buddhist
September 30	Independence Day	Botswana

SEPTEMBER HOLIDAYS WITH NONFIXED DATES

LABOR DAY

• • • •

First Monday in September
United States, Canada

Background

The first Labor Day celebration was held in New York City in 1882 when a number of labor unions participated in a parade and picnic. The idea was proposed by a Knights of Labor leader, P. J. McGuire. It was decided that the first Monday in September, a date halfway between Independence Day and Thanksgiving Day, would be an appropriate date to honor labor. Labor Day is now a legal holiday throughout the United States and Canada.

Activities

• Have the children write letters to community service workers, labor organizations, or businesses whose services they rely on and enjoy—for example, utility or postal workers, park and recreation services, electrical or plumbing unions, toy manufacturing companies, or favorite restaurants and theaters. Communications may be in the form of thank-you notes, wishes for a pleasant Labor Day, or requests for information about careers.

• Organize your class into a "Students' Union." Hold an initial meeting to elect officers and to establish the first priority of the union—a Labor Day celebration. Following this leaders could meet in a collective bargaining session with management (the school administration) to negotiate time off from "work" and funding for the project. At the second union meeting, members could volunteer to work on committees to plan the event, after which spokespersons would negotiate with the cafeteria manager, physical education, music, computer, and/or art teachers to arrange for food for the picnic, recreation and games, music for the parade (this

could be as simple as a boom box playing Sousa marches), and banners or hand-painted signs for the marchers to carry. If you want to carry things a step further, also include program and publicity committees to arrange for speakers and to design invitations for families and/or community leaders. Following the event, conduct a follow-up discussion with the children to evaluate their experience, their knowledge of the collective bargaining process, and their understanding of the purpose of labor unions.

CONFUCIUS'S BIRTHDAY

• • • •

China

Background

Kung Chiu was born about 551 B.C. in northern China in what is now Shantung. He was known by the Chinese as Kung fu tzu (Grand Master Kung), which has been westernized to Confucius. Confucius was the first private teacher in China and the first to devote his whole life to teaching. His teachings were both political and social in nature and strongly supported the institutions that provided his society with order—family, hierarchy, and seniority. He believed that each person had a place and a duty to perform within the society, that individuals were the masters of their own destinies, and that all people were to be respected. Confucius was known as the "Great Sage" and his philosophical teachings influenced China, Japan, Korea, and Vietnam. While religious in nature, Confucianism is a philosophy of life and has never been an institutionalized religion.

Activities

• Have children consider and write or talk about their duties within the society, the school, or the family.

• Define the terms "seniority" and "hierarchy" and have children discuss their superiors and inferiors and how they should act toward both groups. For example, fourth graders have seniority over kindergartners, yet fourth graders should treat kindergartners with kindness and respect and accept the role of mentor for younger students or siblings.

- Discuss the differences between philosophy and religion. Compare the basic teachings of Confucius to the "Golden Rule."

- With older children you could begin a comparative study of the world's great philosophers and their basic beliefs. This might include Confucius, Plato, Aristotle, Socrates, St. Thomas Aquinas, Benedict de Spinoza, John Locke, Jean-Jacques Rousseau.

MOON FESTIVAL
(Mid-Autumn Festival)

• • • •

At Full Moon in September
Hong Kong

Background

The Moon Festival, held in September, is the harvest festival of Hong Kong and one of the biggest of the Chinese festivals. It is also known as the Mid-Autumn Festival. It originated from the ancient tradition of making offerings to the sun in spring and to the moon in autumn. This is a time for families to get together and people often travel long distances to be with their loved ones.

The streets are decorated with lanterns, reminiscent of the moon, and children are permitted to stay up later than usual to go to high places with their families to watch the full moon rise. Girls try to stay awake as late as possible since tradition has it that the later a girl goes to sleep on this night the longer her mother will live. A favorite food is moon cakes, a tribute to the moon as well as a reminder of when wartime messages, hidden inside the cakes, were smuggled past the enemy. Today the cakes are filled with lotus, sesame seeds, a duck egg, or dried fruits. (See also "Tet Trung Thu" below.)

Activities

- Today is a good day to make an exception and to allow children to pass notes to each other during school—as long as the notes are written on moon-shaped paper to represent moon cakes! (Watch what prolific writers you have when children are allowed to write for their own purposes!)

- When you need to communicate with children, smuggle them a note instead. Be creative! Pull apart a sandwich-type cookie and place a note (wrapped in waxed paper) between the layers. Take the "workings" out of a ball point pen, tightly roll your note, and place inside. Write a note on the inside of the outer wrapper of a stick of gum then glue back in place. Palm a note and pass it in a handshake. Write a message on the top page of a pad of paper, pressing hard. Give the children the second sheet from the pad (by rubbing lightly with a pencil, they can make the message appear). Have children brainstorm other ways in which they could secretly pass written messages.

- Use the example of girls staying up late on this night to ensure that their mothers will enjoy a long life to initiate a discussion of the students' own traditions or superstitions.

- Bake fortune cookies (see recipe in Appendix B, "Chinese"). Allow children to write personal messages to put inside. (Be sure to note the placement of the cookies on the cookie sheet before baking so that you will get the correct message to each person!)

- This is a perfect time to study the phases of the moon. Cut a circle from the center of a piece of paper and place the paper on an overhead projector or tape it to a sunlit window to create a circle of light that represents the moon. Move a globe or the circular piece of paper across the circle of light to simulate the way in which the shadow of Earth creates the phases of the moon. Follow up on this lesson by giving the children the homework assignment of observing the moon that evening and drawing a sketch of it. The next day you can discuss what phase the moon is currently in and begin a chart in which the children observe and record the phase of the moon through a full cycle. At the close of the activity you might wish to take it one step further with older children by discussing the differences in lunar and solar calendars or even by having the students project into the future to create their own lunar calendars, naming the months and relating their lunar calendar to our Gregorian calendar.

- Give children plastic knives and moon pies or circular cookies and have them work in pairs or small groups for a hands-on lesson on fractions. "Share and be fair" is a good phrase to teach young children that halves or fourths must be equal in size. Older children might cut their own cookies and then add the fractional parts with those of friends to explore more complex facts—four halves equals two, six fourths equals one and one half, and so on.

- You could also relate this to the lesson on moon phases by giving the children paper circles and having the children move the circles across the cookies before the cookies are cut to illustrate the different phases of the moon.

TET TRUNG THU
(Mid-Autumn Festival)

• • • •

At Full Moon in Late September or Early October
Vietnam

Background

This holiday, which is held to honor the moon, falls at the time of the full moon, on the fifteenth day of the eighth month of the Chinese lunar calendar. Traditional moon cakes are eaten and given to family and friends as gifts, and the children work to create lanterns in the shapes of a variety of animals and other objects. After dark the students place candles in their lanterns and parade through the streets to the sounds of crashing cymbals and drums. (See also "Moon Festival" above.)

Activities

- Give the children scissors, glue, tape, and construction paper and tissue paper in wide varieties of colors and have them create their own paper lanterns. Start with a circular base cut from cardboard or poster board. Cut a construction paper rectangle

about 8 inches tall and wide enough to fit around the diameter of the base. Cut shapes from the construction paper being careful not to get too close to any of the edges and glue tissue paper over these spaces. Curl the construction paper into a cylinder and tape securely onto the base. With a hole punch make four evenly spaced holes around the top of the lantern. Tie string through the holes and attach the lantern to a sturdy dowel. Put a small flashlight or chemical light stick (available in most hardware or camping supply stores) inside for a safer source of light than the traditional candle.

- Study rhythm instruments or learn about different time signatures and beats in musical compositions.

- Put together a simple rhythm band using homemade instruments and have a Tet Trung Thu parade with your paper lanterns and band. Many different rhythm instruments can be made from junk. Give the children glue, scissors, rubber bands, dry beans, string, and paper clips, as well as a wide variety of recyclable junk (egg cartons, boxes, cardboard tubes from paper towels, Styrofoam meat trays, etc.) and have them brainstorm ideas for making their own instruments. If they need help coming up with ideas, try one of the following:

  - Drum: Two aluminum pie plates stapled together make a handheld drum. A pencil can be used as the drumstick.
  - Rattle: Put dry beans inside a cardboard tube and fasten paper over the ends with rubber bands to make a rattle.
  - Guitar: Cut a hole in one side of a shoe box then run different-width rubber bands around the box to make a guitar. Glue a cardboard tube on one end to make the "neck" of the guitar.

ONAM
(Harvest Festival)

• • • •

India, Hindu

Background

This four-day festival occurs at the end of the monsoon season and at the time of the harvest in India. All people, regardless of caste or creed, welcome the sunny weather and join in the celebration by feasting and wearing new clothes. Vegetarian meals are served during the celebration, often on plantain leaves instead of dishes, and Hindu women decorate their homes and courtyards with beautiful floral arrangements. Landlords distribute cloth and rice to their tenants and the peasants in turn offer their landlords gifts of produce from their fields. Everyone participates in the games, music, and dancing. One day is set aside as a special celebration for the children. The children receive from their parents and relatives new clothes or cloth from the shops, and enjoy singing while pushing each other on swings called oonjals.

Activities

- Have the children compose simple songs or poems then go to the playground where they can push each other on the swings while reciting or singing their compositions. With very young children you may just want to teach them a simple song, such as this one, sung to the tune of "Twinkle, Twinkle, Little Star":

  > Swinging up and swinging down;
  > My feet never touch the ground.
  > How I love to swing and sing,
  > How I love to sing and swing.
  > My song makes a happy sound
  > While I'm swinging up and down.

- Draw a line down the middle of a piece of paper. On one side have the children draw a picture of the monsoon season, gluing grains of rice on the paper to represent the rain. On the other side have them draw a picture to represent the harvest—a bowl of rice, people celebrating, or farmers harvesting their crops—again using real rice glued to the picture.

KATHIN
CEREMONY

• • • •

Buddhist

Background

The three-monthlong Buddhist Lent terminates on the first day of the waxing moon of the eleventh lunar month (usually during our month of September) and is marked by the Kathin Ceremony. This ceremony is a time for the people to present rewards to the monks for having spent the Lenten season studying in seclusion. The traditional gift is Kathin robes, new clothing for the monks to wear now that they are free to travel and make pilgrimages. The timing of the Kathin Ceremony varies from monastery to monastery and may take place at any time during the month following Lent. In Buddhism, giving is a spiritual exercise and giving to the monks at this time is not only an act of merit for the giver but also an opportunity to uphold the faith by providing for the monks. (For information about Buddhist Lent, see July.)

Activities

- Discuss in general the reasons people around the world extol and reward higher education. Talk about the similarities between the Kathin Ceremony and a graduation ceremony including the giving of gifts, air of celebration, and wearing of special robes.

- The Kathin Ceremony takes place at the end of the rainy season. Study the water cycle and rain, the formation of clouds, and/or why there is more precipitation in some seasons than in others.

- Discuss the psychological effects of long periods of dreary weather.

- Have the children choose a country that they would like to visit, then use the precipitation and temperature charts found in encyclopedias or travel books to determine which time of the year would provide the most pleasant weather for their trip.

ROSH HASHANAH (NEW YEAR) AND YOM KIPPUR (DAY OF ATONEMENT)

• • • •

Jewish

Background

Rosh Hashanah, which literally translated means "head of the year," is celebrated on the first day of the first lunar month, Tishri, and usually falls in our month of September. The observance begins at sundown with a special evening meal. A blessing, called Kiddush, is recited over wine and everyone eats a piece of challah (egg bread). The challah is round and smooth, symbolic of the wish that the new year go smoothly, and is shaped like a crown, a reminder that God is the king of Heaven. Another special food offered to family and friends during Rosh Hashanah is apple slices dipped in honey—a wish for a sweet and fruitful new year.

On Rosh Hashanah Jewish people the world over attend worship services at synagogues and hear the sounding of the shofar (ram's horn). In ancient times the shofar was blown to call people together in times of trouble; nowadays it is a reminder that we must always help each other and work together.

The days following Rosh Hashanah are called the Ten Days of Repentance, and it is believed that this is when God judges all of mankind. During this time people atone for the wrongs they have done their fellow man and ask forgiveness for their transgressions against God.

The High Holy Days end on Yom Kippur. Yom Kippur means "Day of Atonement" and falls ten days after Rosh Hashanah. This day is spent in fasting and praying and ends with the final sounding of the shofar and the breaking of the fast.

Activities

- The time between Rosh Hashanah and Yom Kippur is a time for reflecting and reminiscing. Have the children use cash register tape or other long strips of paper to make a personal timeline of the past year marking pleasant events, good deeds they performed, and times when other people did things that affected them in a positive way.

- Show a picture or sketch of a shofar. (*We Celebrate New Year* by Bobbie Kalman [New York: Crabtree Publishing, 1985] contains a good sketch; *Jewish Holidays in the Fall* by Dianne M. McMillan [Springfield, N.J.: Enslow Publishers, 1993] includes both a photograph and a woodcut.) Discuss/learn about different kinds of horns. Fasten a piece of tissue paper to the end of a cardboard tube with a rubber band and decorate with paint, markers, or colored paper to make a horn. (Hum into the open end of the tube to make sounds.)

- The final note sounded on the shofar is drawn out as long as possible. Use the horns you made to hold the note; count beats.

- Smell, touch, look at, taste, and listen to the crunch as you enjoy a traditional snack of apples dipped in honey.

- Sample challah bread. (See recipe in Appendix B, "Jewish")

- Read the book *Bread, Bread, Bread* by Ann Morris (New York: William Morrow, 1989). Use this as a starting point for comparing and learning about peoples of other cultures through the foods they eat, and plan to sample many different kinds of bread throughout the year.

YAM FESTIVAL (New Year)

• • • •

Ghana

Background

Ghana's Yam Festival occurs at the time of the harvest in September and marks the start of the new year.

Along with a parade, festivities include dancing, singing, drumming, wearing animal masks, and displaying fetishes. Everyone shows their pleasure in the harvest and, of course, eats plenty of fresh yams!

Activities

- Study the ancient pagan religions including nature worship and animalism and draw some conclusions about the original uses and meanings of the masks. Compare the masks of African tribes, Native Americans, and other cultures of the world. (*Masks Tell Stories* by Carol Gelber [Brookfield, Conn.: Millbrook Press, 1993] and *The Mystery of Masks* by Christine Price [New York: Charles Scribner's Sons, 1978] are both good resources for this activity.)

- Have the children choose their own favorite animal and fashion three-dimensional masks of construction paper. Begin by cutting the shape of the animal face making it slightly larger than the child's face. Cut eyeholes. Decorate by gluing on construction-paper shapes for the features. Curl strips of paper by rolling around a pencil to make wool or fur. Cylinders of different lengths can be used for bulging eyes, ears, or snouts. Cut edges of paper into fringe for eyelashes or shaggy hair or beards. Triangles can be folded in half and two of the edges glued down to make beaks, noses, or horns. Allow the children to be creative and remind them that the colors they choose need not be the realistic colors of the real animals. To finish the mask glue or staple two strips of paper onto the back to fit the child's head. The first strip should go around the back of the head at about eye level. The other strip should be attached to the middle of the first strip and should then be taken up over the top of the child's head and fastened to the mask.

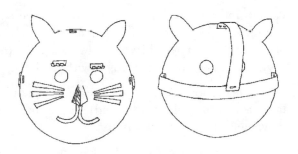

- Beginning with Ghana and its yams, discuss the staples in the diets of various countries and peoples. To make the project manageable, limit the discussion to representative countries or groups of countries, for example: United States/wheat, South America/corn, China/rice, Ireland/potatoes, and so on. Mark these on a world map, then study climate, weather, and growing seasons of the different areas and have the children draw conclusions about the different crops and why they grow well in the different regions.

- Cook some yams then mash with a little milk, butter, salt, and pepper for a treat that the children can see, smell, taste, and touch.

T'BOLI TRIBAL FESTIVAL

• • • •

Third Week in September
Philippines

Background

This thanksgiving festival takes place on the Philippine island of Mindanao. It stems from the T'Boli's belief in an earlier Utopian society that they call Lem-lunay and that they would like to rebuild for themselves. For this festival ten major tribes of the island converge on the city of South Cotabato. In a blend of Catholic ritual and local traditions the festival serves to reenergize the people in their quest for a more perfect life and to make them thankful for what they have. Traditional games, ethnic dances, and staged horse fights add to the excitement of the celebration.

Activities

- Have the children work in small groups to list the qualities that they would attribute to a Utopian society. Spokespersons from each group can then share their ideas with the whole group and similarities can be noted. Children could then divide the characteristics they listed into two categories—those they have no control over (e.g., perfect weather) and those they can influence. Then they can set personal or group goals for improving life within the family or school community.

AMERICAN INDIAN DAY

• • • •

Fourth Friday in September
United States

Background

A number of states currently recognize and celebrate this day in honor of Native Americans. Legislation before Congress could serve to make this a nationally observed day.

Activities

• Construct a simple cloth Indian story bag. Into it put a feather, stone, twig, shell, and other objects from nature. Have the students reach into the bag and choose objects to use as "story starters" for creative writing or storytelling. (For example, the feather could lead to a story about a chief with a feathered headdress, a narrative about a hunting expedition, or a legend about the sky god.)

• If your state has towns, rivers, lakes, parks, or streets that have Indian names, have children list these and do research to find their meanings or origins.

• Provide a brief description of land, climate, and vegetation for a number of different tribes and have children work cooperatively to try to match the tribes with different styles of homes—wigwam, longhouse, tepee, hogan, cliff dwelling, adobe hut, and so on. (*Where Indians Live: American Indian Houses* [Sacramento: Sierra Oaks Publishing, 1989] is a good resource for this activity.)

• Have the children write stories using pictographs instead of words to depict their messages. The pictographs need not be authentic, but if the children are to be able to read each other's stories, they should be uniform. Work as a group to design simple pictographs to be used in the stories—a stick figure for a person, circle with rays emanating from it for the sun, rippled lines for water, a darkened circle for night and hollow circle for day, and simple drawings of animals, mountains, plants, tepees, a bow and arrow, and so on.

• The Native Americans were the first ecologists and conservationists in this country. Have the children discuss/write about the lesson of taking from the earth only what you need and giving back what you can. Brainstorm ways in which children can put the lesson into effect—start a compost pile, volunteer to make animal feeders for a local park, or clean up litter on the school grounds.

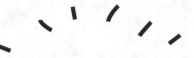

• Young children will enjoy making Native American–style necklaces by stringing beads or tinted macaroni in a color pattern. To dye macaroni, place about 2 tablespoons of rubbing alcohol and the contents of a small bottle of food coloring in a container that can be tightly sealed. Add a box of macaroni (be sure to buy the large type), shake, then spread on newspaper to dry. Repeat with other colors of food coloring to give children a variety of choices. Have children use yarn with large plastic needles for stringing the necklaces or dip about $2\frac{1}{2}$ inches of the end of the yarn in clear nail polish to stiffen it and make a safe "needle," which may be cut off when the stringing is completed.

• Use an Indian tom-tom (or an empty coffee can painted and decorated with Indian designs) to beat out auditory patterns. Have children clap out the rhythms and create dances to go with the beat.

• During classroom transitions use your Indian drum to set a beat (fast, slow, soft, loud) for the students' movement from one activity to another.

• Read and discuss traditional Native American legends and tales. While doing so, softly play Native American music in the background and/or burn mesquite incense.

OKTOBERFEST

• • • •

Begins the Last Week in September and Lasts Two Weeks Germany

Background

Oktoberfest is a tradition that dates back to 1810. The first celebration took place at the time of the autumn marriage of Ludwig I of Bavaria and Therese von Sachsen Hilburghausen. At that time the farmers brought their new crops to the celebration and formed a mound with them. The mound has evolved into an Oktoberfest monument, which differs from year to year but is always erected as part of the celebration and always contains the fruits of the harvest. Another tradition is the parade that kicks off the Oktoberfest celebration and is led by a child, der Munchen Kinder (the Munich child). The child represents the birth of a new Germany—the merger of north and south that took place upon the marriage of Ludwig and Therese. In modern-day Germany people from all over the country, indeed from all over the world, gather in Munich during the end of September and the first part of October to join in festivities that last for two weeks and include sampling the German foods and beers, the playing of music, and dancing.

Activities

- Make your own Oktoberfest monument by stapling a piece of poster board together to form a cylinder or cone. Have children draw fruits and vegetables to glue in place until the poster board is covered. A doll placed on top could represent der Munchen Kinder.

- Discuss the evolution of the English language and the many words that came from German. Learn a few simple German words or phrases: guten morgen (good morning); guten tag (good day; hello); gute nacht (good night); das is gut (that is good); ja (yes); nein (no); schokolade (chocolate); buter kekes (butter cakes; cookies).

- Read/study/compare several of the fairy tales written by the Brothers Grimm. Be sure to preview the fairy tales before reading them to children to ensure that they are age appropriate since some of the tales tend to be quite violent.

- Incorporate dancing or movement activities using German waltzes, polkas, or marches.

- Touch, smell, and taste some German knockwurst, chocolate, or butter cakes (all are readily available in most grocery stores).

- Listen to German music as background for study time, silent reading, or while reading aloud from the Brothers Grimm.

SEPTEMBER HOLIDAYS WITH FIXED DATES

NATIONAL DAY

• • • •

September 2 Vietnam

Background

During the mid-nineteenth century Vietnam fell prey to French colonialism after nearly 1,000 years of independence. Victory in the French-Indochina War (1946–54) won Vietnam the independence it celebrates on this day. The war, however, also led to the partition of the country into North and South Vietnam. For the next two decades Communist North Vietnam fought democratic South Vietnam. The Vietnam War became a limited international conflict with the United States supporting South Vietnam while China and the

Soviet Union backed North Vietnam. American troops withdrew in 1973 and on June 2, 1976, the country was reunited under a Communist regime.

SOMHLOLO
(Independence Day)

• • • •

September 6
Swaziland

Background

Although it is bordered by the country of South Africa on three sides, Swaziland, with British support, resisted annexation by South Africa in the late 1800s. Again in 1949 Britain rejected a South African request for control, and in 1968 granted the Swazi's their independence. Both English and siSwati are spoken in the nation. Christianity and traditional African religions are practiced here.

INDEPENDENCE DAY

• • • •

September 7
Brazil

Background

Sao Paulo, the first permanent European colony in what is now known as Brazil, was established by the Portuguese in 1532. During the next three centuries the rule of Brazil remained primarily in the hands of the Portuguese. In 1807, having been expelled by Napoleon, the royal family of Portugal took refuge in Brazil. When he returned to Portugal in 1821 the king left his son, Pedro, as regent of Brazil. Pedro was ordered to return to Europe the following year but refused and on September 7, 1822, declared Brazil's independence from Portugal. Pedro's Brazilian-born son, Pedro II, brought about the abolition of slavery in the country in 1888.

KITE FESTIVAL

• • • •

September 9
China

Background

Legend has it that about 200 B.C. an inventive dwarf named Han Shin constructed the first kite ever to be seen in the skies of China. Supposedly Han Shin used this kite in a resourceful way to win a battle for his country. Han Shin is remembered on this day in China when kites in his image—that of a fat little man—as well as kites in many other shapes and of all sizes are flown throughout the country by men and boys of all ages. The Kite Festival falls on the ninth day of the ninth moon (or month) of the Chinese calendar. Kites fill the sky from morning to nightfall and thousands of people spend the day outdoors watching the antics of the kites. In attempts to be as clever as Han Shin colorful ingenious kites, some with moving parts, are made and the boys engage in contests trying to cut each other's kite strings and prove the superiority of their kite.

Another version of the story of the origin of this holiday centers around a Chinese farmer named Sun Go. In this legend Sun Go was warned by a witch that a death would occur at his farm on the ninth day of the ninth month. To save his family Sun Go took them to a mountaintop on that day. When they returned all of the animals on their farm were dead, but the family was safe. The Chinese commemorate this event by climbing to high places and flying kites since it is believed that kites can carry one's misfortunes off into the sky. This celebration is also called Double Nine Day or the Festival of High Places.

Activities

- Write a story about Kite Flying Day from the perspective of the kite.

- Do a lesson on basic aerodynamics. How do birds and airplanes fly? What keeps a kite up in the air?

How do gliders work? What makes a pinwheel turn in the same direction every time? Two good resource books are *Flight and Flying Machines* by Steve Parker (Boston: Houghton Mifflin, 1990) and *How Things Work: Flight* by Walter Boyne and others (Alexandria, Va.: Time-Life Books, 1990).

- Many toy stores sell inexpensive kite kits. Purchase several (you may have to buy these in advance as they are usually most readily available in the spring of the year) and have children work cooperatively in groups to read the directions and create kites. Or, find a book on making kites or paper airplanes and make it available to the children. Allow the children to create their own paper kites in different styles and decorate the kites to represent their school, family, self, or community. (*Step-by-Step Making Kites* by David Michael [New York: Kingfisher Books, 1993] is a good book for beginners.) Remember to allow time to celebrate by going outside to fly the kites!

- Create your own windy kite day. Bring several fans to school and position them around the room to create constant breezes. Tie several tiny (1-inch to 2-inch) kites the children have made onto the front of the fans to keep the festive atmosphere going throughout the day.

TEACHERS' DAY

• • • •

September 10
China

Background

In China teachers are held in high esteem. This day is set aside in honor of all those involved in the teaching profession. Schools are closed as are most businesses.

Activities

- Study careers in education. Older children may be interested in learning more about higher education, requirements for admission to college, and so on.

- Have children research the education systems of other countries and compare lengths of school days and years, class sizes, teaching methods (some countries teach by rote and recitation, for example), curricula (differences may include instruction in religion or a traditional native language), attitudes toward teachers, and so on.

- If your school does not celebrate Teacher Appreciation Day, speak to your PTA president about starting this tradition. Your local education association or the National Education Association can provide you with information and materials.

- Have children write thank-you notes/letters to former teachers.

RESPECT FOR THE AGED DAY

• • • •

September 12
Japan

Background

A day set aside to honor aged relatives and family friends.

Activities

- Practice letter-writing skills by writing letters to grandparents. Responses may later be shared with the class.

- Collect books in which grandparents or elderly people are heroes or main characters. Base a language arts unit of study on these books.

- Have children interview a grandparent or another older relative, friend, or neighbor.

- Take a field trip to a nearby retirement community or "adopt" a nursing home. Children might perform or prepare gifts for the residents on Respect for the Aged Day and plan to return throughout the year to celebrate selected holidays with their elderly friends.

INDEPENDENCE DAY

• • • •

September 15
Central America

Background

The area known as Central America consists of the countries of Guatemala, Belize, El Salvador, Honduras, Nicaragua, Costa Rica, and Panama. In 1921 Central America declared its independence from Spain and aligned itself politically with the newly independent Mexico.

HISPANIC HERITAGE MONTH

• • • •

September 15–October 15
United States

Background

Hispanic Heritage Month begins on the day on which Mexicans and Central Americans celebrate their independence. It is dedicated to the study of Hispanic life and culture, and includes the contributions of peoples from Central America, Mexico, much of South America, and a substantial number of the Caribbean nations.

Activities

- Many popular children's books are now printed in Spanish versions. Read both versions of a story to your class. By reading the Spanish translation first you can provide your English-speaking students an opportunity to see what it might be like to try to function in a classroom when you are unfamiliar with the language—thereby helping them to develop understanding and empathy for their non-English-speaking peers. If you are not fluent in Spanish this is not a problem. Students who do not speak the language will not know, and those who do will appreciate that you are willing to try to function in their language (much as they are now trying to learn English). Alternatively, you might ask your Spanish-speaking students to do the reading or to give you a quick reading lesson before you read the book.

- Learn a few simple Spanish words or phrases: hola (hello); adios (good-bye); amiga (friend—girl); amigo (friend—boy); madre (mother); padre (father). Learn to count in Spanish or to say the days of the week or months of the year (many have names similar to those in English). Discuss words that we have "borrowed" from the Spanish language (taco, chili, tortilla, piñata, sombrero, etc.).

- While they share a language, there is much diversity among the Hispanic countries and cultures worth exploring. Prepare a large wall chart listing the names of the countries down the side and aspects of the country or culture across the top (e.g., climate, religion, type of government, population, agriculture, exports, average income). As children read about and study the Hispanic nations they can add information they discover to the chart.

- Learn songs in Spanish. Add maracas, guiros, claves, or other appropriate yet inexpensive rhythm instruments.

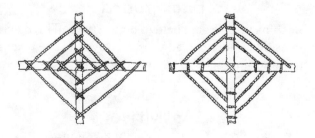

- Even young children can make colorful God's Eyes

(Ojos de Dioses) to decorate their classrooms or homes. To do this you need yarn and Popsicle® sticks. Fasten two sticks together in the center so they are at right angles to each other. Tie a piece of bright yarn to the center of this "X." Wrap the yarn around one arm of the "X" starting at the top, going around under the bottom, and back to the top. Move to the next arm of the "X" and repeat the procedure. Continue in this fashion until the sticks are covered as far as possible with yarn and a square or diamond shape has been completed. By using one color of yarn then tying on other colors (try to keep the knots in the back of the piece) thee decorations will have bright patterns.

- Create your own outdoor marketplace with papier-mâché fruits and vegetables. Rub real fruits and vegetables with petroleum jelly then cover with $\frac{1}{2}$ inch strips of newspaper dipped in a thin paste made of flour and water. Repeat this procedure four more times allowing to dry between each layer. Add a final layer using paper towels or tissue paper for a finer finish. When completely dry, cut the papier-mâché objects in half, remove the real fruits or vegetables, and glue the papier-mâché pieces back together. When glue is dry, paint and, if desired, shellac.

- For a group project make a piñata using a balloon and the papier-mâché technique described above. Instead of cutting the piñata in half, wait until the children have completely decorated it then cut a hole in the top, pop and remove the balloon, and fill with candy and trinkets. Punch two holes near the top and suspend the piñata from a tree. Mak ing sure that the other children stand well back, have one child at a time don a blindfold and swing a stick to try to break the piñata and release the goodies!

- Ask your art teacher to coordinate lessons with your unit of study. The children could make symmetric cutouts such as the ancient Mexicans made from amate bark paper, simple rhythm instruments, or clay pots.

- Work on soccer skills (the game originated in Mexico) or teach the children one of these games which are popular in the Hispanic countries:

"La Thunkna" (Bolivia): Draw a hopscotch board but instead of numbering it write the name of one day of the week in each space—Lunes, Martes, MieRcoles, Jueves, Viernes, Sabado, and Domingo (Monday through Sunday). Each player tosses a flat stone onto each day in turn, hops to that day on one foot, and kicks the stone back over the starting line. Players can continue until they make a mistake (put the other foot down or fail to kick the stone back over the starting line). The first player to reach Domingo (Sunday) is the winner.

"Horse Race" (Panama): Mark a starting and ending line on the playground or sidewalk. Two teams of players line up behind the starting line. The first player in each line is the "horse." The second player in each line holds onto the "horse's" waist and "rides" to the finish line. The second player then lets go of the first player and becomes the new "horse," rushing back to the starting line to get the next "rider." The first team to get everyone to the finish line wins.

"Who Is It?" (Chile): Players form a line with the first person in the line being "It." The game begins by asking questions as follows: It: "Have you seen my friend?" Others: "No, sir (ma'am)." It: "Do you know where my friend is?" Others: "No, sir (ma'am)." "It" then takes nine steps forward without turning. The other players switch places and call out "Who is it?" The player who is "It" may ask three questions (e.g., Is it a girl or boy? Does the person have blond or brown hair? Is the person short or tall?) and then must try to guess who the child immediately behind him is. If "It" is correct, that child gets another turn; if incorrect, the child behind "It" gets a turn to be the guesser.

- Play traditional and contemporary music from the various countries as background music during classroom activities.

- Taste some favorite ethnic foods. If possible cook them in the room so that the children can also enjoy the delicious smells. (See Appendix B, "Hispanic," for recipes.)

- Invite Hispanic-American members of your community to visit your class and talk about their country and culture.

- Take a field trip to a Mexican restaurant or to a Hispanic grocery store or shop. Be sure to arrange this well in advance so that someone will be available to show you around and answer students' questions.

INDEPENDENCE DAY

• • • •

September 16
Mexico

Background

Prior to its conquest by Spain in the early seventeenth century, Mexico was a center of advanced civilizations, primarily the Mayan and Aztec. Mexico is a federal republic that first declared independence from Spain in 1821, but there has been much political upheaval and many forms of government throughout the history of the nation. The principal religion is Catholic, and Spanish is the primary language, although over a million citizens speak Maya or other Native American languages.

INDEPENDENCE DAY

• • • •

September 16
Malaysia

Background

Malaysia lies at the western edge of the South China Sea and consists of the Malay Peninsula and part of the island of Borneo. During the sixteenth and seventeenth centuries both Portuguese and Dutch colonies were established along the coast, but at the end of the eighteenth century, with the coming of the British East India Company, England gained control of the area. The Malay Peninsula achieved independence on August 31, 1957, and Singapore and the Borneal states of Sabah and Sarawak gained independence on September 16, 1963. Together they formed the federation of Malaysia. Singapore seceded from the federation in 1965. The principal language is Malay; religions include Islam and Buddhism.

INDEPENDENCE DAY

• • • •

September 16
Singapore

Background

The island of Singapore, once part of the British Straits Settlements colony, became a self-governing state within the British Commonwealth in 1959 and four years later became a member of the federation of Malaysia. While they still celebrate their independence on the date of the forming of the federation, political strife between the heavily Chinese Singapore and the Malay-dominated mainland caused Singapore to secede in 1965. (See "Independence Day," Malaysia, above.)

INDEPENDENCE DAY

• • • •

September 18
Chile

Background

In 1817 Chilean nationals defeated the Spanish at Chacabuco and military leader Bernardo O'Higgins was declared dictator of Chile. Independence was formally declared in 1818. The 18 de Septembre, Chile's National Day, is a celebration of independence similar to our Fourth of July. Streets are decorated with flags, banners, and lanterns, and outdoor celebrations are held in every village and city. Special foods include chicha, a red wine, and humitas (see Appendix B, "Hispanic," for recipe). Guitar music fills the air and skirts

swirl as dancers holding handkerchiefs in their right hands beat out the rhythm of the Cueca Chilea, the national dance.

FEDERAL THANKSGIVING DAY

• • • •

September 20
Switzerland

Background

Although Thanksgiving Day is not a nationally celebrated holiday in Switzerland, in some of the country's cantons (states) people do get a holiday from work or school to celebrate with their families. On or around this time there are many village celebrations as this is the time of year when local herdsmen make their descent from the Alps bringing their sheep or herds of cows down from their summer alpine pastures. Frequently the cattle are adorned with flowers or decorated tree branches and brought into town in a formal procession, cowbells ringing. This is followed by a fair, feasting, yodeling, and dancing to traditional music. Frequently the festivities continue all night.

Activities

- Learn about mountains and the changing plant and animal life from the base of the mountains to the snowy peaks.

- Have children brainstorm a list of things we get from cows or sheep.

- Discuss the relationship between elevation and temperature, vegetation, and animal life.

- Divide the class into groups and assign each group one mountain in the Swiss Alps. Have them research to find the height of the mountain then work together to convert the height (usually given in feet) to inches, yards, meters, or miles.

- Make a fondue or taste some Swiss cheese or Swiss chocolate.

INDEPENDENCE DAY

• • • •

September 21
Malta

Background

Malta consists of three small islands (Gozo, Comino, and Malta) and lies south of Sicily in the Mediterranean Sea. Throughout history control over Malta changed hands frequently. In 1814 it became a part of the British Empire and self-government, in the form of a diarchy, was introduced in 1921. On September 21, 1964, Malta became an independent monarchical member of the British Commonwealth. Both Maltese and English are spoken on the islands. The primary religion is Roman Catholic.

REPUBLIC DAY

• • • •

September 22
Mali
Background

Archaeologists have found evidence that this area of Africa was inhabited as early as 2000 B.C. During the late nineteenth century the French conquered this territory and made it part of French West Africa. Historically speaking France held its influence for a relatively short time. Mali became a fully independent state on this date in 1960. French remains the official language and the primary religion is Islam.

HIGAN-E

• • • •

September 22 or 23
Buddhist

Background

Higan-E is celebrated twice a year, at the time of the

autumnal equinox in September and then again at the vernal equinox in March. During these two days of the year there is a balance of light and darkness with day and night being of equal length. The balance of these days symbolizes harmony, peace, and equality, important aspects of the teachings of Buddha.

Activities

• See "Higan-E," March 21–22.

INDEPENDENCE DAY

• • • •

September 30
Botswana

Background

Botswana, formerly known as Bechuanaland, was once a British protectorate. It gained independence in 1966 when a new constitution was drawn up and Seretse Khama was elected as the first president of the republic.

10
OCTOBER HOLIDAYS

NONFIXED DATES

Fire Prevention Week	United States	Week in Which October 8 Falls
Thanksgiving	Canada	Second Monday
Navaratri (Doll Festival)	India	
Diwali (New Year, Festival of Lights)	India, Hindu	October or November
Bhau-Beez (Brother and Sister Day)	India, Hindu	
Feast of Lights	Myanmar	
Sukkoth (Harvest)	Jewish	
Simhath Torah	Jewish	
Spring Festival	Peru	
Zolla (Harvest Festival)	Nigeria	

FIXED DATES

October 1	Independence Day	Nigeria
October 1	National Day	China
October 2	Independence Day	Guinea
October 2	Gandhi Jayanti (Mahatma Gandhi's Birthday)	India
October 3	National Foundation Day	North and South Korea
October 3	Republic Day	Germany
October 4	Independence Day	Lesotho
October 4	Feast of St. Francis of Assisi	Christian
October 7–9	Kunchi Festival	Japan
October 9	Independence Day	Uganda
October 10	Sports Day	Japan
October 12	Columbus Day	The Americas
October 20	Bab's Birthday	Baha'i
October 24	Independence Day	Zambia
October 26	International Red Cross Day	International
October 28	Republic Day	Czech Republic and Slovakia
October 29	Republic Day	Turkey
October 31	Halloween	United States, Great Britain, Ireland
October 31	UNICEF Day	United States

OCTOBER HOLIDAYS WITH NONFIXED DATES

FIRE PREVENTION WEEK

• • • •

Week in Which October 8 Falls United States

Background

Fire Prevention Week was first instituted in 1922 by President Warren Harding to commemorate the Great Chicago Fire that began on October 8, 1871. It always takes place during the week in which October 8 falls.

Activities

• Have children generate a fire safety list and inspect their own homes for safety as a homework assignment. Families can also become involved by practicing having fire drills at home.

• Learn emergency phone numbers and role-play what to do in case of a fire.

• Teach children to "Stop, Drop, and Roll." This is a technique used when one's clothing catches on fire. In that situation most children tend to panic and need to be taught to "stop" running, "drop" to the ground, cover their face with their hands and "roll" to smother the flames.

• Sharpen map skills by having children use local maps to find the quickest route from the fire station to a given street or address.

• Begin a career unit on related service professions, such as firefighters, police officers, chimney sweeps, and emergency medical specialists.

• Discuss/research the long-reaching effects forest fires have on plants, animals, and humans.

• Generate a list of inventions that have helped to prevent or control fire damage such as fire-retardant treatments for cloth, smoke alarms, fire extinguishers, and sprinkler systems. If desired the children may work to create inventions or improvements on current devices.

THANKSGIVING

• • • •

Second Monday in October Canada

Background

This national holiday is a celebration of the harvest. Traditions of the holiday are very similar to those of the United States (see November).

NAVARATRI (Doll Festival)

• • • •

India

Background

A nine-day celebration in South India, Navaratri, the Doll Festival, begins with the Hindu month of Ashwin and usually falls in our month of October. It is a time for women and girls to dress in their best clothes and visit one another. As a tribute to the Divine Mother, the Hindu goddess Durga, a copper or silver bowl filled with rice and covered with coconut or mango leaves is placed in each house. The room where the entertaining is to take place is festooned with brightly colored paper and decorated with flowers. Dolls representing animals, people, and gods line the walls. The entertainment consists of much music and dancing including songs to the goddess. As the guests depart the hostess gives gifts to each, possibly coconuts, cakes, or betel nuts.

Activities

- List the qualities that have traditionally been attributed to women and the roles that women have historically assumed. Discuss how and why this is changing.

- Children of both sexes could use their dolls (some boys prefer to call them "action figures") to write stories using the dolls as the main character.

- Trade children (boys for girls) with another teacher for part of the day. While the other teacher does something special with the boys, conduct a Navaratri celebration in your room with the girls. Have the girls in your class send invitations in advance. During the celebration allow the girls to eat coconut macaroons, play with dolls brought from home, and dance to Indian music.

DIWALI
(New Year, Festival of Lights)

• • • •

October or November
India, Hindu

Background

Diwali, also known as Dipavali, marks the beginning of the Hindu new year. The exact date depends on the Hindu calendar, but it usually falls in October or November. Diwali is called the Festival of Lights and is celebrated in honor of Rama-chandra, the seventh avatar (incarnation of the god Vishnu). It is believed that on this day Rama returned to his people after fourteen years of exile during which time he fought and won a battle against the demons and the demon king, Ravana. The people lit their houses in celebration of his victory over evil (light over darkness), thus, the Festival of Lights. The goddess Lakshmi, goddess of happiness and good fortune, also figures into the celebration.

The celebration comes at the end of the monsoon season, when the weather is generally mild and pleasant, and lasts from three to five days. In preparation for the new year people try to pay off their old debts, make or purchase new clothes, and thoroughly clean their houses. The exteriors of the houses are then whitewashed and sometimes decorated with designs drawn in white rice flour and filled in with color. Buildings are traditionally illuminated with oil-burning bowls called *dipa* lights or, more recently, with strings of electric lights. Daughters return home and friends and family are entertained.

On the first day of the festival prayers are said, a special breakfast consisting of fourteen different foods is eaten, and Lakshmi's statue is carried through the streets in a procession. Children enjoy eating sweets, and are sometimes given candies or toys bought from booths set up for the occasion. In South India children wear wreaths of flowers on their heads and anklets of bells. Boys in some areas construct elaborate castles and forts of mud and display them for visiting guests. After dark there are fireworks and people who live near rivers float lighted lamps on tiny rafts.

Activities

- Have children clear all their old "debts" today by turning in any uncompleted homework, paying money owed to the cafeteria, and returning overdue library books. This is also a good day for children to clean out their desks!

- Compare this holiday to new year's celebrations of other countries and cultures.

- Decorate Styrofoam meat trays or milk cartons with the top cut off to make rafts. Add tissue paper flames and float across the nearest body of water (a wading pool, your classroom sink, or a water table borrowed from the kindergarten). Use this as an introduction for a science lesson on objects that sink or float.

- Have the children draw the outline of a house on gray paper then "whitewash" the picture using white tempera paint. Pastel designs may be added if desired.

- Children could make forts or castles using sand, Legos, clay, blocks, or paper. Given equal amounts of the material to be used, children could compete to try to make the tallest, largest, most elaborate, or smallest possible structure.

- Plan a breakfast of fourteen different foods and have each child be responsible for bringing one type of food. In a classroom cold foods such as muffins, cereal, and fruits would work best. If more than fourteen children are involved some could provide Styrofoam bowls, plastic silverware, paper plates and napkins, and other items.

- Taste some sweets.

- Decorate the doorway to your room with a string of lights.

- Listen to representative Indian music.

- Burn an oil lamp to simulate the smell of the *dipa* lights.

BHAU-BEEZ

• • • •

(Brother and Sister Day)
India, Hindu

Background

Bhau-Beez (Brother's Day or Brother and Sister Day) is celebrated on the fifth day of Diwali. Married women return home and all girls and women honor their brothers on this day. A low stool is placed on the floor for the brother to sit on and the sister(s) draws decorative designs on the floor around it. In the evening the brother sits on the stool and a ritual is performed including the sister throwing a few grains of rice on her brother's head to wish him a long and safe life. She waits on him and brings him gifts of food. In return the brother often places a gift for his sister on her serving tray. When a mother has only sons she invites a niece or the daughter of a friend to be the "sister," which often develops relationships that last for life.

Activities

- The girls had their celebration earlier with Navaratri, now have them arrange a celebration for the boys in the class by decorating large sheets of paper for them to sit on and preparing food. While the girls are doing this the boys can use their imaginations to create simple gifts for their "sisters."

- Have the students hold a discussion regarding their siblings. Each child should then write a letter to or a story about a brother or sister that includes characteristics that they admire about that person. Children who do not have siblings could choose a cousin, friend, or classmate.

- Make a graph showing the number of brothers and sisters each child in the group has. Use the graph to write and answer story problems.

FEAST OF LIGHTS

• • • •

Myanmar

Background

This festival is very similar to the celebration of Diwali in the neighboring country of India. Homes are decorated with candles set in colorful cornucopias made of thin paper and fastened to long sticks that are placed in the ground. Children carry paper lanterns shaped like birds, animals, or other objects or push lighted carts. After dark, people walk through this fairyland atmosphere to visit and admire one another's decorations. Sweets made with coconut, raisins, and nuts are enjoyed.

Activities

- To introduce or review solid geometry, have the students wrap colored paper around a pencil leaving the pencil point exposed to form a tall, thin cylinder with a cone (the point) on the end. Use another sheet of colored paper to make a larger paper cone and tape it to the eraser end of the pencil to simulate candleholders. Take the finished products outdoors and place them in the ground arranging them by color to form a pattern.

- Make "trail mix" of raisins, nuts, and shredded coconut for the children to sample (perhaps outside while they are admiring their candleholders!).

SUKKOTH (Harvest)

• • • •

Jewish

Background

The Jewish calendar contains three pilgrimage festivals, so called because in the past on each of these days Israelis would climb the Temple Mount in Jerusalem. Each of these commemorates a historical event as well as marking one of the seasons of the agricultural year in Israel. Sukkoth is the third of these festivals. This is a time to remember the 40 years of wandering in the desert by the Jews following their exodus from Egypt. It is also a time to celebrate the grape harvest. Temporary shelters called sukkahs are built and decorated with leaves, grapes, gourds, cornstalks, and/or cranberries to symbolize the harvest. Families often take their meals in these boothlike constructions. The sukkah represents the tents people erected in the fields and lived in during the grape harvest in ancient Palestine. It is also a reminder of the frail huts that the children of Israel inhabited in the desert before reaching the promised land. Symbols of God's blessings that comprise a part of the Sukkoth celebration include the lemon and palm branch. (See "Passover," April, and "Shavuot," May, for information on the other two pilgrimage festivals.)

Activities

- Do a study of types of temporary housing used by people throughout history. This might include, but need not be limited to, caves, Conestoga wagons, Native American tepees, tents, and modern camping trailers.

- Research desert areas of the world and compare and contrast life in these regions. Be sure to include some deserts that are not arid such as Antarctica.

- Brainstorm to compose a list of fruits or vegetables that grow on vines.

- Construct a small sukkah. This could be done outdoors by hanging old sheets over a clothesline (or better yet, over two parallel clotheslines) and fastening to the ground with nails to form a tentlike structure. Inside, sukkahs could be made in a corner of a room. Two walls of the room form two of the sukkah's walls and the other two walls could be formed by hanging netting from the ceiling. In either case, the sukkah walls should be decorated with leaves, gourds, grapes and grapevines, and cornstalks cut by the children from construction paper. Spray the area with lemon-scented air freshener or slice and smell a real lemon. Allow the children to eat lunch or have snacks inside. Appropriate snacks might include grape jam on crackers and grape juice or lemonade.

SIMHATH TORAH

• • • •

Jewish

Background

This holiday marks the end of the Sukkoth festival and is the day on which the yearly cycle of readings from the Torah ends and begins anew. It is a time of rejoicing characterized by singing, dancing, and processions led by the rabbi who carries the sacred Scrolls of the Law.

SPRING FESTIVAL

• • • •

Peru

Background

Since Peru is located in the Southern Hemisphere, spring arrives in October. October is known as the purple month because the violet blossoms of the jacaranda trees are in bloom. It is also a time to remember Señor de los Milagrous, member of a Catholic brotherhood near Lima who painted an image of Christ on an adobe wall of one of the buildings of the brotherhood. In 1655 a violent earthquake occurred in the area causing many deaths and destroying virtually all of the buildings. Only the wall with the image of Christ remained standing. Today this miracle is remembered and celebrated in conjunction with the spring festival. Women wear purple robes tied with white cords and men wear purple armbands in honor of Señor de los Milagrous.

Activities

- Study earthquakes and their causes.

- Explain and discuss why the seasons are reversed in the Northern and Southern Hemispheres. It's interesting to note that the months of daylight savings time are also reversed. Discuss the reasons for this.

- If you were planning a trip to South America, where would you go to be in the Southern Hemisphere? Northern Hemisphere? To stand with one foot in each hemisphere? Have the students locate the equator on a world map and list South American countries according to these three categories.

- Purple is a secondary color. Mix red and blue colored water or paint to show how these primary colors blend to make purple. Have the children paint spring pictures using only shades of purple. Expand the lesson to include other secondary colors (orange and green). With older children include tertiary colors.

- The traditional pastry of this holiday is called *turron de dona pepa*. Everywhere in the streets of Peru peddlers are seen carrying large wooden boards stacked with this delicious treat. Taste some *turron de dona pepa* (see Appendix B, "Hispanic," for recipe) or substitute a ready-made pastry in its place.

ZOLLA
(Harvest Festival)

• • • •

Nigeria

Background

This harvest festival is celebrated by the Wurkum tribes of northern Nigeria and lasts from five to seven days. It marks the beginning of the new year, and takes place at the time of the new moon, usually in late October. Near sundown an appointed elder of the village climbs to a high vantage point and faces east. Villagers go outdoors and stand in a row with their family and also face east. Everyone stands very quietly and listens for the shouted cry that indicates that the moon has risen, the new year has arrived, and the Zolla festival has begun. At the signal the father begins dancing, children start beating on drums, and there is much joy. A feast is enjoyed after which everyone goes to the village square to dance by the light of torches and a bonfire. The following days are spent visiting and entertaining friends, with music and dancing each evening. One special food that is enjoyed during the festival is Zolla bread, a kind of fried bread made of cornmeal.

Activities

• Develop children's ability to reason logically by discussing the following types of questions: Why did the people face east? Which would begin celebrating earlier, a village in the eastern part of the region or a village in the western part? A village at 10 degrees longitude or one at 6 degrees? Why do we have different time zones? How many time zones are there? Explain why. It's 9:00 here. What time is it in the time zone east of ours? Seven time zones west of ours?

• Have the children write their own math story problems about different time zones to share with the group.

• Bake and eat some cornbread.

OCTOBER HOLIDAYS WITH FIXED DATES

INDEPENDENCE DAY

• • • •

October 1
Nigeria

Background

In 1960 Nigeria became a democracy thus ending a century of British rule. This, the most populous of all African nations, is composed of nearly 250 different ethnic groups. The prevailing religions include Muslim, Christian, and traditional African faiths. English is commonly spoken as well as a number of African languages.

NATIONAL DAY

• • • •

October 1
China

Background

In October 1911 the followers of Sun Yat-sen overthrew the Manchu dynasty in a nearly bloodless rebellion. They first looked to the West for a democratic form of government but later turned toward Russian Marxism. Under the communist government the country is officially atheist, but the religious sects of Taoism and Buddhism still exist as does Confucianism.

INDEPENDENCE DAY

• • • •

October 2
Guinea

Background

After Guinea gained its independence from France in 1958 the rule of a repressive socialist regime plunged the country into a period of economic disaster and reliance on foreign aid, but a more liberal government has reformed banking and trading policies in recent years and greatly improved the economy. Mining is a major industry and bauxite, diamond, and gold mines are all found in Guinea. In addition the country exports coffee, bananas, peanuts, pineapples, citrus fruits, and palm oil. Both French and native languages are spoken. Muslim and traditional African religions are currently practiced.

GANDHI JAYANTI
(Mahatma Gandhi's Birthday)

• • • •

October 2
India

Background

Mohandas Karamchand Gandhi, commonly known as Mahatma ("great soul") was born on October 2, 1869, in Porbander, India. He was the leader of Indian nationalism as well as a social reformer and Hindu religious leader. His philosophy and method of social protest, which he called *satyagraha* (soul force), was a type of passive resistance and greatly influenced civil rights movements. On this day prayers are said and celebrations are held throughout India in remembrance of Gandhi and his contributions to the country.

Activities

- Study the teachings of Gandhi, the part he played in the movement against discrimination of Indians in South Africa, and the impact he had on Martin Luther King Jr. and the civil rights movement in America.

- Discuss the Hindu caste system and Gandhi's success in bringing about the abolition of the practice of untouchability.

NATIONAL
FOUNDATION DAY

• • • •

October 3
North and South Korea

Background

This national holiday commemorates the founding of Korea by Tangun (or Dan-goon) in the year 2333 B.C. According to legend Tangun not only founded the kingdom of Korea, but ruled it for twelve centuries as well. The official Korean calendar is calculated from the time of this traditional founding of the country.

REPUBLIC DAY

• • • •

October 3
Germany

Background

At the close World War II, in May 1945, Germany signed an unconditional surrender to the Allies. In August of the same year the Potsdam Conference put into effect the conditions regarding Germany agreed upon at the earlier Yalta Conference. The conditions were intended to be tentative and to be in effect only until a peace conference was held. Since no such conference ever materialized these conditions shaped the history of Germany for the remainder of the century. Germany was divided into four separate zones to be administered by the United States, the Soviet Union, France, and England. Berlin, although located within the area ruled over by the Soviet Union, was similarly divided and was named as the seat of the Allied Control Council. The council failed to agree on implementation of the conditions of the Potsdam Conference, and separate governments were soon established. A complete split between the Soviet Union and the three other Allied nations occurred in 1948 and Germany was divided into two separate states—the Federal Republic of Germany (West Germany) and the German Democratic Republic (East Germany). By 1952 the East German government had established a guarded zone between the two Germanys to curb the flow of emigrants to West Germany, and in August 1961 the Berlin Wall was built for the same reason. It was not until the political upheavals in East Germany during 1989 and 1990 that reunification seemed feasible. In mid-1991 a number of "two-plus-four" talks between the two Germanys and the four Allied countries took place, and on October 3, 1991, the two Germanys were formally reunited as the Federal Republic of Germany.

INDEPENDENCE DAY

• • • •

October 4
Lesotho

Background

In the early nineteenth century Basuto Chief Moshoeshoe requested that the British administer the kingdom of Lesotho in an effort to provide a buffer against the Boer expansion. The British retained control until Lesotho became independent in 1966. Christianity is the main religion and both the African language, Sesotho, and English are spoken in this southern African nation.

FEAST OF ST. FRANCIS OF ASSISI

• • • •

October 4

Christian

Background

St. Francis, founder of the Franciscan order of the Catholic Church, lived during the late twelfth and early thirteenth centuries in Italy. He is remembered for his generosity to the poor and his willingness to minister to the lepers, but what most people recall first is his love of nature and animals.

Activities

- Take a nature walk. Have the children write about the plants, insects, and animals that you see.

- Give children a list of endangered species and have each choose one to research and report on. In the reports have them include reasons that the animal has become endangered; ways, if any, in which we can help; and the effect that extinction would have on the environment and/or other plant and animal life (e.g., a missing link in the food chain).

- Study careers that relate to animals, such as veterinarian, breeder, and farmer.

- Learn about the Society for the Prevention of Cruelty to Animals and/or the animal rights movement. Possible sources of information include the following:

  ASPCA
  424 East 92nd St.
  New York, NY 10128

  International Society for Animal Rights
  421 S. State St.
  Clarks Summit, PA 18411

  National Anti-Vivisection Society (NAVS)
  53 W. Jackson, Suite 1552
  Chicago, IL 60604

KUNCHI FESTIVAL

• • • •

October 7–9

Japan

Background

The Kunchi Festival of Suwa Shrine in Nagasaki is just one of many local festivals held in Japan. This particular celebration features a parade with decorated floats and a dragon dance. The dragon dance originated in China but has been adopted by the Japanese.

Activities

- Have children write about the personal traditions that their families follow in birthdays, holidays, or other special occasions. Put these together to create a class (or family) book of traditions.

- Compare local Japanese festivals to local celebrations held in our country, such as county fairs, rodeos, and seafood festivals.

- Have children write stories about dragons. Encourage them to use adjectives and descriptive phrases when depicting their dragons. List the words/phrases they used to describe their dragons (these will generally be negative), then generate a list of antonyms. Use the second list to write stories in the Asian tradition in which dragons are both necessary and good.

- Do a dragon dance. Have the children line up, each holding the waist of the child ahead. Have the first child wear a dragon mask (this can be made from a paper plate or large grocery bag) and drape a long piece of brightly colored netting or sheer fabric over the other children to form the body. Stress cooperation as the children weave and turn in their dance.

INDEPENDENCE DAY

• • • •

October 9

Uganda

Background

This Central African country borders on Lake Victoria. Once a British protectorate it became an independent nation in 1962. In this country English and the native languages of Swahili and Luganda are spoken. Likewise, both Christian and traditional religions flourish. Under the regimes of Milton Obote and Idi Amin hundreds of thousands of Ugandans were murdered, but in recent years political changes have brought law and order to the country as well as a greater respect for human rights.

SPORTS DAY

• • • •

October 10
Japan

Background

This relatively new national holiday of Japan was first celebrated in 1966 as a way of encouraging physical activity and a balance between physical and mental health and well-being. October 10 was chosen as the date for the holiday as a means of commemorating the opening of the Olympic games in Tokyo on October 10, 1964.

Activities

• Work with the physical education teacher to plan and execute a physical fitness day for the students. For one day children should write down everything they eat at meal and snack times, hours of sleep, and types and duration of exercise they got. Have them analyze the data, participate in cardiovascular and/or muscle-building exercises, and make commitments for improving their physical fitness.

• Using Olympic athletes as examples discuss the importance of both physical and mental fitness and self-discipline.

• Baseball is a popular sport in Japan. Organize children into groups and play a game of baseball, softball, or T-ball.

COLUMBUS DAY

• • • •

October 12
The Americas

Background

Financed by both private sources and the royal treasury of Spain Christopher Columbus, commanding a fleet of three ships—the Niña, the Pinta, and the Santa Maria—set sail on August 3, 1492, from Palos on a voyage intended to establish a new route to Japan and the East Indies. Having crossed the Atlantic he first sighted land on October 12 at San Salvador (Watlings Island). Before returning to Spain he established a post on Hispaniola (Santo Domingo). Columbus has been given credit for the discovery of the "New World"— all of the Western Hemisphere. In fact, in the Bahamas this date is known as Discovery Day. His "discovery" radically affected the lives of Native Americans, Europeans, and Africans and in recent years this celebration has drawn mixed reactions.

Activities

• We have all read accounts of Columbus's first sighting of land. Ask your students to write an account of the first sighting of Columbus's ships from a Native American's viewpoint.

• Read aloud and discuss *The Tainos: The People Who Welcomed Columbus* (see Appendix A, "Native American").

• Make a grid with "sugar," "horses," "potatoes," "disease," and "corn" written across the top and "Europeans," "Native Americans," and "Africans" written down the side. Have students work in groups to fill in the grid telling how each of the items affected each of the cultures. For example, sugar plantations brought wealth to the Europeans, but because of the need for cheap labor in the form of African and Native American slaves, the production of sugar had a serious negative affect on these two cultures.

• It took Columbus and his men 70 days to sail from Spain to Hispaniola. Use a map to calculate the distance in miles, then have children figure the average distance per day. Older children may enjoy converting land miles to nautical miles. (A nautical mile equals 6,076 feet, or about 1.15 land miles.)

• The invention of the magnet compass was a boon to Columbus and other explorers. Today is a good day to study compasses, Earth's poles, or magnets and magnetic field

- The stars were also used for purposes of navigation in early times. Find the North Star and discuss its significance to sailors. Use this as a starting point for a lesson on astronomy.

BAB'S BIRTHDAY

• • • •

October 20
Baha'i

Background

It is the belief of people of the Baha'i faith that Muhammad was the last prophet of the Age of Promise. Bab, born on October 20, 1819, is believed to be the first prophet of the Age of Fulfillment, and the forerunner of the great prophet, Baha'Allah.

INDEPENDENCE DAY

• • • •

October 24
Zambia

Background

On this date in 1964 Zambia gained independence from Great Britain. Originally known as a copper mining center, in recent years Zambia's economy is becoming more dependent on agriculture. Bantu languages are spoken here along with English, and both traditional and Christian religions are followed.

INTERNATIONAL RED CROSS DAY

• • • •

October 26
International

Background

The Red Cross was established in 1864 as a result of the Treaty of Geneva. It was drawn up to assure the protection of the wounded and those who cared for them in time of war. Later it was extended to include naval warfare, prisoners of war, and civilians in time of war. The United States became the 32nd nation to sign the Geneva Convention in 1881 when the American Association of the Red Cross was founded with Clara Barton as its first president. In 1919 the League of Red Cross Societies was established to promote mutual aid and cooperation among the Red Cross societies of various nations during peacetime.

Activities

- Have the children research and report on various medical professions or invite a doctor, nurse, or medical technician to visit and speak to your class. Visit your local fire department or medical emergency squad. Unless there is a crisis these people will usually be glad to allow you and your children to view the ambulance and will take time to explain various pieces of equipment. It is considered courteous, however, to phone ahead.

- Study the role of the International Red Cross following natural disasters.

- Study basic first aid and methods for handling emergency situations. All children should memorize emergency phone numbers and should be able to deal with minor cuts, scrapes, bumps, and nosebleeds.

- Children who participate in sports need to know how to avoid heatstroke and what to do if it occurs.

- Examine different types of natural disasters.

REPUBLIC DAY

• • • •

October 28
Czech Republic and Slovakia

Background

The union of the Czech lands and Slovakia was first proclaimed in 1918. In 1938 Czechoslovakia became the first non-Germanic nation to be subjugated by Adolf Hitler. The Czechs and Slovaks began a resistance movement abroad and a provisional government was established and located in London. After liberation by U.S. troops the government moved to Prague where a provisional national assembly was formed on October 28, 1945. Today celebrations of the liberation include fireworks displays and *lampion* processions in which hundreds of people march through the streets carrying *lampions* (paper lanterns) lit by candles and held high on sticks.

Activities

- Using current sources have the students research and report on the dissolution of the Federation of Czechoslovakia into the Czech Republic and Slovakia that took effect on January 1, 1993.

- Use a historical atlas to see how the political boundaries of countries have changed over the years.

- Study and compare other satellite countries of the former Soviet Union and their current status.

- Make paper lanterns (see "Tet Trung Thu," September).

REPUBLIC DAY

• • • •

October 29
Turkey

Background

For 600 years, until World War I, Turkey was the center of the vast Ottoman Empire that spread across southeastern Europe, northern Africa, and southwestern Asia. In 1923 Mustafa Kemal was responsible for the founding of the Republic of Turkey. He became known as Ataturk, Father of the Turks. Languages of Turkey include Turkish, Kurdish, and Arabic. Sunni Muslim, a conservative Islamic religion, unites the vast majority of the people.

HALLOWEEN

• • • •

October 31
United States,
Great Britain, Ireland

Background

Originally, Halloween, or Samhain as it was then called, was the eve of the Celtic New Year. On this day tribute was paid to Samhain, the lord of death, in honor of the dying year and of those souls who were no longer among the living. It was believed that the veil between the worlds of the living and the dead was the thinnest on this night. The sun god was also honored in thanksgiving for the harvest, and a central part of the festival was the lighting of a bonfire, a reflection of the sun. During early Christian times the date became known as All Hallows' Eve and remained a time to pray for the dead and honor the saints.

Today we light candles in jack-o'-lanterns rather than bonfires. We retain other elements of the pagan celebration as well: Halloween is still a night for spirits, and both children and adults enjoy dressing as witches, ghosts, and goblins and celebrating.

Activities

- Using chalk on black paper draw human skeletons and study the functions of various bones.

- Make a list of fears, then divide the list into those that are real (such as fire and being abandoned) and those that are imaginary (such as ghosts, skeletons, and monsters). Discuss constructive ways to deal with both kinds of fears.

- At this time of year children's thoughts turn to witches, vampires, mummies, and zombies. Researching the origins of such monsters will take your children back in time to central Europe, ancient Egypt, and the Caribbean islands where they will learn about rare diseases, religious practices, and the fear of the unknown.

- Carve the flesh of a pumpkin into different shapes and use tempera paint to make pumpkin prints on paper. (If you are planning to carve a jack-o'-lantern save the pieces you cut out for this purpose.)

- Show the students a pumpkin and have them estimate how many seeds are inside. Cut the pumpkin open and count the seeds to see whose guess was the closest. (Encourage the children to work cooperatively and to group the seeds and count by twos, fives, or tens.) Dry the seeds to plant in the spring or wash, salt, and bake them for a snack. Carve the pumpkin into a jack-o'-lantern using geometric shapes.

- Make pumpkin bread or cookies. (See recipes in Appendix B, Halloween.) Allow the children to measure the ingredients, determine the time when the food will finish baking, and figure out how much each person will get to eat.

UNICEF DAY

• • • •

October 31
United States

Background

The United Nations International Children's Emergency Fund (UNICEF) was established in December 1946. It was designed to provide for children and mothers in underdeveloped nations. October 31, Halloween, became UNICEF Day as part of a design to have children help children. On Halloween night, as children went about trick-or-treating, they would carry small cardboard boxes with the UNICEF logo on them instead of treat bags and collect coins in place of the usual candy. The money collected would then be turned in to the UNICEF office and used to help needy students the world over. This practice is dying out as fewer and fewer parents allow their children to trick-or-treat from house to house, but the intent has not changed. This is a good day for us all to count our blessings and perhaps to do something for those less fortunate whether at home or abroad.

Activities

- Plan and execute a Halloween party. Charge small fees for snacks and to play games. Give the proceeds to UNICEF or to a local charity.

- Celebrate UNICEF Day in your class, rather than Halloween. Have children come to school in costumes from various countries. Older children could write reports on the country they chose, younger ones could be ready to tell about it.

- Brainstorm or use newspapers and magazines to create a list of common acronyms and what they stand for.

- Have children plan and carry out a "Children Helping Children" fund raising activity for which they make and sell a product and donate the proceeds to UNICEF. This could involve a bake sale featuring pumpkin cookies or bread, the children making greeting cards or gift wrap from pumpkin prints, or some other product the children think up.

11

NOVEMBER HOLIDAYS

NONFIXED DATES

Htamane-hto (Harvest)	Myanmar	
Festa dos Tabuleiros (Festival of the Trays)	Portugal	
Father's Day	Sweden	Second Sunday
Thanksgiving	United States	Fourth Thursday
Umoja Karamu	African American	Fourth Sunday
Loy Krathong	Thailand	Mid-November

FIXED DATES

November 1	All Saints' Day	Roman Catholic, Anglican
November 1–2	El Dia de los Muertos (The Day of the Dead)	Mexico
November 2	All Souls' Day	Roman Catholic
November 3	Independence Day	Panama
November 5	Guy Fawkes Day	England
November 9	Independence Day	Cambodia
November 10 or 11	St. Martin's Day	Europe
November 11	Veterans Day	United States
November 11	Remembrance Day	Canada
November 11	Independence Day	Poland
November 12	Baha' Allah's Birthday	Bahai
November 14	Children's Day	India
November 15	Shichi-go-san (7-5-3 Festival)	Japan
November 18	Birth of Guru Nanak	Sikh
November 19	National Celebration	Monaco
November 22	Independence Day	Lebanon
November 22	St. Cecilia's Day	Christian
November 28	Independence Day	Mauritania
November 30	Independence Day	Barbados
November 30	St. Andrew's Day	Europe

NOVEMBER HOLIDAYS WITH NONFIXED DATES

HTAMANE-HTO
(Harvest)

• • • •

Myanmar

Background

Following the first harvesting of the rice crop, usually sometime in November, the people of Myanmar celebrate with a festival called Htamane-hto. The farmers send packets of pickled tea leaves (called *la-hpet*) to all the men in the neighborhood along with an invitation for them to come and help in the husking of the rice. Toward dusk the men arrive and enjoy a bit of socializing and tea before settling down to work. They then take out their mortars and pestles and work on husking the rice while a party atmosphere continues with stories, singing, and eating of *la-hpet* (which helps to keep everyone awake). While the men are doing this the women are busy preparing onion, ginger, coconut, and sesame seeds, which they then mix with the prepared rice to make a dish called *htamane*. After it is cooked everyone enjoys eating some of the fresh *htamane*, and the girls, dressed in their finest clothes, visit their friends and neighbors and present them with gifts of *htamane*. The following day the boys accompany their fathers to the monastery where they present lacquered boxes full of *htamane* and baskets of rice to the Buddhist monks.

Activities

• Compare religions and the different types of gifts people offer to churches. Discuss when and how the gifts are given today and how that has changed over time.

• Discuss and compare different kinds of "work parties" (e.g., quilting bees, barn raisings, moving parties, corn-husking bees) and why these are more prevalent and important in agrarian cultures.

• Study different kinds of grain (rice, wheat, oats, etc.) and how they grow.

FESTA DOS TABULEIROS
(Festival of the Trays)

• • • •

Portugal

Background

The Festa dos Tabuleiros, the Festival of the Trays, is a Portuguese harvest festival based in the city of Tomar. Because the citizens cannot always afford a yearly celebration they save their money and conduct the festival every two or three years. For several days before the festival the people work on making elaborate hats called *tabuleiros*, which are decorated with bread and flowers. On the day of the festival the girls don long white dresses and their *tabuleiros* and lead a procession through the town carefully balancing the tall, heavy hats. They are followed by priests, brass bands, and cattle. Even the cattle wear flowers on their horns or heads. When the procession ends the cattle are roasted and there is a great feast. Much of the beef, as well as the bread from the *tabuleiros*, is given to the needy. What is left is auctioned off and the money used to help the poor of Tomar.

Activities

• Compare this festival to our Thanksgiving holiday. Discuss how the two are alike and how they are different.

• Using paper plates as bases have the students design *tabuleiros* using paper, egg cartons, Styrofoam, and other items. Have a contest and give awards for the tallest, fanciest, most colorful, and so on.

• At the children's level discuss financial planning, savings accounts, or budgeting.

FATHER'S DAY

• • • •

Second Sunday
in November
Sweden

Background

The celebration of Father's Day in Sweden is based on the traditions of the American holiday, and the customs, including the almost compulsory gift of a necktie, are nearly identical. The main difference is that in Sweden the day is celebrated in November whereas in the United States the celebration falls in June.

THANKSGIVING

• • • •

Fourth Thursday
in November
United States

Background

Tradition has it that the first Thanksgiving in North America was held during the autumn of 1621 at Plymouth Colony, Massachusetts, when the colonists and Native Americans sat down together to give thanks for the harvest and to feast on wild turkey and venison. In recent years there has been debate over the legitimacy of this claim with Virginia maintaining that a harvest celebration was first held in that state. In all probability both groups of colonists, unbeknownst to each other, held feasts of thanksgiving that were quite similar (not to mention that the Native Americans held harvest ceremonies in both areas long before the arrival of the Europeans!). Since that time autumn harvest festivals have become a tradition, and to allow for uniformity the date was eventually set, by presidential proclamation, as the fourth Thursday of November. On this date schools and businesses are closed, many churches hold services to give thanks for the blessings of the past year, and families gather together to visit and feast.

Activities

- Brainstorm a list of holidays that are neither political nor religious in nature. Discuss reasons the list is so limited.

- Compare this holiday to harvest festivals celebrated in other countries of the world.

- Begin a unit of study on Native Americans. Learn about their seasonal rites and celebrations.

- Brainstorm a list of foods that may have been enjoyed at the first Thanksgiving and then have children research to find out if the foods really were available to the first settlers (remember, the early settlers had no cows and no sugar). After this is completed, generate a second list of foods, this time noting the foods that the children's families prepare for their Thanksgiving dinners. Compare the two lists. Depending on the social and cultural backgrounds of the children in the group they may be very similar or very different. Discuss the reasons for this.

- Based on the research the children did earlier, plan and enjoy a feast of traditional foods (e.g., cornbread, honey, turkey, nuts, fruits, etc.).

- Have the children choose whether they want to be Pilgrims or Native Americans and make costumes to wear to the feast. Play Native American drum or flute music in the background.

- Use a Native American drum to set the beat for the children's movement around the room when making transitions from one activity to another.

UMOJA KARAMU

• • • •

Fourth Sunday in November
African American

Background

Literally translated the Kiswahili words "umoja" and "karamu" mean "unity feast." This African-American celebration was first introduced in 1971 by Edward Simms Jr. The spirit of the day is one of family and of striving together in harmony.

Five periods of African-American life are represented in the ceremony of Umoja Karamu in the forms of literature, music, food, and colors. The five periods and their colors are as follows: (1) before slavery = black, (2) during slavery = white, (3) emancipation = yellow, (4) struggle for liberation = green, and (5) looking to the future = orange or gold. During the ceremony narratives of each historical period are read as music of the period is played. Decorations in the five colors as well as foods in each of the colors are part of the celebration.

Activities

• Have children discuss or write about gatherings that their families have, such as family reunions, birthdays, and holidays. Talk about traditions of individual families and of cultural groups.

• Plan and carry out a classroom unity feast. Ask children to discuss the word unity and how it pertains to your class "family." Ask the children to bring in favorite snacks for that day and to attribute meaning to the colors of the food (the color might signify a certain period of the school year, a quality that the children think they should be working toward, or a characteristic of the class).

• Have children write nonfiction stories about examples of times when they witnessed classmates working together and helping each other. Place the stories in a scrapbook that can be added to throughout the year. Pages of the scrapbook might be different colors to represent different times of the year (orange for fall, white for winter, green for spring, yellow for summer). Periodically throughout the year "unity hours" could be held during which pic-

tures from the scrapbook would be viewed, stories read orally, and seasonal snacks enjoyed.

• Listen to different kinds of music associated with African Americans, from traditional African music to spirituals, blues, jazz, reggae, or steel drum bands. Learn about famous black musicians and the contributions they have made.

• Divide the class into five cooperative work groups. Have each group research and report on one of the five periods of African-American history. As an alternative, individual children could interview members of their families to trace their histories as far back as possible and then could write about the different periods of their family's history.

• Study the symbolism of colors—white/purity, red/anger, blue/ depression, purple/royalty, and so on.

• Have children draw or paint pictures using only the five colors that are associated with Umoja Karamu/white, black, yellow, green, and gold or orange. Older children may want to choose their own colors to use symbolically in their pictures of their families or class. Later their classmates can try to interpret the symbolism they intended.

LOY KRATHONG

• • • •

Mid-November
Thailand

Background

Loy Krathong takes place at the time of the full moon in the twelfth lunar month (usually in mid-November). It comes at the end of the rainy season and at a time when the farmers' work in the fields is mostly completed and they have time to relax and celebrate before harvesting their crops. The festival is of Brahminical origin and traditionally is a time to offer thanks to the god of water. On the night of Loy Krathong, Thais meet on the banks of rivers and canals to float elaborate boats illuminated with candles or joss sticks and frequently decorated with flowers and leaves. The boats were originally made of banana leaves ("Krathong" means a bowl made of a banana leaf), but today wood, cardboard, and plastic are frequently used instead. The boats often contain offerings of coins or betel nuts, and symbolically the floating of the boat or bowl with its offerings is a way of dispelling sins and bad luck.

Activities

- Do a lesson on water—its importance to plants, its essential role to human and animal life, or a study of the different types of bodies of water.

- Give the children a variety of "junk" (such as large plastic lids, Styrofoam sandwich containers, small cardboard boxes, wood scraps, poster board) and allow them to invent their own boats. Unlit birthday candles as well as paper or real flowers and leaves can be added for a festive touch. Provide a water table, wading pool, or sink full of water for the children to use in testing, and later sailing, their Loy Krathong boats.

- Compare to other similar festivals (such as Holi, see March, and Pimia, see March 21–22) that center around water.

NOVEMBER HOLIDAYS WITH FIXED DATES

ALL SAINTS' DAY

• • • •

November 1
Roman Catholic, Anglican

Background

This festival, also known as All-Hallows-Tide, is dedicated collectively to all of the saints. It was first celebrated in the seventh century and was made an authorized holiday by Pope Gregory IV in 837.

EL DIA DE LOS MUERTOS
(The Day of the Dead)

• • • •

November 1–2
Mexico

Background

El Dia de los Muertos, the Day of the Dead, is a somber yet playful holiday in Mexico during which time it is believed that spirits return to Earth. Preparations are made days in advance. An altar is set up in each house, upon which are set pictures of relatives who have died, and the house is stocked with food so that the returning ghosts will not become angry at the lack of hospitality and play nasty tricks on the family. Bakeries sell a sweet bread called *pan de los muertos*, which is shaped in the form of bones or skulls, and street vendors and stores carry chocolate ghosts and whimsical skeleton-shaped toys and jewelry. On the night of November 1 families visit cemeteries bearing food for their departed loved ones, burn incense, pray, and illuminate the graves with candles. Fireworks explode to light the path homeward for the departed. Following the visits to the graves there is feasting, music, and games.

Activities

- Compare El Dia de los Muertos to Halloween (see October 31), All Souls' Day (see below), and/or the Japanese Bon Festival (see July 13–15).

- Make bread dough ornaments in shapes appropriate for El Dia de los Muertos or in other whimsical shapes of the children's choosing. To make the dough, blend together 1 cup of salt and 2 cups of flour then add 1 cup of water a little at a time. Knead for 7–10 minutes. Form into desired shapes (they should be fairly thin, no more than $1/2$ inch) and bake on a cookie sheet at 325°F for about 30 minutes. Test for hardness by tapping lightly with a spoon. If you wish to make hanging decorations, push a paper clip into the finished piece until only one loop of metal is showing or poke a hole in the dough with a pencil point to put a string through later. After baking, the decorations may be painted with bright colors and, if desired, shellacked.

- Burn some incense, listen to Mexican music, or have a "feast" of traditional Mexican foods.

ALL SOULS' DAY

• • • •

November 2
Roman Catholic

Background

This holiday was first instituted at the monastery in Cluny in 993 and quickly spread throughout the Christian world. It is a day of alms giving and prayers for the dead. The intent is for the living to assist those in purgatory.

INDEPENDENCE DAY

• • • •

November 3
Panama

Background

In 1717 Panama became a part of the Spanish territory of New Granada (Panama, Colombia, Venezuela, and Ecuador). Independence was gained from Spain in 1819 and eventually Panama became a part of the republic of Colombia. In 1903 representatives of Colombia and the United States agreed on a treaty allowing the United States to build a canal through Panama. The Colombian senate refused to ratify the treaty, however, so in November 1903 the Panamanians declared and won their independence from Colombia in a bloodless revolution.

GUY FAWKES DAY

• • • •

November 5
England

Background

In 1605 a group of aggrieved Catholic landowners banded together in a conspiratorial plot to blow up the English houses of Parliament and King James I on the opening date of Parliament, November 5. Guy Fawkes, one of the conspirators of what came to be

known as the Gunpowder Plot, spent nearly a year filling a rented cellar below the House of Lords with gunpowder. The plot was discovered on the day before it was to have been carried out and Guy Fawkes and his confederates were captured and hanged.

The incident is commemorated by the searching of the vaults below Parliament before the opening of each session as well as by the celebration of Guy Fawkes Day. On this day bonfires are lit throughout England, Guy Fawkes and his coconspirators are hanged or burned in effigy, and everywhere there are huge displays of fireworks. Before the bonfire is lit children carry the "Guy" through the streets shouting "A penny for the Guy!" Onlookers can hurl rotten vegetables, sticks, and insults at the effigy of Guy Fawkes. They also throw coins, which the children collect and later use to purchase refreshments. Potatoes and chestnuts are often roasted in the bonfire.

Activities

- Examine terrorist activity in the past and present. Discuss appropriate and inappropriate methods of bringing about changes in governmental policies.

- Begin with Parliament and discuss/compare different systems of government.

- Consider the symbolism of fireworks in the celebration of this and other holidays.

INDEPENDENCE DAY

• • • •

November 9
Cambodia

Background

In 1863 France made Cambodia a protectorate thereby ending the encroachment of Vietnam and Thailand upon Cambodian soil. In 1953, as a result of the Geneva Declaration, Cambodia gained its independence. The country is primarily Buddhist and the language spoken is Khymer.

ST. MARTIN'S DAY

• • • •

November 10 or 11
Europe

Background

St. Martin's Day, or Martinmas, was originally a thanksgiving festival in honor of St. Martin, or Tours, a fourth-century bishop and patron of the harvest. The focus of this holiday now varies greatly from country to country. In Great Britain this date is now most closely associated with the signing of the armistice of World War I, which occurred on November 11, 1918 (see Remembrance Day below). Following the Reformation, much of Germany began to celebrate St. Martin's Day on November 10, the date of Martin Luther's birth. (Martin Luther was baptized on November 11, St. Martin's Day, and that is how he came to be a Martin.) A relatively new custom in Germany and the Netherlands is that of parades featuring schoolchildren carrying lanterns made of paper or carved from harvest vegetables. Many countries enjoy feasts on this day, frequently featuring goose. This custom was probably influenced by the legend that St. Martin, who felt that he was unworthy of being made the Bishop of Tours, hid in a flock of geese until their squawking and cackling gave him away.

VETERANS DAY
(United States)
and
REMEMBRANCE DAY
(Canada)

• • • •

November 11

Background

Formerly known as Armistice Day, this holiday was first celebrated at the close of World War I to honor those who fought in the war and to commemorate the armistice that ended the war. Because of World War II and the Korean conflict the name was changed in the United States and Canada so that all veterans would be remembered and honored. In some European countries, however, this date is still a legal holiday commemorating the signing of the armistice at the end of World War I, and is still known as Armistice Day.

INDEPENDENCE DAY

• • • •

November 11
Poland

Background

On the night of November 10, 1918, just hours before the armistice that ended World War I was signed, Polish troops disarmed the German garrison in central Poland. A provisional government was set up and the country of Poland as we now know it was born. It took several years for the boundaries of the nation to be established and many years for Poland to get out from under the Communist control of the Soviets, but Poland is now a free and independent nation. Poles celebrate the date that ended World War I as their national Independence Day.

BAHA'ALLAH'S BIRTHDAY

• • • •

November 12
Bahai

Background

According to Baha'i tradition Baha'Allah was a descendant of Abraham. He was born on November 12, 1817, in Persia (now Iran). When he was still a child a soothsayer interpreted a dream of his father's to mean that Baha'Allah would someday achieve "supreme ascendancy" over the world of people. Originally a follower of the Bab, Baha'Allah was persecuted, jailed, reduced to poverty, and banished from his native land to Iraq for his religious teachings. During the ten years he spent in Baghdad his personal influence and fame reached a peak, and on April 21, 1862, he instituted the feast of Ridvan and assumed his position as the prophet of God. (See also notes for "Ridvan," April 21–May 2.)

CHILDREN'S DAY

• • • •

November 14
India

Background

November 14, the anniversary of the birth of Jawaharlal Nehru, the first premier of India, is celebrated throughout India as Children's Day. On this day children gather to perform in cultural programs and to participate in rallies.

Activities

- Have the children work cooperatively in groups to research the art, music, literature, and theater of India and plan their own cultural program.

SHICHI-GO-SAN
(7-5-3 Festival)

• • • •

November 15
Japan

Background

This is a special day set aside for girls who are seven years old, boys who are five, and three years olds of both sexes. On this day those children are dressed in their finest clothes—frequently traditional costumes—and taken by their parents to the shrine. There the guardian spirits are thanked for the children's good health and prayers are said for their future growth and development. Later the children receive presents, candy, and money and have parties with their friends. This tradition probably goes back to the times when there was a much higher rate of infant mortality and these were significant milestones in children's lives.

Activities

- Have the children bring pictures of themselves at the ages of three, five, and seven. Ask them to discuss with their families what they did that was memorable at each age, to write a paragraph to go with each picture, and to present their abbreviated autobiographies to the class.

- Do a lesson on odd numbers.

- Practice counting by threes and/or fives.

- Play a game of "Buzz." The children sit in a circle. They start with the number 1 and, with each child in turn saying a number, count as high as they can. The catch is that they cannot say any number that is divisible by 7 or has a 7 in it (e.g., 7, 14, 72) but must say "buzz" instead. Children who make a mis-

take are out of the game. The game can also be played with 5 or 3 as the "buzz" number with younger children.

- Brainstorm a list of medical advances that have improved children's chances for good health (such as regular checkups, vaccinations, prenatal care, and the development of penicillin and other drugs). Older children could do research projects on these advances and/or the people who brought them about. With younger children discuss what they can do on their own to stay healthy.

BIRTH OF GURU NANAK

• • • •

November 18
Sikh

Background

Nanak, born in India in 1469, was a Hindu religious leader who came to be known as Guru (teacher). By establishing Sikhism he attempted to reconcile the Hindus and Muslims and to bring them together under a new religion with one god, Sat Nam (True Name). As a concession to the Muslims Guru Nanak rejected the Hindu caste system, and as a concession to the Hindus he retained the idea of reincarnation. Preceding the *gupurb* (anniversary of his birth) is the continuous reading of the teachings of the Guru Granth Sahib, which takes about two full days. On the morning of the *gupurb* religious services are held. Because hospitality is of great importance to the Sikhs most *gurdwaras* (temples) have an attached communal kitchen. Following the service food is shared.

NATIONAL CELEBRATION

• • • •

November 19
Monaco

Background

Monaco is a tiny independent principality bordering the Mediterranean. Its total area is 1.9 square kilometers. During the fourteenth century the Grimaldis, a Genoese family, established control over Monaco. In 1450 Monaco came under Spanish rule and in 1641 it was taken under the protection of France. The Treaty of Paris, signed in 1814, returned the principality to the Grimaldi family.

INDEPENDENCE DAY

• • • •

November 22
Lebanon

Background

The Ottomans ruled Lebanon until the end of World War I when the League of Nations mandated the country to France. In 1920 the French established Lebanon as a separate state. Following the fall of France in World War II the Vichy regime held control of the country until British and Free French forces occupied it in the summer of 1941. Independence was proclaimed on November 22, 1941. Approximately 60 percent of the Lebanese people are members of Shiite, Sunni, or Druze Islamic sects while the remainder of the population is primarily Christian. Under a constitution that guaranteed Christian domination, civil war broke out in the 1970s and strife continues to this day. Both French and Arabic are spoken in the country.

ST. CECILIA'S DAY

• • • •

November 22
Christian

Background

St. Cecilia was a third-century Roman martyr who is credited with the invention of the organ. According to legend she had a great musical talent and praised God with both vocal and instrumental music thereby causing an angel to fall in love with her. St. Cecilia is considered the patron saint of musicians.

Activities

• John Dryden was inspired to write an ode about St. Cecilia which Frideric Handel set to music in 1736. Ask your music teacher if a recording is available, or order it through a local music store and play it for the class (G. F. Handel, *Ode for Saint Cecilia's Day*, Laserlight; order # 15 607). Discuss the elements that make classical music distinctive.

• Have a musical talent show and invite all of the children to perform their favorite piece of music on an instrument or vocally.

• Listen to recorded organ music.

• Make children aware of classical music by having them listen for its use as background music as they watch movies and TV shows. Discuss the use of such music to affect the emotions of the viewer.

• Provide the children with empty milk cartons, paper plates, string, cardboard tubes, and other items, and have them invent musical instruments. Form a class rhythm band. (See activity for "Tet Trung Thu," September.)

• Discuss careers in the field of music.

• Have the children write simple songs in praise of nature, your school, or a special person. Combine this with a language arts lesson on rhyming words and poetry.

INDEPENDENCE DAY

• • • •

November 28
Mauritania

Background

The Portuguese explored in the fifteenth century the area that is now Mauritania. In the nineteenth century it was seized by the French and became part of what was known as French West Africa. It became a protectorate of France in 1903, a colony in 1920, and a French overseas territory in 1946. On November 28, 1960, Mauritania became an independent republic. The country has been influenced by French, Arabic, and African cultures. Both Arabic and French are spoken on the island.

INDEPENDENCE DAY

• • • •

November 30
Barbados

Background

The first British settlers arrived on this, the most easterly of the Caribbean islands, in 1627. Of the former Caribbean colonies Barbados is the only one that never changed hands. Barbados was granted a distinct government in 1937 and by 1961 had achieved full internal self-government. On November 30, 1966, Barbados was proclaimed an independent state within the British Commonwealth. The religion of the country is Protestant and both Creole and English are spoken on the island.

ST. ANDREW'S DAY

• • • •

November 30
Europe

Background

Traditionally St. Andrew is the saint to whom young unmarried women appeal when seeking a husband. St. Andrew's Day is a time for parties, fortune-telling, and participation in superstitious rituals. Two popular ways of determining one's future mate come to us from Poland. The first involves pouring melted wax on water and trying to divine from the resulting shapes who one's future husband will be. The second requires the woman to peel an apple leaving one long, unbroken piece of peeling. The peeling is then thrown over the left shoulder and the letter it forms when it lands is said to be the initial of the woman's future spouse.

Activities

- Instead of an apple peel, have the children (both male and female) take turns throwing a length of red ribbon over their shoulders. Next they need to take a good look at the resulting shape and write a creative story about what they saw.

- Pour melted wax from a candle or other source onto a bowl of water. Discuss why the two do not mix.

- Learn about the different melting points of wax, ice, steel, and other substances.

12

DECEMBER HOLIDAYS

NONFIXED DATES

Hanukkah (Festival of Light)	Jewish
Pikkujoulu	Finland

FIXED DATES

December 4	St. Barbara's Day	Poland
December 5	Sinterklaas Day	Netherlands
December 6	St. Nicholas Day	Europe
December 6	Independence Day	Finland
December 9	Independence Day	Tanzania
December 10	Constitution Day	Thailand
December 12	Independence Day	Kenya
December 12	Day of Our Lady of Guadalupe	Mexico
December 13	Feast of Santa Lucia	Sweden
December 16	Bijoy Dibash (Victory Day)	Bangladesh
December 16	National Day	Bahrain
December 16–24	Nine Days of Posada	Latin America
December 18	Republic Day	Niger
December 21 or 22	Mother Night (Winter Solstice)	International
December 24	Independence Day	Libya
December 25	Christmas	Christian
December 26	Boxing Day	Europe
December 26	St. Stephen's Day	Czech Republic and Slovakia
December 26	Junkanoo	Bahamas
December 26–January 1	Kwanzaa	African American
December 28	Childermas	Europe, Mexico
December 31	Birth of Guru Gobind Singh	Sikh
December 31	New Year's Eve	International
December 31	Festival of Iemanja	Brazil

DECEMBER HOLIDAYS WITH NONFIXED DATES

HANUKKAH
(Festival of Light)

• • • •

Jewish

Background

Hanukkah, a minor Jewish festival, is an eight-day celebration beginning on the 25th day of the Hebrew month of Kislev, near the time of the winter solstice. It honors a victorious battle for religious freedom that occurred more than 2,100 years ago. In 168 B.C. Jerusalem was ruled by the Greek king, Antiochus, who worshipped a different deity and tried to force the Jews to worship his gods. In his attempt he captured the great temple of Jerusalem, condemned Jewish scholars to death, and had their holy books burned. When his soldiers entered the village of Modin a group of Jewish men who came to be known as the Maccabees refused to obey his orders. They fought with and killed the soldiers, then fled to the mountains from which they raided and fought with the king's men for years.

When their victories enabled them to return to Jerusalem, Judas, their leader, vowed to cleanse the temple and rededicate it to Jehovah, the god of the Jews. They prepared to rekindle the eternal light in the temple but found only a small vial of consecrated oil. Eight days would be required to prepare more holy oil, and the amount they had was not even enough to burn for one day yet somehow the small amount of oil burned for eight days until more consecrated oil was prepared.

The Jews believed that this could only have occurred through a miracle so they made a great celebration. The celebration of the Festival of Light, or Hanukkah, has been observed by the Jewish people every year since that date in 168 B.C. and has come to commemorate the victory of good over evil and the bringing of light to dark places. Modern celebrations include the lighting of the menorah, games, feasting, and the exchange of gifts.

Activities

• Discuss the symbolism of the eight-branched candelabra called the menorah. Some menorahs have a ninth branch in the center that holds the shammes, the "helper" candle that is used to light the other candles. Discuss how this candle represents the small amount of oil that provided light for eight days.

• Compare the Maccabees to people in other cultures who fought for religious freedom.

• Paint cardboard tubes to make a menorah and the candles that go in it. A long tube, such as the kind you get with gift wrap, can be the menorah and an egg carton or flat box can be the base. Paper towel–sized cardboard tubes can form the candles. The menorah and candles may be affixed to a wall or chalkboard with masking tape or magnetic strips. Add one candle each day of Hanukkah and light it with a tissue paper flame.

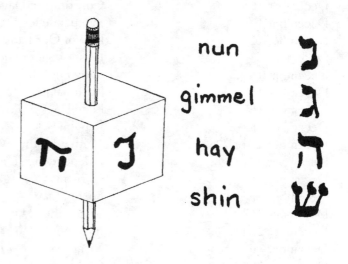

nun   gimmel   hay   shin

• At Hanukkah children enjoy playing with a special four-sided top called a dreidel. Each side of the top has a Hebrew, letter printed on it. These letters signify words, which, when translated, mean "a great miracle happened here." The children use the dreidel to play a "give and take" game in which the letters on the sides have a different meaning as listed above. A simple dreidel can be made by cutting and taping the bottom of a quart-sized milk carton to form a cube or using a cube of Styrofoam. A sharpened pencil can then be stuck through the center of the top of the cube all the way through to the bottom. The dreidel is then decorated with the four Hebrew letters—one on each side—and spun on the point of the pencil. To play children are given equal numbers of peanuts, candies, Hanukkah gelt (chocolate coins wrapped in gold foil), or even plastic markers. The game starts with each child placing one object in the "pot." They then take turns spinning the dreidel and doing what the letter facing up indicates: nun = nothing; gimmel = all (take everything in the "pot"); hay = half (take half of the "pot"; if number of objects is uneven, take half plus one); shin = put in (add one object to the "pot").

- Purchase or make a dreidel and have the children play the dreidel game to sharpen their math skills.

- Make potato latkes (see recipe in Appendix B, "Jewish") or buy frozen ones at the grocery store. Prepare/cook them at school and serve them with sour cream or applesauce.

- Give the children gifts of Hanukkah gelt (gold foil-covered chocolate coins) to taste and enjoy.

PIKKUJOULU

• • • •

Finland

Background

Pikkujoulu, or "Little Christmas," is a holiday of Finnish invention. Although it originally fell on the night of the first Sunday of Advent it currently has no fixed date and refers to any of a great number of celebrations of offices, businesses, schools, and so on. A Pikkujoulu celebration may fall at anytime during the month preceding Christmas. This celebration is a blending of the customs of the pagan harvest festival and Christian Christmas, both of which fell at about the same time. In fact, the Finnish word for Father Christmas is "joulupukki," which literally translated means "Christmas goat." This came from the straw goat of the ancient harvest festival and indicates that, before the influence of the German St. Nicholas, Father Christmas was associated with an animal figure rather than a human one. Today straw goats are frequently seen as tree decorations and centerpieces on tables.

Activities

- After discussing Finland's straw goat decorations talk about other traditional Christmas decorations from around the world (e.g., stars, angels, candy canes, candles, mistletoe, holly) and what they symbolize. Children may also enjoy bringing in and showing decorations that have symbolic significance for their families.

- Finland's northern third lies above the Arctic Circle and during this time of year the country is predominantly in darkness. Discuss the reasons for this. Mention that candles and lanterns are an important part of Pikkujoulu and Christmas celebrations in Scandinavian countries.

- Thoughts of harvest festivals commonly focus on the crops. This holiday affords an opportunity to discuss the importance of goats and other animals to farming communities and the products we get from animals.

DECEMBER HOLIDAYS WITH FIXED DATES

ST. BARBARA'S DAY

• • • •

December 4
Poland

Background

Coal mining is of vital importance to the economy of Poland, and in this country coal miners are held in great esteem. St. Barbara is revered as their patron saint and her name day is the traditional holiday of miners. On this day mass is said in the aspiration of attaining safety in the coal mines. Afterward, coal miners, dressed in full uniforms, participate in much celebration and merrymaking.

Activities

- Research coal and other fossil fuels. From this you can move into a study of alternative energy sources and/or conservation.

- Brainstorm a list of different things that are mined, such as ores, gems, and minerals. Research to find out the countries where different kinds of mining take place.

- Begin with a study of mining as a career and branch off to other related jobs and industries—refining, manufacturing, design, and so on.

SINTERKLAAS DAY

• • • •

December 5
Netherlands

Background

On this day children in the Netherlands put out their shoes before going to bed with the expectation that they will be filled with presents by that jolly old elf, Sinterklaas. Our name for Father Christmas, "Santa Claus," comes from the Dutch "Sinterklaas."

ST. NICHOLAS DAY

• • • •

December 6
Europe

Background

St. Nicholas was born in the third century in Turkey. He has become the patron saint of Christmas, of gift giving, and children. The celebration of his death is still observed in a number of European countries.

In Belgium, St. Nicholas, accompanied by his manservant, arrives on donkeyback from Spain some weeks before this date. He then sits on a throne in stores where children come to tell him what toys they most desire and to promise to be good. On the eve of December 6 they put their shoes near the hearth, sometimes along with a snack for the donkey. During the night St. Nicholas rides on the rooftops and drops the children's toys down the chimney so that they land in the waiting shoes.

The celebration differs in the Czech Republic and Slovakia. Here December 6, St. Nicholas Day, marks the start of the month long Christmas season. On the evening of December 6, St. Nicholas, accompanied by an angel and the chief devil, Lucifer, pays visits to all of the families that have children. St. Nicholas asks the children what gifts they would most like to receive. The angel writes the answers down in a golden book, and the devil growls "Be good or else … !" St. Nicholas may then give the children a piece of fruit or some sweets, but the real gifts are delivered by the baby Jesus on December 24.

Activities

- Compare Christmas holiday customs of different countries. Make a data retrieval chart to show how practices in varying countries are alike and how they differ. Another option would be to compare different winter holidays (e.g., Hanukkah, Kwanzaa, Christmas). The chart below is one possibility.

- Older children may like to research the life of the real St. Nicholas and to categorize their sources as fact or legend.

- Show pictures of Santa as he is depicted in various countries. Have children try to use clues in the pictures or verbal clues to match each with the name of the correct country.

DECEMBER HOLIDAYS	Who?	When?	food?	candles?	gifts?	decorations?	music?
Hanukkah							
Christmas							
Mother Night							
Kwanzaa							

INDEPENDENCE DAY

• • • •

December 6
Finland

Background

Up until 1809, when the Russians invaded and annexed Finland, the country was an integral part of Sweden. After the annexation Czar Alexander I set up an independent government in Finland but later in the century Russification began to undermine Finland's autonomy and Finnish nationalists began to work toward independence. In January 1918 Russia voluntarily recognized Finland's independence but opposing factions within Finland led to a bitter war for independence, a war that, despite the involvement of Russian and German troops, was in essence a civil war. The pro-Communist faction was defeated and a proclamation of independence was issued on December 6, 1917. Both Finnish and Swedish are spoken in the country. The vast majority of Finns belong to the Lutheran Church.

INDEPENDENCE DAY

• • • •

December 9
Tanzania

Background

Tanzania consists of the spice islands of Pemba and Zanzibar as well as the large area of East Africa formerly known as Tanganyika. As many as 2,000 years ago this area had already established contact with Arabia. In the late fifteenth century the Portuguese arrived and gradually superseded the Arabs along the coast. By the mid-nineteenth century explorers and missionaries from Europe had moved inland and by the end of that century Germany ruled the area. Following World War I the League of Nations gave Britain a mandate to rule Tanganyika and British influence continued until independence was achieved on December 9, 1961. Several years later the United Republic of Tanganyika and Zanzibar (Tanzania) was formed. (See "Union Day," April 26.)

Activities

• Have students use a historical atlas to explore how the world's political boundaries have changed through the centuries. It would be appropriate to begin with Tanganyika, Zanzibar, and Arabia, but interested children may also wish to study old maps of Europe, Africa, and other areas of the world.

• Do a geography lesson on early trade routes and the importance of the spice islands.

CONSTITUTION DAY

• • • •

December 10
Thailand

Background

The government of Thailand was an absolute monarchy until June 24, 1932, at which time a constitutional monarchy was established through a bloodless coup d'état. On December 10 of that year King Rama VII signed the National Constitution at the Throne Hall in Bangkok. Today the holiday is marked by a royal ceremony, presided over by the king, at the Parliament building in Bangkok. Businesses, homes, and government buildings are decorated with flags and buntings, and all of Thailand celebrates the date on which the people first achieved the right to take part in the governing of the nation.

INDEPENDENCE DAY

• • • •

December 12
Kenya

Background

Although Arab traders sailed to the coast of Kenya as early as the seventh century, European influence was not established until 1888 when the Imperial British East Africa Company was founded. By the middle of the twentieth century African resentment of British rule was high and in 1952 took violent form as the Mau Mau, a terrorist society of the Kikuyu tribe, brutally killed European settlers and sympathetic Africans. The uprising was put down, but the sentiments remained and the first election with limited suffrage for Africans took place in 1957. From there Kenya moved rapidly toward independence, which was realized on December 12, 1963. Since that time Kenya has been one of the most stable of the African nations. Kenyans are primarily Christian. English, Swahili, and other African languages are spoken in the country.

DAY OF OUR LADY OF GUADALUPE
• • • •
December 12
Mexico

Background

Originally Our Lady of Guadalupe was the patron saint of Mexico but her fame spread and by 1910 she had become the patroness of all of Latin America. On her day Hispanic Catholics celebrate in a subdued manner with the sharing of food and chanting and singing before an altar beautifully decorated with flowers and images of the Virgin of Guadalupe.

According to legend the Virgin Mother first appeared to an Indian, Juan Diego, on a hill near Mexico City in 1532. She instructed him to charge the bishop with the task of building a shrine to her on the spot where she had appeared and told him to take some flowers that were growing nearby to the bishop as proof of her existence. When Juan Diego gave the flowers to the bishop the Virgin again appeared. The sanctuary was built and a church has stood on the spot from that day to this. This holiday is also known as the Feast of Tonantzin because it is believed by some that it was the ancient goddess Tonantzin who appeared to Juan Diego as the manifestation of the Virgin Mary and that the site where she appeared, on Tepayak Hill, was the site on which her pagan temple had originally stood.

FEAST OF SANTA LUCIA
• • • •
December 13
Sweden

Background

Lucia was a Sicilian saint of the third or fourth century. Tradition has it that a heathen of noble birth was attracted to her by the beauty of her eyes. To preserve her chastity, she had herself blinded, supposedly on the shortest and darkest day of the year, the date of the winter solstice. Because she chose to sacrifice her vision and live in darkness she has come to represent the precious gift of light, and is sometimes equated with Lucina, the sun goddess. In some historically unknown fashion the saint became a favorite of the Swedes and her feast day moved forward a week or two.

Santa Lucia, or St. Lucy's Day, now marks the start of the Christmas season in Sweden. Early on the morning of this day the eldest daughter of the household dresses in white, adorns her head with a wreath decorated with burning candles, and offers coffee and sweet rolls or gingersnap cookies to the members of the family. The practice has spread to schools and places of business where a young girl is chosen to act as Lucia and distribute the treats, spreading cheer much as the sun goddess spreads cheer with her rays of light.

Activities

• Have children work in groups and use their knowledge of liquid and dry measurement to mix up dough for cookies or rolls.

• Make Santa Lucia wreaths of cardboard or poster board to use as centerpieces. Decorate them with leaves cut from green paper and painted cardboard tube "candles" with tissue paper "flames."

- Do a lesson on blindness and/or other handicaps and the effects they have on people's lives. Have children take turns wearing blindfolds and, working in pairs, explore and try to understand what it would be like to live in total darkness.

BIJOY DIBASH
(Victory Day)

• • • •

December 16
Bangladesh

Background

Following its nine-month War of Liberation against West Pakistan, Bangladesh (formerly known as East Pakistan) gained its independence and emerged as a sovereign state on December 16, 1971. Bengali is spoken throughout this country, which is populated primarily by Sunni Muslims and Hindus.

NATIONAL DAY

• • • •

December 16
Bahrain

Background

In 1507 the Portuguese occupied this island nation and held it for about a century. At that time Persian invaders took and held control until 1783 when Arabs from the mainland took over the island. By treaty in 1861 the Bahrain Islands came under British protection. Currently the country is ruled by Sunni Muslims although the majority of the population is Shiite Muslim. The national language is Arabic.

NINE DAYS OF POSADA

• • • •

December 16–24
Latin America

Background

The Spanish word "posada" means lodging. This nine-day ceremony commemorates the journey of Joseph and Mary from Nazareth to Bethlehem and their search for lodgings. Each evening of the celebration villagers walk in torch-lit processions led by images of Joseph and Mary. They strum guitars and sing as they march along from house to house seeking lodging for Mary. A predetermined member of the congregation opens his home to the Christ child (usually represented by a doll) for the night. The procession files into the house where there are readings from the scriptures, refreshments, and Christmas carols. In Mexico the celebration would probably include a piñata as well. On the following evenings the ritual is repeated, stopping at a different house for each night's celebration, as the people open their homes, and symbolically their hearts, to Jesus.

Activities

- Have the children use papier-mâché to make a piñata. (See "Hispanic Heritage Month," September 15–October 15, for instructions.)

- Sing some songs (Christmas or otherwise) with guitar accompaniment.

- Learn about stringed instruments or about instruments of Spanish origin.

- Read aloud a version of the Christmas story to gain background information. This is especially useful if there are non-Christian children in the class.

- Read *Nine Days to Christmas: A Story of Mexico* (see Appendix A, "Christmas," for more information) then discuss the traditions outlined in the book.

- Discuss other holidays during which historical events are reenacted to keep them fresh in our memory (e.g., Fourth of July, Thanksgiving).

REPUBLIC DAY

• • • •

December 18
Niger

Background

This landlocked African nation, two-thirds of which is desert, became a French colony in 1922. In 1960 Niger declared itself an independent republic. The people of Niger are principally Sunni Muslims. In addition to French, the African languages of Hausa and Djerma are spoken in the country.

MOTHER NIGHT
(Winter Solstice)

• • • •

December 21 or 22
International

Background

Tonight is the night of the winter solstice, the longest night of the year and, according to ancient beliefs, the mother of all other nights. It also marks the depth of winter—from here on out the days will get progressively longer, and Mother Earth will give birth to new life in the spring!

Activities

• On this longest and most magical night of the year do a little "magic" of your own—crayon resist style! Have the students draw landscapes with brightly colored crayons then brush over the whole picture with black tempera paint thinned with water to turn it into a nighttime scene in honor of the solstice.

• Study the rotation of the earth and explanation for the seasons.

• Do a lesson on astronomy and the constellations.

INDEPENDENCE DAY

• • • •

December 24
Libya

Background

The Phoenicians first linked Libya with the civilized world in about 800 B.C. by establishing trade centers and founding the city of Tripoli. Later the area came under the control of Rome. The Romans ruled for nearly five centuries until the Arab conquest of Libya in A.D. 642. In the fifteenth century Western Christendom initiated raids against Libya and Arab power began to decline. Finally, in 1911, Italy invaded the country and ruled for more than 30 years. In 1951 Libya gained independence and became one of the "new states" of Africa. In view of its history it is not surprising that Arabic, English, and Italian are all spoken in the country. The major religion is Sunni Muslim.

CHRISTMAS

• • • •

December 25
Christian

Background

The word "Christmas" comes from the Old English "Cristes maesse," the mass of Christ. It is the celebration by Christians of the birth of Jesus Christ. At the beginning of the Christian era the date of Christ's birth was a matter of speculation and no reference to a celebration of the event on the 25th of December can be found prior to the year 363. It is probable that this date was chosen to offset the pagan celebrations of Saturnalia and Natalis Invicti. It may also be that the celebration of the birth of "the true light of the world" may have been set at the time of the winter solstice because this is the time when days in the Northern Hemisphere begin to lengthen. The customs of the holiday come from a wide variety of sources—Teutonic, Celtic, Roman, West Asian, and Christian.

Activities

- Brainstorm a list of possible differences in Christmas celebrations in our country and in a country in the Southern Hemisphere (where it is summer). Research to see how accurate the speculations were.

- Have the children choose different holiday customs and symbols and research their origins.

- Read and discuss the legends surrounding Christmas, such as the legends of the Christmas tree, the poinsettia, and holly.

- Older children might be interested to discover that there really was a St. Nicholas and could compare the different forms he has taken in different cultures and countries. Following exposure to this knowledge, through fiction and/or nonfiction books, the children could choose a Santa Claus to use as a character in a creative writing assignment. (Stories might be shared with younger children.)

- Use "The Night before Christmas" and/or seasonal songs to teach rhyming. Have children write song lyrics to familiar tunes.

- Much greenery is used in decorating for this holiday. Do a lesson or unit on different kinds of evergreens.

- String popcorn, cranberries, beads, or colored macaroni in patterns to decorate a Christmas tree. Have children estimate how many of each they will need to make a string of a given length, then complete the project and check to see how close their estimate was.

- Mary and Joseph were going to Bethlehem to pay their taxes. Discuss modern taxes and do a lesson on percentages.

- Use stars to teach the concept of multiplication (four-pointed stars for the four tables, five-pointed stars for the five tables, etc.).

- Give each child a given dollar value and use newspaper ads to have children make gift lists within their "budget."

BOXING DAY

• • • •

December 26
Europe

Background

In days gone by wealthy landowners expected their servants to work on Christmas Day, preparing and serving the food, driving the carriage, and performing other services that would assure that the family had a pleasant celebration. The servants were, however, given a holiday on the following day, December 26, as well as boxes containing gifts from their employers. In present-day Europe few people have servants but the custom continues.

Activities

- Brainstorm a list of community helpers and the services they provide. Use this as a basis for a unit on careers.

- Consider the many people who work daily to keep your school running smoothly, such as cafeteria workers, bus drivers, and custodial staff. Have the children make cards or simple gifts for them as a way to say "thanks!"

- Have the children select a day they have especially enjoyed. This could be anything from a trip to an amusement park to a birthday celebration. Have them consider the people who worked to make that day possible, and write a story from the point of vew of one of those people.

ST. STEPHEN'S DAY

• • • •

December 26
Czech Republic and Slovakia

Background

On the day following Christmas groups of children in villages in the Czech Republic and Slovakia go from house to house caroling and wishing everyone well. They are rewarded with coins, candy, or fruit.

Activities

• Compare this custom to the practice of going trick-or-treating at Halloween.

• Discuss the major role that music plays during the holiday season. Brainstorm a list of all places where seasonal music is heard (e.g., in stores, on the radio, in churches). Talk about the different kinds of music played in these various places, the reason each is appropriate, and how they make people feel—sentimental, jolly, devout.

JUNKANOO

• • • •

December 26
Bahamas

Background

The Bahamian culture is showcased through costumes, music, and dance on this, the most celebrated day in the Bahamas. Junkanoo is an African-derived celebration that dates back to early colonial times and the days of slavery. At that time slaves were expected to work every day including Christmas Day. To compensate for this they were given off the following day (Boxing Day) and New Year's Day. Instead of resting on these days the slaves used them to celebrate and to recall their African ancestral traditions.

The central activity of these days is the Junkanoo parade, which begins very early in the morning, about 3:00 A.M., and lasts for hours. During the parades the spectators enjoy colorful floats and cheer for their favorite band. Marching groups wearing garish papier-mâché and crepe-paper costumes, masks, and headdresses dance frenetically to the beat of goatskin drums, cowbells, whistles, and conch shells as they compete for prizes.

Activities

• Listen to Caribbean music or have the children work in groups to form rhythm bands.

• Make papier-mâché masks. Use the directions for papier-mâché under Hispanic Heritage Month (see September 15–October 15). Use balloon or playground balls covered with petroleum jelly for the base, covering only one half. After the first layer of papier-mâché is dry, a three-dimensional effect can be created by taping poster board or cardboard ears and noses to the mask and covering with additional layers of papier-mâché. Cut eyeholes before painting or decorating.

• Explore African influences on modern-day life, including art, music, foods, clothing, and literature.

KWANZAA

• • • •

December 26–January 1
African American

Background

The seven-day celebration of Kwanzaa is an African-American holiday. It was created in 1966 by Maulana Karenga, an African-American teacher, who wanted to educate his people about their history. It is a time to celebrate kinship with family gatherings and reunions. The holiday is an attempt to bind the African harvest customs to the cultural and social history of

African Americans. The East African Swahili phrase "Matunde ya kwanza" means "the first fruits." From this the word "kwanza" (first) was taken as the name of the holiday; the extra "a" in "Kwanzaa" was added to give the name seven letters. This represents the seven principles of Kwanzaa, one of which is stressed on each of the seven days as follows:

1. umoja (oo-MO-jah): unity
2. kujichagulia (koo-jee-cha-goo-LEE-ah): self-determination
3. ujima (oo-JEE-mah): collective work and responsibility
4. ujamma (oo-JAH-mah): cooperative economics
5. nia (NEE-ah): purpose
6. kuumba (koo-OOM-bah): creativity
7. imani (ee-MAH-nee): faith

There are also seven symbols of Kwanzaa as listed below:

1. mkeka (mm-KEH-kah): the woven place mat, a symbol of history (the other symbols of Kwanzaa stand on the mkeka as our present life stands upon our history)
2. kikombe cha umoja (kee-KOH-beh chah oo-MOH-jah): a large cup that symbolizes staying together
3. mazao (mah-ZAH-oh): fruits and vegetables, symbolic of the harvest and of all work

4. muhindi (moo-HIN-dee): ears of corn, representative of the children
5. kinara (kee-NAH-rah): candleholder that contains seven candles, symbol of history and the people who lived in Africa many years ago
6. mishumaa saba (mee-SHOO-mah SAH-bah): the candles that represent the seven principles of Kwanzaa

7. zawadi (zah-WAH-dee): gifts for children that are usually handmade and are given as rewards for promises kept during the previous year

Activities

• Compare this celebration to other, older harvest festivals.

• Read some African folktales or an Uncle Remus story. Discuss the influences of African literature on the culture of the United States.

• Learn some Swahili words. In addition to the words listed above these two phrases, associated with Kwanzaa, are appropriate: Harambee! (hah-RAHM-bee): "Let's pull together!" and Kwanzm Yenu Iwe Na Heri! (KWAH-nzah YEH-NOO ee-WEH nah HEH-ree): "May your Kwanzaa be happy!"

• Have each child weave a mat of colored construction paper. Fasten them all together to form a large mat to accommodate your class "family."

• Paint or draw kinaras. The three candles on the left are red (representing the struggle), the middle candle is black (representing the people), and the three candles to the right are green (representing the future).

• On the day when you discuss creativity have the children make a gift (draw a picture, write a story, etc.) to present to a classmate whose name they drew in a classroom gift exchange.

• Have a discussion or lesson about one of the principles of Kwanzaa during each day of the holiday. Relate these principles to life in your community.

• Have each child bring in mazao (a vegetable or piece of fruit) on the last day of Kwanzaa. Discuss nutrition, then place the foods on your class mkeka and have a feast!

• Listen to some jazz or rap and discuss the influence of black musicians on the music of today.

• During your lessons on Kwanzaa play African music in the background.

CHILDERMAS

• • • •

December 28
Europe, Mexico

Background

Childermas, also known as Holy Innocents' Day, is a commemoration of King Herod's slaughter of the infants in an attempt to kill the baby Jesus. Because his plan was foiled, this day has come to be a time when children are permitted to play tricks on their elders and perform pranks. It is most common in Western Europe and in Mexico where it has become the equivalent of our April Fools' Day.

BIRTH OF GURU GOBIND SINGH

• • • •

December 31
Sikh

Background

Initially a totally religious movement, toward the end of the seventeenth century Sikhism became more political and military in nature. Guru Gobind Singh, tenth and last of the Sikh gurus, is responsible for uniting the Sikhs into a strong group known as the *Khalsa*. As a sign of brotherhood all males are given the surname Singh (lion); all females, kaur (princess). Guru Gobind Singh also established the code of dress that identifies all Sikhs, the most notable feature of which is the long uncut hair. The *gupurb* (anniversary) of Guru Gobind Singh is celebrated with prayer, meditation, and the reading of the Granth. Following the religious services food is shared and gifts may be exchanged.

NEW YEAR'S EVE

• • • •

December 31
International

Background

Just as our calendar came from the Romans, so did many of the customs surrounding modern celebrations of New Year's Eve and New Year's Day. The Romans were very superstitious and believed in magic and omens. New Year falls at the darkest and bleakest time of the year. Our custom of sounding noisemakers and setting off fireworks probably originated in the belief that this would scare off the old, dying year and make way for the new year. In Hungary the old year is "burned out" with great bonfires, and in Germany and Greece it is traditionally "cracked out" with whips. Our practice of making New Year's resolutions is most likely traceable to ancient beliefs that one's behavior on New Year's Day could bring good or bad luck for the year. People show their friendship by sharing a drink and toasting one another's good health in the new year. (See also "New Year's Day, January 1.")

Activities

• Compare this celebration to other new year's celebrations (see index for listing). This could be done in the form of a data retrieval chart such as the one suggested for St. Nicholas Day (see above) and could be added to throughout the year.

• Research new year customs of specific cultures or countries.

• Study or review concepts of time, such as the months of the year and telling time.

- Research calendars of the past, why changes were made, the role of calendars both past and present, and/or how the months got their names.

- Write New Year's resolutions for school or home.

- Learn to say "Happy New Year" in different languages: German, "Prosit Neujahr"; French, "Bonne Année"; Spanish, "Feliz Ano Nuevo."

FESTIVAL OF LEMANJA

• • • •

December 31
Brazil

Background

In Brazil December 31 marks not only the start of a new calendar year but also the ancient ritual celebration of Lemanja, the spirit of the sea. On this night people who wish to demonstrate their devotion and respect for Lemanja dress in white and gather on the beaches. They bring offerings of flowers and food that they throw into the ocean or send out into the sea on small rafts. Candles are pressed into the sand, often in patterns, and lit to display more offerings of food or flowers. People sing and dance on the beach far into the night.

Activities

- Brainstorm a list of ways in which we are dependent upon the world's oceans. Have children choose an area of interest and do further research.

- Do an ecology lesson on water pollution.

- Study different forms of marine life.

- Compare this holiday to Diwali (see October) and Loy Krathong (see November).

Appendix A: Trade Books Arranged According to Topic

Africa/African American

A

Aardema, Verna. *Bringing the Rain to Kapiti Plain.* New York: Dial Books, 1981.

An African tale told in rhyme. Caldecott winner.

_____. *Traveling to Tondo: A Tale of the Nkundo of Zaire.* New York: Alfred A. Knopf, 1991.

In this folktale Bowane, a civet cat, is traveling to Tondo to claim a wife and invites his three loyal friends to accompany him. The friends accommodate each others' needs to the point where they take several years to make the journey and arrive only to find the intended bride married to another.

_____. *Why Mosquitoes Buzz in People's Ears: A West African Tale.* New York: Dial Press, 1975.

When the mosquito starts chattering, the iguana puts sticks into his ears rather than listen. This begins a long chain of events, which ultimately ends in disaster. Aardema's retelling of this West African folktale earned the Caldecott Award.

Adler, David A. *A Picture Book of Harriet Tubman.* New York: Holiday House, 1992.

This story of Harriet Tubman, who led more than 300 slaves to freedom on the Underground Railroad, begins with her childhood, spent in slavery, and follows her life through 1913 when she died at the age of 90.

_____. *A Picture Book of Jesse Owens.* New York: Holiday House, 1992.

A biography of the famous Olympic runner in picture book form.

Angelou, Maya. *My Painted House, My Friendly Chicken, and Me.* New York: Clarkson Potter, 1994.

Meet Thandi, an eight-year-old South African girl, her village, and her best friend—a chicken. Brilliant photographs by Margaret Courtney-Clarke enhance Angelou's delightful story.

B

Burden-Patmon, Denise. *Imani's Gift at Kwanzaa.* Cleveland: Modern Curriculum Press, 1992.

Young Imani, whose name comes from the Swahili word for faith, learns firsthand some of the important principles of Kwanzaa.

C

Chocolate, Deborah M. Newton. *Kwanzaa.* Chicago: Children's Press, 1990.

Told in the first person by a young boy, this story clearly explains the traditions and customs of Kwanzaa.

_____. *My First Kwanzaa Book.* New York: Scholastic, 1992.

This simple picture book, suitable for the very young, contains a wealth of definitions and information for use by parents and teachers.

D

Dayrell, Elphinstone. *Why the Sun and the Moon Live in the Sky: An African Folk Tale.* Boston: Houghton Mifflin, 1968.

Long ago the sun and the moon, who were married, invited their friend, water, to come and visit. But there were so many water people that the sun and moon were first forced out of their house, onto the roof, and finally into the sky.

F

Feelings, Muriel. *Jambo Means Hello: A Swahili Alphabet Book*. New York: Dial Books, 1974.
> Children review the alphabet and learn about African culture at the same time.

French, Fiona. *Anancy and Mr. Dry-Bone*. New York: Scholastic, 1991.
> In this original story, based on the Anansi character of African and Caribbean folktales, Anancy takes on the form of a man who must make his ladylove laugh in order to win her hand.

G

Greenfield, Eloise. *Nathaniel Talking*. New York: Black Butterfly Children's Books, 1988.
> A collection of poems and raps about life from the point of view of Nathaniel, a nine-year-old black child.

H

Haley, Gail E. *A Story a Story*. New York: Macmillan, 1970.
> Traditional African tale of how the first stories came to Earth.

Himler, Ronald. *Nettie's Trip South*. New York: Macmillan, 1987.
> In 1859 Nettie, a young, white Northerner, takes a trip south where she witnesses the horrors of slavery and writes home an account to her dear friend. Based on a true story.

I

Isadora, Rachel. *Ben's Trumpet*. New York: William Morrow, 1989.
> The story of a young black boy growing up in the city during the 1920s. A Caldecott Honor book.

J

Jackson, Garnet Nelson. *Selma Burke, Artist*. Cleveland: Modern Curriculum Press, 1994.
> The biography of the sculptor whose most well known accomplishment is the image of President Franklin D. Roosevelt on the U.S. dime. In picture book form.

Jones, Kathryn. *Happy Birthday, Dr. King!* Cleveland: Modern Curriculum Press, 1994.
> A young boy's father and grandfather help him to solve his school problems through the stories of Rosa Parks and Martin Luther King Jr.

K

Kimmel, Eric A. *Anansi and the Moss-Covered Rock*. New York: Holiday House, 1988.
> Anansi discovers a magic rock and uses it to trick his friends, the other animals, but in the end the tables get turned.

L

Lowrey, Linda. *Martin Luther King Day*. Minneapolis: Carolrhoda Books, 1987.
> Tells of the life, work, and death of Dr. King and of the establishment of the holiday in his honor in a style young children can understand.

M

Marzollo, Jean. *Happy Birthday, Martin Luther King*. New York: Scholastic, 1993.
> A biography suitable for young children.

McDermott, Gerald. *Anansi the Spider: A Tale from the Ashanti*. New York: Henry Holt, 1972.
> A beautifully illustrated book in which Anansi gets into trouble and is saved by his sons, each of whom has a unique ability. A good book to compare to the Chinese tale *The Five Chinese Brothers* listed below.

McKissack, Patricia. *Flossie and the Fox*. New York: Dial Books for Young Readers, 1986.
Flossie is entrusted with the job of delivering a basket of fresh eggs but has to outwit the fox to get them safely to their destination.

Mendez, Phil. *The Black Snowman*. New York: Scholastic, 1989.
The dirty, black snow of the city streets depresses a young boy until the snowman he and his brother have made comes to life to teach him values, history, and tradition.

Monjo, F. N. *The Drinking Gourd: A Story of the Underground Railroad*. New York: Harper Trophy, 1993.
Easy-to-read and fast-paced historical fiction. Written at about a second-grade level.

R

Ringgold, Faith. *Aunt Harriet's Underground Railroad in the Sky*. New York: Scholastic, 1992.
In her fantasies a modern-day girl dodges bounty hunters, searches for her little brother, and meets "Aunt Harriet" on her ride to freedom.

S

Seeger, Pete. *Abiyoyo*. New York: Macmillan, 1987.
The boy and his father are ostracized until they find a way to save the villagers from the giant, Abiyoyo, in this adaptation of a South African tale. Scholastic offers a paperback version and an audiotape in which the story is narrated by James Earl Jones.

Steptoe, John. *Mufaro's Beautiful Daughters: An African Tale*. New York: William Morrow, 1987.
The African version of the Cinderella story. Caldecott winner.

T

Towle, Wendy. *The Real McCoy: The Life of an African-American Inventor*. New York: Scholastic, 1993.
In the mid-1880s Elijah McCoy invented a device to oil locomotives. His invention was so superior to anything else available at the time that it is said that the engineers would ask for "the real McCoy."

W

Winter, Jeanette. *Follow the Drinking Gourd*. New York: Alfred A. Knopf, 1988.
The story of how a young Quaker boy discovers and helps runaway slaves on the Underground Railroad. Includes the words and music for the traditional song of the same name.

Cambodia

S

Sothea Chiemroum. *Dara's Cambodian New Year*. New York: Modern Curriculum Press, 1992.
The family has fled Cambodia in search of a better life, but Grandfather is homesick and Dara has a plan to cheer him up on Songkran, the Buddhist New Year.

China

B

Bishop, Claire Huchep. *The Five Chinese Brothers*. New York: Sandcastle Books, 1989.
Five identical brothers use their exceptional qualities to outwit the executioner.

H

Hong, Lily Toy. *Two of Everything.* Morton Grove, Ill.: Albert Whitman, 1993.
> In this Chinese folktale a poor farmer finds a magic pot that creates two of everything placed inside it. But when his wife falls into the pot things begin to get complicated.

L

Louie, Ai-Ling. *Yeh-Shen: A Cinderella Story from China.* New York: Philomel Books, 1982.
> A version of the Cinderella story that predates European versions by centuries. Beautifully illustrated by Ed Young.

M

Mahy, Margaret. *The Seven Chinese Brothers.* New York: Scholastic, 1990.
> The story of seven brothers, each with a superhuman ability, who use their talents to work together. (A good book to compare and contrast with *The Five Chinese Brothers* listed above.)

R

Reddix, Valerie. *Dragon Kite of the Autumn Moon.* New York: Lothrop, Lee, and Shepard Books, 1991.
> When Grandfather is too ill to go with him on Kite Day, young Tad-Tin, in an effort to help his grandfather get well, uses all of his strength to fly the kite on his own then cuts the string so that the kite will carry away their bad fortune.

S

Sing, Rachel. *Chinese New Year's Dragon.* New York: Modern Curriculum Press, 1992.
> The story of a family's preparations for the Lunar New Year and a young girl's dream about the New Year dragon.

W

Waters, Kate. *Lion Dancer: Ernie Wan's Chinese New Year.* New York: Scholastic, 1990.
> This nonfiction story of a young boy's first opportunity to join in the lion dance in New York City's Chinatown is illustrated with actual color photos of his experience.

Y

Yolen, Jane. *The Emperor and the Kite.* New York: Putnam and Grosset, 1988.
> This Caldecott Honor book, illustrated by Ed Young, is a good way to tie in literature with the study of the Chinese Kite Festival.

Young, Ed. *Lon Po Po: A Red-Riding Hood Story from China.* New York: Philomel Books, 1989.
> In this story it is the mother who has to go away, leaving the children to deal with the wolf when he comes calling.

Christmas

B

Brett, Jan. *Christmas Trolls.* New York: G. P. Putnam's Sons, 1993.
> When the trolls become jealous and steal the family's gifts, Christmas pudding, and treetop angel Treva decides that she needs to teach them the real meaning of Christmas. Beautifully detailed illustrations.

_____. *The Wild Christmas Reindeer*. New York: G. P. Putnam's Sons, 1990.
> Teeka learns the hard way that bossing and yelling is no way to get Santa's reindeer ready for Christmas Eve. In addition to the beautifully detailed main pictures on each page, Brett shows a month's preparation for Christmas on the part of the elves in pictures that border the pages.

Bruna, Dick. *Christmas*. Garden City, N. Y.: Doubleday, n.d.
> The story of Christmas told in rhyme with simple line drawings filled in with bright colors.

D

dePaola, Tomie. *Jingle the Christmas Clown*. New York: G. P. Putnam's Sons, 1992.
> When the little clown is left in an economically depressed Italian town he plans a very special Christmas Eve performance for the villagers.

_____. *The Legend of the Poinsettia*. New York: G. P. Putnam's Sons, 1994.
> When the little girl brings the only gift she has, an armful of weeds, into the church on Christmas Eve a miracle turns them into beautiful flowers. A Mexican legend.

E

Ets, Marie Hall, and Aurora Labastida. *Nine Days to Christmas: A Story of Mexico*. New York: Viking Press, 1959.
> This story of a young Mexican girl's first posada (Christmas party) and her first piñata is a delightful introduction to Mexican Christmas traditions.

F

Forest, Heather. *The Baker's Dozen: A Colonial American Tale*. New York: Harcourt Brace Jovanovich, 1988.
> Based on a true story this legend of a baker in Beverwyck (now Albany), New York, and his famous Christmas cookies explains how thirteen came to be known as a "baker's dozen" and how the baker came to understand the true spirit of Christmas.

S

Soto, Gary. *Too Many Tamales*. New York: G. P. Putnam's Sons, 1993.
> Maria thinks she has lost her mother's ring in the masa while making tamales for the Christmas celebration so she and her cousins eat all of the tamales to try to find it.

V

Van Allsburg, Chris. *The Polar Express*. Boston: Houghton Mifflin, 1985.
> Is there really a Santa Claus? When the young storyteller wakes up on Christmas morning to find the bell from one of Santa's reindeer under the tree he knows that his trip to the North Pole was real.

Z

Ziefert, Harriet. *A New Coat for Anna*. New York: Alfred A. Knopf, 1986.
> In England during World War II new clothes were hard to come by, but Anna's ingenious mother finds a way to get her a beautiful new coat for Christmas. A warm Christmas story, a look at another period of history, and an opportunity for children to trace a coat from sheep to finished product. Based on a true story.

Earth/Environment

B

Buscaglia, Leo. *The Fall of Freddie the Leaf*. New York: Holt, Rinehart and Winston, 1982.
> Told from the point of view of a single leaf this book explains the natural cycle of life and death.

C

Cherry, Lynne. *The Great Kapok Tree*. New York: Harcourt Brace Jovanovich, 1990.

A man sent to chop down trees in the rain forest falls asleep under a kapok tree and dreams of all of the creatures who depend upon the trees for their existence. When he awakens he looks at the rain forest through new eyes.

_____. *A River Ran Wild*. New York: Harcourt Brace Jovanovich, 1992.

View the Nashua River from the time of the first Native Americans through settlement by the English, industrialization, pollution, and finally one woman's successful campaign to clean up and restore the river to its original grandeur. Based on a true story.

D

Donahue, Mike. *The Grandpa Tree*. Boulder, Colo.: Roberts Rinehart, 1988.

The story of the life cycle of a tree from seed to compost in which the new seedlings sprout.

E

EarthWorks Group. *50 Simple Things Kids Can Do to Save the Earth*. Kansas City, Mo.: Andrews and McMeel, 1990.

A collection of activities and experiments that actually get children involved in turning around such harmful things as pollution, the damage to the ozone layer, endangered species, acid rain, and the greenhouse effect.

H

Halpern, Shari. *My River*. New York: Scholastic, 1992.

An easy-to-read picture book whose characters are all animals, insects, and plants that call the river their home.

L

Luenn, Nancy. *Mother Earth*. New York: Macmillan, 1992.

A delightful picture book that likens Earth to a human mother, outlines the gifts that we receive from her, and speaks to the kindnesses we can do her in return.

_____. *Song of the Ancient Forest*. New York: Macmillan, Atheneum, 1993.

Long ago Raven had a dream of a time when the ancient forests would be destroyed. When he sees the horror becoming a reality he finds a young girl, daughter of a logger, to take his message to the world.

M

McLerran, Alice. *The Mountain That Loved a Bird*. Saxonville, Mass.: Picture Book Studio, 1985.

A story of the interdependence of life on our planet. Beautifully illustrated by Eric Carle.

R

Rose, Deborah Lee. *The People Who Hugged Trees*. Niwot, Colo.: Roberts Rinehart, 1990.

This legend from India tells of a young girl who persuaded the people of her village to hug the trees in order to save them from the axmen of the maharajah.

S

Say, Allen. *The Lost Lake*. Boston: Houghton Mifflin, 1989.

The story of a young boy who hikes through the mountains of Japan in search of an unspoiled part of nature.

Shaw, Kiki, and Katherine Shaw. *Maya and the Town That Loved a Tree*. New York: Rizzoli International Publications, 1992.

> The city had torn down its parks to build skyscrapers and polluted its air with industrial waste, killing everything green. Then one day a little girl appeared with a tree and taught the people how to clean up the air and care for their environment.

Silverstein, Shel. *The Giving Tree*. New York: Harper and Row, 1964.

> A simple story that tells of many of the things we get from trees and the importance of not taking them for granted.

T

Thompson, Colin. *The Paper Bag Prince*. New York: Alfred A. Knopf, 1992.

> Twenty years ago, when his farm burned down, the city paid off the man, moved him to a housing project, and turned his farm into a dump. Every day he would bicycle out to the place, sift through the trash, recycle what he could, and watch his land suffer until the day when the city finally decided to close the dump in favor of a more efficient form of waste removal.

W

Wood, Douglas. *Old Turtle*. New York: Scholastic, 1992.

> Old turtle speaks to Earth and its inhabitants telling them that God is everywhere, in everything and everyone, and that we must learn to respect and care for each other and for our home, Earth. Magnificently illustrated with watercolors by Cheng-Khee Chee.

Easter

P

Polacco, Patricia. *Chicken Sunday*. New York: Philomel Books, 1992.

> Miss Eula has her eye set on a new Easter bonnet and the children set out to raise the money to buy it for her. The story combines several ethnic traditions related to the Easter season.

Egypt

C

Climo, Shirley. *The Egyptian Cinderella*. New York: HarperCollins, 1992.

> Set in sixth-century Egypt, this story, a mix of fact and fiction, tells of how the Pharaoh chose Rhodopis, a slave girl, to be his queen.

H

Heide, F. P., and J. H. Gilliland. *The Day of Ahmed's Secret*. New York: William Morrow, 1990.

> The city of Cairo comes alive in the story of young Ahmed's day and the secret he shares with his family at the end of the day.

Greek Mythology

G

Gibson, Michael. *Gods, Men, and Monsters from the Greek Myths.* New York: Peter Bedrick Books, 1991.
Background on the gods and their relationships as well as most of the more popular myths. A good read-aloud book with colorful two-page illustrations.

L

Low, Alice. *The Macmillan Book of Greek Gods and Heroes.* New York: Macmillan, 1985.
The chronology of events from Mother Earth to the Titans to the gods of Mt. Olympus as well as a collection of the myths that surround them is presented at a readability level suitable for children in intermediate grades.

M

McCaughrean, Geraldine. *Greek Myths.* New York: Margaret K. McElderry Books, 1993.
A collection of sixteen Greek myths with appealing illustrations.

Hispanic

A

Aardema, Verna. *Borreguita and the Coyote.* New York: Alfred A. Knopf, 1991.
Brains triumph over brawn as the little lamb outwits the coyote time after time in this Mexican folktale.

B

Burden-Patmon, Denise. *Carnival.* Cleveland: Modern Curriculum Press, 1992.
When a young girl from Trinidad moves to Brooklyn she is sure that the celebration of Carnival will not compare to those she has enjoyed in her native country, but she ends up participating in the parade, playing in a steel band, and enjoying herself very much.

D

Delacre, Lulu. *Arroz Con Leché: Popular Songs and Rhymes from Latin America.* New York: Scholastic, 1989.
Colorful illustrations enhance this collection of twelve traditional children's rhymes and songs from Puerto Rico, Mexico, and Argentina. A tape is also available (see Appendix C).
_____. *Vejigant.* NewYork: Scholastic, 1993.
The touching story of a young Puerto Rican boy's perseverance in making his dream to become a masquerader during Carnival come true.

M

Martel, Cruz. *Yagua Days.* New York: Scholastic, 1976.
When Adan makes his first visit to his relatives in Puerto Rico he discovers the joy of rainy days and sliding down the wet, grassy slopes on a palm frond.
Martinez, Alejandro Cruz. *Woman Who Outshone the Sun.* New York: Scholastic, 1993.
From the oral tradition of the Zapotec Indians of Oaxaca, Mexico, comes this legend of Lucia Zenteno, a stranger who came to the town and taught the villagers the valuable lesson of learning to treat all people with respect and kindness. Adapted from Martinez's poem.

McNaught, Harry. *500 Palabras Nuevas Para Ti: 500 Words to Grow On*. New York: Random House, 1982.
    A picture dictionary that labels items in both Spanish and English.

R

Rohmer, Harriet, and Mary Anchondo. *How We Came to the Fifth World*. San Francisco: Children's Book Press, 1987.
    The Aztecs of ancient Mexico believed that there had been four "worlds" or historical ages, each destroyed by natural elements, before the one in which we now live. Text in both English and Spanish enhances this story of how we came to the present day.

Z

Zapater, Beatriz McConnie. *Fiesta!* New York: Modern Curriculum Press, 1992.
    A family from Colombia celebrates its first Hispanic fiesta in the United States.
_____. *Three Kings Day*. New York: Modern Curriculum Press, 1992.
    In this story of Día de los Reyes Magos, a young Hispanic girl's dream comes true when she finds the gift left for her by the Three Kings.

India

M

Martin, Rafe. *Foolish Rabbit's Big Mistake*. New York: G. P. Putnam's Sons, 1985.
    This ancient folktale about fears and rumors is possibly the oldest version of the "sky is falling" story.

R

Rose, Deborah Lee. *The People Who Hugged Trees*. Niwot, Colo.: Roberts Rinehart, 1990.
    This legend from India tells of a young girl who persuaded the people of her village to hug the trees in order to save them from the axmen of the maharajah.

Japan

S

Say, Allen. *Tree of Cranes*. Boston: Houghton Mifflin, 1991.
    An American-born mother blends the traditions of Japan and the United States by creating a very special Christmas tree for her son.

Y

Yashima, Taro. *Crow Boy*. New York: Viking Press, 1965.
    The story of a young boy who is misunderstood and ignored by his classmates until a compassionate teacher draws him out and helps the other students to understand and accept him. A Caldecott Honor book.
_____. *Umbrella*. New York: Viking Penguin, 1986.
    On her third birthday Momo receives her first umbrella and impatiently waits for her first chance to use it "like a grown-up lady." A Caldecott Honor book.

Jewish

A

Adler, David A. *A Picture Book of Hanukkah.* New York: Holiday House, 1982.
An explanation of the historical significance of the holiday.

G

Gilman, Phoebe. *Something from Nothing.* New York: Scholastic, 1992.
Adapted from a Jewish folktale, this touching story tells of a young boy's attachment to his grandfather and to his baby blanket, which grandpa keeps altering and changing into new things as he grows up until finally there is nothing left of the blanket but this story.

Goldin, Barbara Diamond. *Cakes and Miracles: A Purim Tale.* New York: Viking, 1993.
Because he is blind Hershel's mother does not want him to help with the hamantashen, but Hershel, who knows that he can see in his dreams and with his hands, fashions the most fanciful and sought-after cookies in the marketplace. Includes a recipe for these delicious cookies.

K

Kimmel, Eric A. *The Chanukkah Guest.* New York: Holiday House, 1988.
Bubba Brayne, whose eyesight is failing, mistakes a bear for the rabbi and before the real guests arrive has shared all of her delicious potato latkes with him, and given him the rabbi's Chanukkah gift.

_____. *Hershel and the Hanukkah Goblins.* New York: Holiday House, 1989.
When Hershel finds out that the goblins have canceled Hanukkah he breaks their spell by facing a different goblin each night of the holiday and tricking the head goblin into lighting the menorah on the eighth night.

Krulik, Nancy E. *Penny and the Four Questions.* New York: Scholastic, 1993.
When a Russian family, new to the United States, joins her family for the first night of Passover, Penny learns the true meaning of the holiday.

M

Manushkin, Fran. *Latkes and Applesauce.* New York: Scholastic, 1990.
The deep snow makes it impossible to dig the potatoes for the Hanukkah latkes or to pick the apples for the applesauce until a stray dog and cat show up at the family's doorstep.

S

Swartz, Leslie. *A First Passover.* New York: Modern Curriculum Press, 1992.
Life is not easy for Jews in the Soviet Union and Jasha cannot experience this celebration of freedom until he and his family find their own freedom in the United States.

W

Wax, Wendy. *Hanukkah, Oh, Hanukkah.* New York: Parachute Press, 1993.
A collection of stories, songs, dances, and games.

Wild, Margaret, and Julie Vivas. *Let the Celebration Begin!* New York: Orchard Books, 1991.
The women are planning a very special celebration and are making gifts for the children from rags and scraps, waiting for the day when the soldiers will come and liberate them from the concentration camp. A story of hope based on fact.

Wohl, Lauren L. *Matzoh Mouse*. New York: HarperCollins, 1991.
When Sarah's family gathers on the first night of Passover they have a lovely seder, but no chocolate-covered matzoh for dessert. Then Aunt Anne remembers a similar problem they had when Sarah's father was a little boy.

Korea

S

Suyenaga, Ruth, and Young Sook Kim. *Korean Children's Day*. New York: Modern Curriculum Press, 1992.
Young Soo invites his American friend, Jeremy, to go with him to the Korean Institute for the Korean celebration of Children's Day.

Laos

X

Xiong, Blia. *Nine-in-One, Grr! Grr!: A Folktale from the Hmong People of Laos*. San Francisco: Children's Book Press, 1989.
When the great god Shoa tells tiger that she will have nine cubs each year, the Eu bird sees disaster for the other animals and devises a plan to limit the tiger population.

Multicultural

D

Dooley, Norah. *Everybody Cooks Rice*. Minneapolis: Carolrhoda Books, 1991.
When Carrie's mother sends her to find her brother and bring him home for dinner she stops at every house in her multiethnic neighborhood and finds that everyone is cooking rice for dinner. In addition to the story, this book contains recipes for rice dishes from seven different countries.

J

Jackson, Ellen. *The Winter Solstice*. Brookfield, Conn.: Millbrook Press, 1994.
Ancient Scottish, Scandinavian, Native American, Peruvian, Roman, and British rituals of the winter solstice are explored and related to customs of contemporary winter holiday celebrations.
Jenness, Aylette. *Who Am I?* Cleveland: Modern Curriculum Press, 1992.
When his school plans a Family Heritage Day, David, an American boy, traces his family to six different nationalities.

M

Marden, Patricia C., and Suzanne I. Barchers. *Cooking Up World History*. Englewood, Colo.: Teacher Ideas Press, 1994.
Recipes, annotated lists of related trade books, and ideas for student research for 22 different countries.
Morris, Ann. *Bread, Bread, Bread*. New York: William Morrow, 1989.
Dozens of full-color photographs show people around the world baking, selling, and eating different kinds of bread.

S

Spier, Peter. *People*. New York: Doubleday, 1980.
> A celebration of Earth's people and their diversity.

W

Williams, Vera B. *"More More More," Said the Baby*. New York: William Morrow, 1990.
> A simple picture book that shows that all babies, regardless of culture or ethnic background, love to be played with and cuddled.

Native American

C

Caduto, Michael J., and Joseph Bruchac. *Keepers of the Animals*. Golden, Colo.: Fulcrum Publishing, 1991.
> Children learn to respect and appreciate the animal kingdom through the Native American stories, guided fantasies, science and art projects, and creative language activities. An excellent resource for anyone who works with children.

_____. *Keepers of the Earth*. Golden, Colo.: Fulcrum Publishing, 1989.
> Native American folktales and environmental activities for children of all ages. Another valuable resource for parents and teachers.

_____. *Keepers of the Night*. Golden, Colo.: Fulcrum Publishing, 1994.
> A collection of Native American tales regarding the moon, the stars, and nocturnal animals, each with a selection of hands-on activities for children.

Cohlene, Terri. *Dancing Drum: A Cherokee Legend*. Vero Beach, Fla.: Watermill Press, 1990.
> When Grandmother Sun becomes angry with the people Dancing Drum is sent to set things right. Following the story is a nonfiction section on the Cherokee.

D

dePaola, Tomie. *The Legend of the Bluebonnet*. New York: G. P. Putnam's Sons, 1983.
> The bluebonnet, state flower of Texas, comes into existence only after a young Comanche girl sacrifices her most prized possession to save her people.

_____. *The Legend of the Indian Paintbrush*. New York: Macmillan, 1988.
> Little Gopher painted many pictures for his people and kept striving to paint the perfect sunset. With the aid of a dream vision his goal is accomplished after which his brushes take root to become the beautiful wildflowers known ever since as Indian paintbrushes.

J

Jacobs, Francine. *The Tainos: The People Who Welcomed Columbus*. New York: G. P. Putnam's Sons, 1992.
> When Columbus's ships arrived in the Caribbean the Tainos, peaceful farming people, were the first to have contact with the Spaniards. Within 50 years they were virtually wiped out through mistreatment, starvation, and disease. A good book to read aloud and discuss with intermediate or middle-school students.

Jeffers, Susan. *Brother Eagle, Sister Sky: A Message from Chief Seattle*. New York: Dial Books, 1991.
> Susan Jeffers's magnificent illustrations make the famous speech of Chief Seattle understandable even to young children.

Joose, Barbara M. *Mama, Do You Love Me?* San Francisco: Chronicle Books, 1991.
> Story of a little Alaskan Indian girl who plays the game of "but what if ..." with her mother and learns that mother love is unconditional.

K

Kendall, Russ. *Eskimo Boy: Life in an Inupiaq Eskimo Village.* New York: Scholastic, 1992.
Enhanced with beautiful photographs of life in a modern-day village located on a small Alaskan island.
Krensky, Stephen. *Children of the Earth and Sky.* New York: Scholastic, 1991.
Stories of Native American children of five different tribes—the Hopi, Comanche, Mohican, Navajo, and Mandan.
_____. *Children of the Wind and Water.* New York: Scholastic, 1994.
Stories of Native American children of five different tribes—the Muskogee, Dakota, Huron, Tlingit, and Nootka.

L

Longfellow, Henry Wadsworth. *Hiawatha.* New York: Dial Books for Young Readers, 1983.
Susan Jeffers's beautiful illustrations bring Longfellow's poem to life for young readers.

M

Martin, Rafe. *The Rough-Face Girl.* New York: G. P. Putnam's Sons, 1992.
An Algonquin Indian version of the Cinderella story.
Matthiessen, Peter. *Indian Country.* New York: Viking Press, 1984.
This nonfiction adult book chronicles ten different instances of European encroachment on Indian tribal grounds from the point of view of the Native Americans.
Medearis, Angela Shelf. *Dancing with the Indians.* New York: Holiday House, 1991.
Every year a young black girl's family travels to Oklahoma to join in the powwow of the Seminoles who took in her grandparents when they escaped from slavery. Based on a true story.

N

Nabokov, Peter, ed. *Native American Testimony: A Chronicle of Indian-White Relations from Prophecy to the Present, 1492–1992.* New York: Penguin Books, 1991.
A collection of more than 100 short narratives collected from primary sources, official documents, and Native American tradition. Perfect for reading aloud to older children.
Nashone. *Where Indians Live: American Indian Houses.* Sacramento: Sierra Oaks Publishing, 1989.
Photos show both traditional and contemporary housing for representative Native American tribes.

O

Osofsky, Audren. *Dreamcatcher.* New York: Orchard Books, 1992.
The story of the Ojibwa dreamcatcher, which was originally made and hung on the cradleboard to assure that an infant had pleasant dreams rather than nightmares.

S

Steptoe, John. *The Story of Jumping Mouse.* New York: Lothrop, Lee, and Shepard Books, 1984.
This Native American legend tells of a small mouse who gives everything to help others and is justly rewarded. A Caldecott Honor book.

St. Patrick's Day

B

Bunting, Eve. *St. Patrick's Day in the Morning*. New York: Houghton Mifflin, 1980.
When Jamie is told that he is too little to march in the St. Patrick's Day Parade he stages a parade of his own.

D

dePaola, Tomie. *Jamie O'Rourke and the Big Potato: An Irish Folktale*. New York: G. P. Putnam's Sons, 1992.
Jamie O'Rourke is so lazy that he would rather starve than work for his food, but when he gets a magic seed from a leprechaun and grows a potato so large that it blocks the road to the town the villagers devise a new plan to keep him from going hungry.

K

Kroll, Steven. *Mary McLean and the St. Patrick's Day Parade*. New York: Scholastic, 1991.
Story of an Irish-American girl whose dream of being in the St. Patrick's Day parade comes true.

M

McDermott, Gerald. *Tim O'Toole and the Wee Folk*. New York: Puffin Books, 1990.
The leprechauns help Tim to outwit the evil Mr. and Mrs. McGoon.

S

Shute, Linda. *Clever Tom and the Leprechaun*. New York: William Morrow, 1988.
A traditional Irish folktale of a man who catches a leprechaun only to be outsmarted and tricked out of the promised pot of gold.

Vietnam

D

Dyer, Lynette Vuong. *The Brocaded Slipper and Other Vietnamese Tales*. New York: Addison-Wesley, 1982.
A collection of five Vietnamese fairy tales.

S

Shalant, Phyllis. *Look What We've Brought You from Vietnam: Crafts, Games, Recipes, Stories, and Other Cultural Activities from New Americans*. New York: Julian Messner, 1988.
A collection of independent and adult-supervised activities for children.

Surat, Michele Maria. *Angel Child, Dragon Child*. Milwaukee: Raintree Publishers, 1983.
Ut arrives in the United States with her father, brother, and sisters, but there is not enough money for mother to follow them until the children who first teased her for being different learn to accept and sympathize with her and organize a fund-raiser.

T

Tran, Kim-Lan. *Tet: The New Year*. New York: Modern Curriculum Press, 1992.
Huy is homesick for Vietnam and does not want to join in the New Year celebration but his friends find a way to cheer up both Huy and his father.

Women's History Month

B

Barchers, Suzanne I. *Wise Women: Folk and Fairy Tales from around the World.* Englewood, Colo.: Libraries Unlimited, 1990.

> Dozens of traditional tales in which brave girls, resourceful wives, and clever women prevail. Contains many stories not included in standard collections of folktales and fairy tales.

C

Cole, Babette. *Princess Smartypants.* New York: G. P. Putnam's Sons, 1986.

> Princess Smartypants does not want to get married, so she sets impossible tasks for her suitors. When Prince Swashbuckle is able to meet all of her demands she gives him a magic kiss that turns him into a frog and manages to stay single and happy after all.

M

Munsch, Robert N. *The Paper Bag Princess.* Toronto, Canada: Annick Press, 1980.

> When a dragon destroys her castle and carries off Prince Ronald, Princess Elizabeth dons a paper bag and rushes to his rescue. However when Ronald is more concerned about her appearance than her bravery she leaves him in the dragon's cave and skips off into the future without him.

R

Riordan, James. *The Woman in the Moon and Other Forgotten Heroines.* New York: Dial Books for Young Readers, 1985.

> A collection of thirteen folktales, each from a different country, which dispel the stereotype of heroines as helpless and meek.

Appendix B: Recipes

African

COCADA AMARELA

Coconut pudding from Angola.

Ingredients:

1 cup sugar
6 whole cloves
1 cup water
meat from 1 fresh coconut (grated in blender or food processor)
6 eggs
$\frac{1}{4}$ teaspoon cinnamon

Directions:

Place sugar, cloves, and water in large saucepan and boil until candy thermometer reads 230°F (about 7 to 8 minutes). Remove and discard cloves. Reduce heat and gradually stir in coconut. Simmer until coconut becomes translucent (about 10 to 12 minutes). Remove from heat. Place eggs in large bowl, add cinnamon, and beat well. Slowly add coconut mixture to the eggs, stirring well after each addition. Return to the saucepan and cook over medium heat until mixture thickens (12 to 15 minutes). Serve hot or chilled.

KARRINGMELKBESKUIT

South African sweet buttermilk biscuits. A tasty snack with milk or coffee!

Ingredients:

3 cups white flour
2 cups whole wheat flour
$\frac{1}{2}$ cup sugar
1 tablepoon baking powder
$\frac{1}{2}$ pound butter
1 egg
about 1 $\frac{1}{2}$ cups buttermilk

Note: Karringmelkbeskuits are intended to be hard and crunchy, more like cookies than the baking powder biscuits you may be used to!

Directions:

Sift together flours, sugar, and baking powder. Cut butter into small pieces then add to flour mixture and mix with fork or pastry blender until mixture has a gritty texture. Beat the egg, then add to mixture. Add 1 cup buttermilk. Continue adding buttermilk, a few spoonfuls at a time until mixture has the consistency of biscuit dough. Flour hands and roll one heaping tablespoon of the batter at a time into a ball. Place on greased baking sheet and bake in preheated 350°F oven for about 20 minutes (a toothpick inserted in the center of the dough should come out clean and the Karringmelkbeskuits should be golden brown). Let oven cool to 200°F. Pile baked biscuits onto baking sheets and place in the oven overnight to dry. Let cool, then store in an airtight container. (Makes about two dozen.)

KULIKULI

Ground nut balls. A Nigerian snack.

Ingredients:

1 pound roasted peanuts
1 small onion, minced
1 teaspoon cayenne pepper
1 teaspoon salt
peanut oil for frying

Directions:

Place the peanuts (or "ground nuts" as they are known in Africa) in a blender or food processor and blend with just enough oil to make a smooth paste. Moisten hands and squeeze excess oil from peanut paste. Season onions with salt and cayenne pepper then sauté in small amount of peanut oil. When onions are golden remove from pan and knead into peanut paste. Roll into round balls, flatten into small patties, and fry in hot oil until outsides are crisp—about 2 to 3 minutes. Place on paper towels to absorb excess oil.

MAFE

Ground nut stew. A favorite in Mali and neighboring Senegal.

Ingredients:

1 chicken, cut into pieces
6 tablespoons peanut oil
1 large onion
2 tablespoons tomato paste
$\frac{1}{4}$ cup water
1 large ripe tomato
$\frac{1}{2}$ teaspoon salt
4 cups boiling water
$\frac{1}{2}$ cup peanut butter
2 cups chopped cabbage
2 small sweet potatoes
3 carrots
3 turnips
6 okra
$\frac{1}{4}$ teaspoon cayenne pepper

Directions:

Brown chicken in oil. Chop half of the onion, add to chicken, and cook until onion is golden brown. Thin tomato paste with $\frac{1}{4}$ cup water and add. Peel tomato, chop, and add. Add salt and 4 cups boiling water. Thin peanut butter with liquid from pot and add gradually. Reduce heat and simmer for 30 minutes. Chop all other vegetables except remaining onion and add about 1 cup of vegetables at a time so that broth remains hot. Cook until chicken and all vegetables are tender. Place remaining onion in blender or food processor and blend. Mix cayenne pepper with onion and add to stew during last 10 minutes of cooking.

Arabic
MA'AMUL

Date cookies.

Ingredients:

1 cup unsalted butter, room temperature
1 $\frac{1}{2}$ cups sugar
2 teaspoons brandy
2 teaspoons orange blossom water*
1 egg
3 cups flour
1 cup semolina
$\frac{1}{8}$ teaspoon salt
powdered sugar

Date Filling:
$\frac{1}{2}$ pound pitted dates
1 tablespoon butter, room temperature
2 teaspoons orange blossom water (optional)*

Note: If orange blossom water is not readily available, mix 1 tablespoon water and 1 teaspoon orange extract as a substitute.

Directions:

Prepare filling. Cut up dates and process in blender to make a paste. Add butter and orange blossom water (if desired) and blend again. Set aside.

For dough, combine butter, sugar, and cream until light and fluffy. Stir in brandy and orange blossom water. Beat in egg. Gradually add flour, semolina, and salt. Knead until smooth (about 5 minutes). Shape dough into balls about 1 $\frac{1}{2}$ inches in diameter. Pat each ball into a 3-inch circle. Place 1 tablespoon of filling in center of each circle. Pull edges of circle of dough over filling and pinch to seal. Shape into patties or balls or place in a *tabi* (a decorative cookie mold available in most Middle Eastern grocery stores). Place on a buttered baking sheet. Bake in a preheated 350°F oven for about 20 minutes. (Tops of cookies should not be brown, but bottoms will be light golden brown.) Sprinkle with powdered sugar while still warm then cool on a rack. Makes about eighteen cookies.

Chinese
DIM SUM

Sweet dumpling snacks.

Ingredients:

Filling:
$\frac{3}{4}$ cup sesame seeds
$\frac{1}{4}$ cup + 2 tablespoons chopped cashews
1 tablespoon butter
1 $\frac{1}{2}$ teaspoons flour
$\frac{3}{4}$ cup extra fine (powdered) sugar

Dough:
$\frac{1}{2}$ cup rice flour
2 cups glutinous rice flour
$\frac{1}{2}$ cup sugar
1 $\frac{1}{2}$ cups shredded coconut

Directions:

Make filling ahead of time. Place sesame seeds in a saucepan and place over low heat. Stir constantly until lightly browned. Repeat browning process with cashews. Allow seeds and nuts to cool completely. Place sesame seeds in blender and blend on high speed for 6 to 8 minutes. Add cashews and continue to blend until a thick paste is formed. Melt butter in saucepan. Add flour and stir until mixture bubbles. Remove from heat and stir in powdered sugar. Stir in sesame and cashew mixture. Chill until firm (about 2 hours).

Directions:
DIM SUM
(continued)

Mix rice flours in bowl. Make a well and add $\frac{1}{2}$ cup boiling water. Stir. Add $\frac{1}{2}$ cup cold water. Stir together then knead for about 5 minutes. Let rest, covered with a damp towel, for 10 minutes. Divide sesame-cashew paste into 24 equal parts and roll into balls. Divide dough into 24 equal parts. Work with one at a time keeping others covered. Roll dough into a ball (dust hands with flour if necessary) then flatten ball into a 2 $\frac{1}{2}$-inch circle. Place a ball of the sesame-cashew filling in the center of the dough circle. Bring up edges of dough and pinch or twist to seal. Roll between hands to make a round dumpling. Place dumplings on lightly greased steaming plate and steam in wok (over high heat) for about 7 minutes. Mix sugar with $\frac{1}{2}$ cup water and bring to a boil. After steaming, dip dumplings in sugar water then roll in coconut. Serve hot or cold.

FORTUNE COOKIES

These were first introduced in Chinese restaurants in the United States so they are not authentic Chinese cuisine, but they are lots of fun!

Ingredients:

$\frac{1}{2}$ cup margarine
$\frac{1}{4}$ cup sugar
1 egg white
1 $\frac{1}{2}$ cups flour
1 teaspoon vanilla extract
$\frac{1}{4}$ teaspoon baking soda

Directions:

Mix margarine, sugar, and egg white until smooth. Add all other ingredients and mix until smooth. Form into a ball and place on a lightly floured surface. Using a rolling pin, roll dough very thin and cut into circles about 2 $\frac{1}{2}$ inches across (a large drinking glass works well for this). Place a fortune written on a 2-inch by $\frac{1}{2}$-inch strip of paper off to one side of each circle. Fold circle gently in half then hang over the rim of a cup or glass to make second fold and traditional fortune cookie shape. Bake on a greased cookie sheet at 425°F for about 10 minutes until lightly browned.

SWEET ALMOND TEA

Ingredients:

$\frac{1}{4}$ cup long-grain rice
3 ounces almonds
1 $\frac{1}{2}$ quarts water
1 cup sugar

Directions:

Rinse rice. Cover with water, soak for 4 hours. Soak almonds in boiling water for 10 minutes. Remove skins. Place rice, almonds, 2 cups water in blender; puree. Add 1 more cup of water and blend for about 1 more minute. Line a colander with cheesecloth, set in a large pan. Pour puree into colander then pour remaining water over the mixture. After mixture has drained, gather cheesecloth and squeeze out any remaining liquid. Place pan over medium heat. Stir constantly until tea begins to bubble. Add sugar, stir until dissolved. Serve hot.

France

CREPES

Ingredients:

1 cup flour
pinch of salt
1 egg, beaten
1 1/4 cups milk
vegetable oil for frying

Possible Fillings:
Cottage cheese with chopped walnuts
Cherries and sour cream
Cream cheese mixed with peach or blueberry pie filling

Directions:

Mix flour and salt in a bowl and make a well. Beat egg and milk together, pour into well in flour mixture, then beat to a smooth batter. Heat a little oil in a crepe pan or frying pan. Pour in about 2 tablespoons of batter, tilting pan so that batter spreads as thinly as possible. Cook until browned on the bottom then flip and brown other side. Layer the crepes between sheets of waxed paper and keep warm while you fry the remaining batter. Serve with filling of your choice.

Greek

GREEK SPAGHETTI

Ingredients:

1/2 pound butter
7–8 cloves garlic, minced
1 pound feta cheese
1 pound thin spaghetti

Directions:

Sauté garlic in butter until soft. Crumble feta and add to butter and garlic mixture. Continue to cook over low heat while you cook the spaghetti. Pour sauce over cooked, drained spaghetti and serve hot.

KOURAMBIETHES

Powdered sugar cookies.

Ingredients:

1/2 pound butter at room temperature
powdered sugar
3 1/4 cups cake flour

Directions:

Whip butter with an electric mixer and add 6 table-spoons powdered sugar. Mix at low speed for at least 30 minutes. Mix in the flour by hand and knead until a soft dough is formed. Take about 1 heaping tablespoon of dough at a time, roll between your hands to form logs or plump circles, and place on ungreased baking sheet. Bake at 350°F for about 25 minutes. Edges should be slightly brown. Remove from baking sheet while still hot, place on waxed paper, and sift powdered sugar over cookies. Allow to cool, then store in airtight container. Makes about three dozen.

YIAHNI

Greek green beans with tomatoes.

Ingredients:

2 cups chopped onion
1/2 cup olive oil
16-ounce can tomatoes
2 pounds green beans, cleaned and cut in pieces
salt, pepper, garlic salt to taste

Directions:

Sauté onions in oil until yellow. Add tomatoes and cook over low heat for 30 minutes. Add beans and seasonings to taste. Continue to cook until beans are soft but not mushy.

HALLOWEEN
PUMPKIN BREAD

Ingredients:

2 2/3 cups sugar
2/3 cup shortening
4 eggs
1 16-ounce can pumpkin
2/3 cup water
3 1/3 cups flour
2 teaspoons baking soda
1 1/2 teaspoons salt
1/2 teaspoon baking powder
1 teaspoon cinnamon
1 teaspoon ground cloves
2/3 cup chopped walnuts
2/3 cup raisins (optional)

Directions:

Preheat oven to 350°F. Mix shortening and sugar until fluffy. Add eggs, pumpkin, and water. Blend in dry ingredients, then stir in nuts and raisins by hand. Pour into two greased loaf pans and bake about 50 to 60 minutes. Test doneness by inserting a toothpick into the center of the loaf. It should come out clean.

PUMPKIN COOKIES

Ingredients:

2 1/4 cups sifted cake flour
2 1/4 teaspoons baking powder
1/4 teaspoon nutmeg
1/2 teaspoon cinnamon
1/4 teaspoon ground cloves
1/2 cup shortening
1 1/2 cups sugar
1 egg
1 1/3 cups cooked mashed pumpkin
1 cup chopped raisins
1/2 cup chopped walnuts (optional)

Directions:

Preheat oven to 375°F. Sift together flour, baking powder, nutmeg, cinnamon, and cloves. Set aside. Cream shortening and sugar until fluffy. Add egg and beat until smooth. Alternately add pumpkin and flour mixture beating well after each addition. Stir in raisins and walnuts. Drop dough by tablespoons, about 2 inches apart on greased baking sheets and bake for 15 minutes.

PUMPKIN SEEDS

Ingredients:

seeds from fresh pumpkin
$1/_4$ cup butter
dash Worcestershire sauce
salt

Directions:

Rinse seeds and pat dry. Melt butter in a pan and add Worcestershire sauce. Remove from heat and toss seeds in butter mixture. Spread seeds on a baking sheet and sprinkle with salt. Bake at 350°F until seeds are lightly browned.

Hispanic

CAMOTE (SWEET POTATO CANDY)

Most closely associated with the Mexican holiday of Cinco de Mayo.

Ingredients:

1 20-ounce can crushed pineapple
1 16-ounce can sweet potatoes
4 cups sugar
$1 1/_4$ cups flour
powdered sugar

Directions:

Cook pineapple over medium heat until tender (about 15 minutes). Cool slightly then place in blender and blend on high for 10 seconds. Pour into mixing bowl. Drain sweet potatoes, place in blender, and puree. Heat sweet potato mixture thoroughly then stir in sugar and flour. Bring to a boil, stirring constantly. Allow to boil for 1 minute, then remove from heat. Mix together sweet potatoes and pineapple. Pour into 9-inch by 13-inch pan and refrigerate for several hours. When mixture is firm enough to mold, roll spoonfuls into log shapes. Roll in powdered sugar. Refrigerate.

CHICKEN TACOS

A Mexican favorite with an accompanying mild sauce children love.

Ingredients:

1 3-pound chicken
4 cloves minced garlic
salt and pepper to taste
2 tablespoons chopped onion
3 tablespoons chopped, peeled tomato
1 tablespoon cooking oil
12 prepared taco shells
shredded lettuce
grated cheese
sour cream
Salsa Para Los Niños (recipe on following page)

Directions:

Cut chicken into pieces, place in large saucepan, and add garlic, salt, and pepper to taste. Cover with water. Simmer 35–40 minutes. Let cool in own broth then remove skin from the chicken and shred. Sauté onion and tomato in oil. Add shredded chicken and cook about 1 minute.

Serve hot in taco shells with lettuce, cheese, sour cream, and salsa.

FLAN

Caramel pudding.

Ingredients:

²/₃ cup sugar
1 14-ounce can condensed milk
1 12-ounce can evaporated milk
4 eggs
¹/₂ teaspoon vanilla
¹/₂ teaspoon almond extract
¹/₄ teaspoon salt
1 teaspoon Amaretto (optional)

Directions:

To make caramel, heat sugar over medium heat. When it begins to melt, lower heat. Continue cooking until sugar is completely melted and browned. Quickly pour into 1 ¹/₂-quart baking dish tilting dish to coat bottom and sides. Place all remaining ingredients in blender and blend well. Pour into cooled caramel-coated baking dish. Cover with foil and place in a larger pan of warm water. Bake at 325°F for 1 ¹/₂ hours (a knife inserted in the center should come out clean). Chill for at least 1 hour. Invert onto a platter immediately before serving.

HUMITAS

Humitas is the name used in Argentina, Bolivia, and Chile for tamales. This dish is traditionally served in Chile on Independence Day.

Ingredients:

8–10 ears of corn
1 tablespoon + 1 teaspoon strained bacon fat or butter
¹/₃ cup finely chopped onion
1 small tomato, peeled, seeded, and finely chopped
³/₄ teaspoon salt
¹/₃ cup corn flour

Directions:

Cut off "stem" end of corn and carefully remove husks. Save the tender husks without tears. Clean corn and grate kernels off cobs (about 2 ¹/₃ cups grated corn). Set corn aside. Heat fat and sauté onion over medium heat until translucent but not brown. Add chopped tomato and cook for several more minutes. Remove from heat. Add grated corn and salt. Sprinkle with corn flour, mix thoroughly. Let sit for 30 minutes, stirring occasionally. On work surface overlap two corn husks, pointed ends facing in opposite directions. Place a third husk in the center of the first two. Place a heaping tablespoon of corn mixture in the center of the husks, wrap securely folding in all four sides, and tie with strips of corn husk or kitchen string. Repeat until all humitas are assembled. Place humitas in a steamer for 45 minutes. Let cool slightly, remove strings, and open husks before serving. (Note: Humitas store well and can be kept in the refrigerator for several days. Steam for about 10 minutes to reheat.)
Variation: In Bolivia it is common to add finely grated cheese (about 2 tablespoons) after adding the corn flour.

SALSA PARA LOS NIÑOS

Sauce for the Children. A mild salsa.

Ingredients:

1 28-ounce can crushed Italian-style tomatoes
¹/₄ cup finely chopped onion
¹/₂ cup ice water
1 tablespoon vinegar
1 tablespoon vegetable oil
1 tablespoon oregano
salt to taste

Directions:

Mix together all ingredients. Serve with tacos (above), nachos, or corn chips.

TURRON DI DONA PEPA

The traditional pastry of Peru's October "Purple Spring" Festival.

Ingredients:

Syrup:
$^1/_2$ cup orange juice
juice of half a lemon
$^3/_4$ cup firmly packed brown sugar
$^1/_4$ cup sugar

Pastry:
2 tablespoons sugar
1 tablespoon anise seed
$^1/_2$ cup water
2 cups flour
$^1/_2$ teaspoon salt
$^1/_4$ cup shortening
$^1/_4$ cup butter
3 egg yolks
colored candy sprinkles

Directions:

Syrup: Combine juices and sugars in a saucepan. Place on very low heat and cook without stirring until a candy thermometer registers 260°F (about 1 hour). Cool until syrup starts to thicken.

Pastry: Place 2 tablespoons sugar, anise seed, and $^1/_2$ cup water in a small saucepan. Cook over low heat until mixture has reduced by half. Strain and chill thoroughly. Sift flour and salt into a bowl. Mix in shortening and butter. In a small bowl beat together egg yolks and the anise syrup made earlier. Make a well in the center of the flour mixture, pour in egg mixture, and work the dough to a smooth consistency. Divide into eighteen equal pieces. On a floured surface flatten each piece of dough, one at a time, into a 5-inch by 2-inch rectangle. Flour hands and roll dough like a jelly roll into a 5-inch by $^1/_2$-inch piece. Place the pastry sticks on a nonstick baking sheet and bake at 350°F for 40–45 minutes. (Sticks should be lightly browned.) Cool on rack.

Assembly: Place six pastry sticks on a serving plate, sides touching. Spoon enough syrup over top to coat. Place the next six pastry sticks on top of the first six but in the opposite direction. Coat with syrup. Place the last six sticks on top in the direction of the first layer. Spoon remaining syrup over top and sprinkle with candies. Let stand for several hours before cutting into individual portions.

India
POORI

Deep-fried bread.

Ingredients:

1 cup sifted whole wheat flour
1 cup white flour
$^1/_2$ teaspoon salt
2 tablespoons oil
$^1/_2$ cup milk
oil for frying

Directions:

Sift flours and salt into a bowl. Drip 2 tablespoons oil over flour mixture and mix to coarse crumb consistency. Slowly add milk to form a stiff dough. Knead until smooth (10–12 minutes). Roll dough into a ball. Oil hands and rub over ball. Place in plastic bag and allow to sit for 30 minutes. Knead dough again then divide into twelve equal pieces. Roll one piece of dough into a ball then flatten into a 5-inch round. Cover with plastic wrap while you form the other dough rounds. Put about 1 inch of oil in a wok or deep frying pan over medium heat. Gently place one poori at a time in the hot oil. Use a slotted spoon to tap the poori down into the oil. Within a few seconds it should puff up. Turn and cook other side for about 10 seconds then remove with slotted spoon and drain on paper towels. Serve hot.

Jewish
CHALLAH BREAD

Ingredients:

3 cups flour
1 $\frac{1}{2}$ teaspoons salt
1 teaspoon active dry yeast
$\frac{1}{4}$ cup + 2 tablespoons warm (not hot) water
3 eggs
2 tablespoons vegetable oil
1 $\frac{1}{2}$ teaspoons honey

Directions:

Place flour and salt in bowl. Dissolve yeast in the warm water. Break 2 eggs into large measuring cup and add water to make 1 $\frac{1}{4}$ cups. Make a well in the dry ingredients and pour in yeast, egg mixture, vegetable oil, and honey. Knead the dough until very springy—about 20 minutes—lightly flouring hands as needed. Form the dough into a ball and place in a bowl, covering with a damp cloth. Let rise for about 30 minutes. Knead dough slightly then let rise as before, this time for about 15 minutes. Divide the dough into three equal balls. Roll each into a long stick (about 18 inches long). Lightly dust each stick with flour, place next to each other, and braid loosely. (It is sometimes easier to braid from the center out to each end.) Place on greased baking sheet. Mix the remaining egg with 2 tablespoons water and brush over top of loaf being careful to cover all areas. Do not allow egg mixture to collect in low areas of the braid. Bake at 350°F for approximately 40 minutes. (Long, skinny loaves will take less time; short, fat loaves, longer.)

CHEESE LATKES

A fast and simple variety of latke.

Ingredients:

3 eggs
1 cup cottage cheese
$\frac{1}{4}$ cup milk
$\frac{1}{4}$ teaspoon salt
1 cup flour
vegetable oil for frying

Directions:

Blend eggs, cottage cheese, milk, and salt in a blender. Add flour and continue to blend. Drop by spoonfuls onto a hot, greased frying pan. Turn to cook other side. Cook until golden brown. Makes about eighteen latkes.

HAMANTASHIN

A three-cornered pastry served at Purim.

Ingredients:

1 cup softened butter
1 cup sugar
3 eggs
$\frac{1}{4}$ cup orange juice
$\frac{1}{2}$ teaspoon salt
4 cups flour
1 tablespoon baking powder
prune, strawberry, or other preserves for filling

Directions:

Cream together butter and sugar. Add eggs and orange juice and mix well. Sift together dry ingredients and add to mixture. Refrigerate dough for one hour. Roll out on floured piece of waxed paper (dough will be very soft) using a floured rolling pin until $\frac{1}{4}$-inch thick or less. Use a floured glass or cookie cutter to cut $2\frac{1}{2}$ inch to 3-inch circles. Place a scant teaspoon of preserves in center of each cookie. Fold up three sides of the cookie and pinch edges together firmly so pastry will not open during baking. The cookie should resemble a tricorn hat with a triangle of jelly showing in the center. Place on a greased cookie sheet about 1 inch apart and bake at 350°F for 10 to 12 minutes, until edges are lightly browned. Cool on wire rack. (Makes about five dozen.)

POTATO LATKES

Traditional Jewish treat served during the Hanukkah celebration.

Ingredients:

5 or 6 peeled, grated potatoes
2 large eggs
1 teaspoon salt
dash pepper
1 medium onion, minced
2 teaspoons lemon juice
3 tablespoons flour
1 tablespoon parsley flakes (optional)
oil for frying

Directions:

Squeeze as much liquid as possible from potatoes. Beat eggs. Combine potatoes and eggs, then add all other ingredients except oil. Heat $1/_2$ inch of oil in a skillet. Drop mixture into hot oil by heaping tablespoons. Flatten with a spatula. Cook until brown on both sides, turning once. Drain on paper towels. Serve with applesauce, sour cream, or jam.

Native American
INDIAN FRY BREAD

Ingredients:

1 cup whole wheat flour
1 cup white flour
$\frac{1}{2}$ teaspoon salt
2 teaspoons baking powder
2 tablespoons vegetable oil
about $\frac{1}{2}$ cup water
oil for frying
fruit pie filling or jam

Directions:

Sift together dry ingredients. Add oil and enough water to make a soft dough. Knead 5 minutes. Let stand 30 minutes at room temperature. Divide into twelve balls then roll each out into a 4- to 5-inch circle. Heat 1 inch of oil in frying pan and fry dough circles for 15 to 20 seconds each. (Bread should puff up during frying.) Drain on a paper towel then cut open and place filling inside.

Southeast Asian
PITA BREAD

Ingredients:

1 ¹/₄ cups lukewarm water
1 teaspoon dry yeast
2 ¹/₂ to 3 cups flour (white, wheat, or half and half)
1 ¹/₂ teaspoons salt
1 ¹/₂ teaspoons olive oil

Directions:

Place water in a large bowl, sprinkle yeast over top, and stir to dissolve. Add 1 ¹/₂ cups of flour, half cup at a time, then stir mixture by hand for about 1 ¹/₂ minutes.

Cover bowl with a damp cloth and let stand for 1 to 2 hours. Sprinkle salt over the mixture and add oil. Mix well. Add remaining flour as needed until dough is too stiff to stir. Turn onto lightly floured surface and knead until smooth and elastic (about 10 minutes). Place dough in a large oiled bowl, cover with plastic wrap, and let sit until double in size (about 1 ¹/₂ hours). Place baking sheet on bottom oven rack and preheat oven to 450°F. Gently punch down dough and divide into eight equal pieces. Roll each piece into an 8- to 9-inch circle, ¹/₄-inch thick or less. Place one at a time on heated baking sheet and bake for 3 to 5 minutes or until bread has puffed up completely.

Turkey

APPLES WITH WHIPPED CREAM

Ingredients:

6 apples
24 whole cloves
juice of 1 lemon
1 cup sugar
1 cup water
whipped cream

Directions:

Peel and core apples; cut into quarters. Stick one clove into each quarter. Pour lemon juice over apples; set aside. Mix sugar and water, place in heavy saucepan, and cook until sugar is dissolved, stirring constantly. Place apples in pan; stir gently to coat with syrup. Simmer for about 6 minutes, basting two or three times during cooking time. Serve hot with whipped cream on top.

LOKMA

Small sweet fritters. Served on special occasions.

Ingredients:

1 ¹/₂ cups sugar
2 cups water
1 teaspoon lemon juice
1 teaspoon active dry yeast
¹/₈ teaspoon sugar
1 ¹/₂ cups warm water
2 cups flour
1 tablespoon butter, melted
pinch of salt
peanut oil for deep frying

Directions:

Make the syrup. Simmer 1 ¹/₂ cups sugar in 2 cups water for 5 minutes. Add lemon juice, bring to boil, and set aside. Place yeast and ¹/₈ teaspoon sugar in 1 ¹/₂ cups warm water. Allow to sit for 10 minutes. Place flour in large bowl. Make a well in the center and put in the yeast mixture, butter, and salt. Stir for 5 minutes. Cover with a damp cloth and let rise for 1 to 2 hours. Drop by teaspoonfuls into hot oil. Lokmas should rise to the top and puff up almost immediately and should be brown in 3 to 4 minutes (adjust heat if they are cooking too slowly or too quickly). Drain on paper towels. Dip in syrup. Serve hot or cold.

United States
KING CAKE

A traditional cake served in New Orleans during Mardi Gras.

Ingredients:

$1/2$ cup warm water
2 packages dry yeast
2 teaspoons sugar
4 to 5 cups flour
$1/2$ cup sugar
2 teaspoons salt
1 teaspoon nutmeg
1 teaspoon grated lemon rind
$1/2$ cup warm milk
$1/2$ cup butter, melted and cooled
5 egg yolks
$1/2$ cup finely chopped candied citron (optional)
1 pecan half
purple, green, and gold sugar crystals

Glaze:
2 cups powdered sugar, sifted
2 tablespoons lemon juice
1 tablespoon + 2 teaspoons water

Directions:

Combine $1/2$ cup warm water, yeast, and 2 teaspoons sugar in a small bowl. Mix well and let sit for 10 minutes. Combine 4 cups flour, $1/2$ cup sugar, salt, nutmeg, and lemon rind; add warm milk, butter, egg yolks, and yeast mixture. Beat until smooth. Place dough on lightly floured surface and knead in enough of the remaining cup of flour so that dough is no longer sticky. Continue to knead until dough is elastic and smooth (about 10 minutes). Place dough in greased bowl, cover with a damp towel, and allow to rise until doubled in bulk (about $1 1/2$ hours). Place dough on lightly floured surface, punch down. If desired sprinkle on citron and knead until citron is evenly distributed. Shape dough into a 30-inch cylinder. Put a well-greased 2-pound coffee can in the center of a buttered baking sheet; form cylinder of dough around the coffee can into a ring. Pinch ends together to seal. Gently press pecan half into the dough from the bottom making sure that it is completely surrounded by dough. Cover and let rise until doubled in bulk (about 45 minutes) then bake at 350°F about 30 minutes or until golden brown. Remove coffee can at once and allow cake to cool. When completely cooled make glaze by combining powdered sugar, lemon juice, and water and stirring until smooth. Drizzle over cake and sprinkle with sugar crystals.

YEAST BREAD

My Grandma Hankins's special recipe. I have made it with children as young as five years old and it has never failed to be fun and delicious!

Ingredients:

1 package dry yeast
2 tablespoons sugar
1 tablespoon + 1 teaspoon salt
3 pints warm (not hot) water
1 cup shortening
5 pound flour + a little extra for use when kneading

Directions:

Dissolve yeast, sugar, and salt in warm water in a large container (a roasting pan works well). Add shortening.

Plunge your hands right on in and squish it all up. Add flour, a part at a time, and keep mixing with your hands. Put dough on a floured surface and knead until your arms hurt (at least 10 minutes). Place dough back in container and cover with a damp cloth. Let rise until double in size. Knead again, then form into three loaves and place in greased bread pans. Poke the top of each loaf several times with a dinner fork to let any large bubbles escape. Let rise until double again then bake at 350°F until golden brown. Remove from pans to cool.

Appendix C: Music

African

A

Amoaku, W. K. *African Songs and Rhythms for Children*. Smithsonian/ Folkways Records (distributed by Rounder Records, One Camp St., Cambridge, Mass. 02140) SF 45011.
   Audiocassette. Prepared under the direction of Carl Orff, this recording uses drums, bells, and voice to introduce children to the musical tradition of a number of African cultures.

Chinese

C

Chinese Music of the Han and the Uighurs. World Music Library. King Records KICC 5141.
   Compact disc. This collection of folk songs played on traditional Chinese instruments sets the mood for study or celebration of holidays from China.

German

O

Oktoberfest in Germany. LaserLight Digital International Passport 15 181.
   Compact disc. A festive collection of German marches, waltzes, and polkas with a nice mix of instrumental and vocal selections.

Hispanic

M

Michael, Sarah. *Fiesta! Mexico and Central America*. Fearon Teacher Aids (P.O. Box 280, Carthage, Ill. 62321) FE-4232.
   Audiocassette. Seventeen songs that appeal to children are performed instrumentally on one side of the tape and with vocals in Spanish on the other.

S

Shaylen, Carl, and Jennifer Shaylen. *Arroz Con Leché: Popular Songs and Rhymes from Latin America Selected by Lulu Delacre*. Scholastic 0-590-60034-6.
   Audiocassette. Selections sung in Spanish on this short (8 1/2-minute) tape complement Delacre's book, *Arroz Con Leché* (see Appendix A, Hispanic), or can stand alone.

Indian

M

Music from India. LaserLight Digital International Passport 15 439.
   Compact disc. Indian classical music featuring Ram Chandra on the sitar. Works well as background music for activities associated with India.

Irish

C

Celtic Twilight. Hearts of Space (P.O. Box 31321, San Francisco, Calif. 94131) HS11104.
   Compact disc. In this collection of instrumental music from Ireland and Scotland contemporary arrangements combine with traditional instruments—the bodhran, pennywhistle, bagpipes, and fiddle.

The Chieftains, with James Galway. *Over the Sea to Skye*. RCA 60424-4.
   Audiocassette. Traditional Celtic music including Galway on the flute and pennywhistle.

N

Noonan, Paddy. *Irish Dew*. Compose (distributed by PPI, Newark, N.J. 07105) 9059-2.
   Compact disc. Includes "The Unicorn," "Whistling Gypsy," "When Irish Eyes Are Smiling," and other great sing-along songs.

Jewish

S

Schreiner, Elissa, and others. *Let's Celebrate Hanukkah*. Astor Books/Astor Music.
   Audiocassette. This collection of sing-along songs comes with a book containing words and music for eight songs. It is available in children's bookstores.

Multicultural

B

Beall, Pamela Conn, and Susan Hagen Nipp. *Wee Sing around the World*. Price Stern Sloan 0-8431-3729-0.
   Audiocassette. Forty-two children's songs, each from a different country, are performed on this tape that comes with a songbook with lyrics in both English and the language of the country from which the song comes.

Native American

D

The Dawning: Chants of the Medicine Wheel. Bear Tribe Medicine Society (P.O. Box 9167, Spokane, Wash. 99209). Audiocassette. Contains sixteen Native American chants, many of which are simple enough to teach to children.

N

Nakai, R. Carlos. *Desert Dance.* Celestial Harmonies (P.O. Box 30122, Tucson, Ariz. 85751). Audiocassette. Music of the traditional nose flute enhanced with Native American drum, rawhide rattles, and vocals. Excellent background music.

Bibliography

A

Anyike, James C. *African American Holidays*. Chicago: Popular Truth, 1991.

Armstrong, Karen. *Muhammad: A Biography of the Prophet*. New York: HarperCollins, 1992.

B

Bancroft-Hunt, Norman, and Werner Forman. *The Indians of the Great Plains*. New York: Peter Bedrick Books, 1989.

Black, Naomi. *Celebration: The Book of Jewish Festivals*. Middle Village, N.Y.: Jonathan David, 1989.

Bracher, Peter, and others. *Public Education Religion Studies: Questions and Answers*. Lawrence, Kans.: National Council on Religion and Public Education, 1986.

Brazil. London: Brazilian Embassy, 1975.

Brotman, Charlene, and Barbara Marshman. *Holidays and Holy Days: A Whole Year of Celebrations*. Lexington, Mass.: Brotman-Marshall, 1983.

Budapest, ZsuZsanna E. *The Grandmother of Time*. New York: Harper and Row, 1989.

C

Caballero, Jane. *Children around the World Today*. Atlanta: Humanities Limited, 1990.

Chase, William. *Chase's Annual Events: The Day-to-Day Directory to 1992*. Chicago: Contemporary Books, 1991.

Chaudhry, Rashid Ahmad. *Muslim Festivals and Ceremonies*. Tilford, England: Islam International Publications, 1988.

China's Folk Festivals. Beijing, China: Foreign Languages Press, 1988.

Cohen, Hennig, and Tristam P. Coffin. *The Folklore of American Holidays*. Detroit: Gale Research, 1987.

E

Everix, Nancy. *Ethnic Celebrations around the World*. Carthage, Ill.: Good Apple, 1991.

G

Groh, Lynn. *A Holiday Book: New Year's Day*. Champaign, Ill.: Garrard, 1964.

H

Hertzberg, Arthur. *Judaism.* New York: Goerge Braziller, 1961.

J

Josephy, Alvin M. *The American Heritage Book of Indians.* New York: American Heritage Publishing, 1961.

Josephy, Alvin M., and others. *The Native Americans.* Atlanta: Turner Publishing, 1993.

K

Kalman, Bobbie. *We Celebrate New Year.* New York: Crabtree, 1985.

L

Laubin, Reginald, and Gladys Laubin. *Indian Dances of North America.* Norman: University of Oklahoma Press, 1989.

Lester, Robert C. *Buddhism.* New York: HarperCollins, 1987.

Linse, Barbara, and Dick Judd. *Fiesta! Mexico and Central America.* Carthage, Ill.: Fearon Teacher Aids, 1993.

M

MacDonald, Margaret Read. *The Folklore of World Holidays.* Detroit: Gale Research, 1992.

Medicine Hawk, and Grey Cat. *American Indian Ceremonies.* New Brunswick, N.J.: Inner Light Publications, 1990.

Morris, Richard B. *Encyclopedia of American History.* New York: Harper and Row, 1976.

Mossman, Jennifer. *Holidays and Anniversaries of the World.* New York: Gale Research, 1990.

Myers, Robert J. *Celebrations: The Complete Book of American Holidays.* Garden City, N.Y.: Doubleday, 1972.

N

National Geographic Atlas of the World. Sixth Edition. Washington, D.C.: National Geographic Society, 1990.

P

Polon, Linda, and Aileen Cantwell. *The Whole Earth Holiday Book.* Glenview, Ill.: Scott Foresman, 1983.

S

Schiffman, Lawrence H. *Judaism: A Primer.* New York: Anti-Defamation League of B'nai B'rith, 1986.

Sen, K. M. *Hinduism.* Middlesex, England: Penguin Books, 1991.

Shalant, Phyllis. *Look What We've Brought You from Vietnam.* New York: Julian Messner, 1988.

Sports and Cultural Calendar 1992—Barbados: Cole's Printery, 1992.

Syme, Daniel B. *The Jewish Home. A Guide for Jewish Living.* New York: UAHC Press, 1988.

T

Townshend, George. *Christ and Baha'u'llah.* London: Lowe and Brydone, 1974.

V

Von Grunebaum, G. E. *Muhammadan Festivals.* New York: Olive Branch Press, 1988.

W

Ward, Hiley H. *My Friends' Beliefs: A Young Reader's Guide to World Religions.* New York: Walker, 1988.

Westridge Young Writers' Workshop. *Kids Explore America's Hispanic Heritage.* Santa Fe: John Muir Publications, 1992.

Bibliography

Index of Holidays

A

Afghanistan
    Independence Day, 103
African American
    Juneteenth, 79
    Kwanzaa, 156–157
    Umoja Karamu, 138
African Liberation Day, 68
Algeria
    National Day, 78–79
All Saints' Day, 139
All Souls' Day, 140
All Souls' Day, Buddhist, 89–90
Alp Feast, 84
Amaterasu-o-Mi-Kami, Festival of, 91
American Indian Day, 112
Angel Day, Be An, 103
Angola
    Feast of Nganja, 42
    Feast of Okambondando, 23
ANZAC Day, 51
April Fools' Day, 46
Arbor Day, International, 2
Argentina
    National Day, 68
Armistice Day, 142
Asalaha Puja Day, 84–85
Ash Wednesday, 22
Asian-Pacific Month, 60–61
Assumption Day, 101
Australia
    ANZAC Day, 51
    Independence Day, 13
Autumn celebrations
    American Indian Day (United States), 112
    Dia de los Muertos (Mexico), 139–140
    Guy Fawkes Day (England), 140–141
    Halloween, 133–134
    Hispanic Heritage Month (United States), 116–118
    Htamane-Hto (Myanmar), 136
    Moon Festival (China), 107–108
    Oktoberfest (Germany), 113
    Onam (India), 109
    Sukkoth (Jewish), 125–126
    Tet Trung Thu (Vietnam), 108
    Thanksgiving Day (Canada), 122
    Thanksgiving Day (Switzerland), 119
    Thanksgiving Day (United States), 137
    Umoja Karamu (African-American), 138
    Zolla (Nigeria), 127

B

Bab, Birthday of, 132
Baha'i
    Birth of Bab, 132
    Birth of Baha'Allah, 142
    Ridvan, 50
Baha'Allah, Birthday of, 142
Bahamas
    Discovery Day, 131
    Emancipation Day, 96–97

Fox Hill Day, 96–97
Independence Day, 88
Junkanoo, 156
Labour Day, 72
Bahrain
National Day, 153
Bangladesh
Bijoy Dibash (Victory Day), 153
Shaheed Dibash (Martyrs' Day), 29–30
Swadhinata Dibash (Independence Day), 40
Barbados
Crop Over Festival, 86
Independence Day, 145
Kadooment Day, 96
Bastille Day, 90
Baswant, 42
Bean Throwing Day (Setsubun), 27
Belgium
National Day, 91–92
St. Nicholas Day, 150
Bevrijdingsdag, 62
Bhau-Beez, 124
Bijoy Dibash, 153
Bird Week (Japan), 56–57
Black History Month, 25
Bolivia
National Day, 99
Bon Festival, 89–90
Botswana
Independence Day, 120
Boxing Day, 155
Boys' Day (Kodomono-Hi), 63
Brazil
Carnaval, 9–10
Festival of Iemanja, 159
Independence Day, 114
St. John's Eve, 80
Brother and Sister Day (India), 124
Brotherhood Week, 21
Brunei
National Day, 69
Buddhist holidays
Asalaha Puja Day, 84–85
Hanamatsun (Birth of Buddha), 47

Higan-E (Fall), 120
Higan-E (Spring), 39
Kathin Ceremony, 109
Magha Puja, 24–25
Songkran, 48
Visakha Puja Day, 73–74
Bun Hill Festival, 55–56
Burma—see "Myanmar"

C

Cambodia
Constitution Day, 65
Independence Day, 141
Cameroon
Independence Day, 13
Canada
Dominion Day, 85
Labor Day, 106
Remembrance Day, 142
Thanksgiving Day, 122
Victoria Day, 54
Candlemas, 26–27
Carnaval, 9–10
Carnival, 9–10
Celtic
Feast of Epona, 77
Lammas (Festival of the New Bread), 98–99
Central America
Independence Day, 116
Chakri Day, 47
Cherry Blossom Festival, 44
Childermas, 158
Children's celebrations
Angola (Okambondondo), 23
Feast of Nganja, 42
Feast of Okambondando, 23

Finland and Sweden (St. Knut's Day), 16–17
India (Children's Day), 142–143
India (Navaratri—Doll Festival), 122–123
Japan (Boys' Day), 63
Japan (Girls' Day), 34
Japan (Shichigosan/Seven-Five-Three Day), 143
Korea (Children's Day), 64
Taiwan (Youth Day), 40
Urini Nal (Korea), 64
Chile
    Independence Day (18 de Septembre), 119
China
    Bun Hill Festival, 55–56
    Confucius's Birthday, 106–107
    Dragon Boat Festival, 56
    Kite Festival, 114–115
    Lantern Festival, 11
    Lich'un, 43
    Moon Festival, 107–108
    National Day, 127–128
    New Year, 8–9
    Teachers' Day, 115
Chinese New Year, 8–9
Christian holidays
    All Saints' Day, 139
    All Souls' Day, 140
    Ash Wednesday, 22
    Assumption Day, 101
    Candlemas, 26–27
    Christmas, 154–155
    Corpus Christi, 58–59
    Easter, 33
    Epiphany, 14–15
    Flores de Mayo, 60
    Good Friday, 32
    Palm Sunday, 32
    Pentecost, 58
    St. Andrew's Day, 145
    St. Cecilia's Day, 144
    St. Christopher's Day, 93
    St. Francis of Assisi, Feast of, 129–130
    Trinity Sunday, 58
    Whitsunday, 58
Christmas, 154–155
Cinco De Mayo, 62–63
Colombia
    Independence Day, 91

Columbus Day, 131–132
Confucius's Birthday, 106–107
Congo
    Independence Day, 102
Constitution Day
    Cambodia, 65
    Norway, 67
    Philippines, 66
    Puerto Rico, 93
    Thailand, 151
Corpus Christi, 58–59
Crop Over Festival, 86
Cyprus
    Green Monday, 23
Czech Republic
    Republic Day, 133
    St. Nicholas' Day, 150
    St. Stephen's Day, 156
    Teachers' Day, 40

D

Dead, Day of the, 139–140
Dead, Feast of the, 89–90
Denmark
    St. John's Eve, 80
Dia de los Muertos, 139–140
Dia de Los Reyes Magos, 15–16
Discovery Day, 131
Diwali, 123–124
Dodenherdenking, 62
Doll Festival (India), 122–123
Doll Festival (Japan), 34
Dominican Republic
    Independence Day, 30
Dominion Day, 85
Double Nine Day, 114–115

Dragon Boat Festival, 56
Dyngus, 33

F

E

Earth Day, 50–51
Easter, 33
Egypt
    Birth of Isis, 101
Eid-Milad-Un-Nabi, 6
Eid-ul-Adhia, 5
Eid-ul-Fitr, 3–4
Emancipation Day (Bahamas), 96–97
Emancipation Day (United States), 12
England
    Guy Fawkes Day, 140–141
    May Day, 61
Epiphany, 14–15
Epona, Feast of, (Celtic), 77
Ethiopia
    New Year, 104
Europe
    Boxing Day, 155
    Childermas, 158
    Fasching (Carnival), 9–10
    Feast of Lanterns, 89–90
    Labor Day, 61
    Liberation Day, 65
    St. Andrew's Day, 145
    St Nicholas Day, 150

Fasching (Carnival), 9–10
Father's Day (Nepal), 97
Father's Day (Sweden), 137
Father's Day (United States), 72
Fatima, Celebration of Our Lady of, 89
Feast of Epona (Celtic), 77
Feast of Lights (Myanmar), 125
Feast of Nganja (Angola), 42
Festa dos Tabuleiros, 136
Festas Junina, 79–80
Festival of Amaterasu-o-Mi-Kami (Japan), 91
Festival of High Places (China), 114–115
Festival of Lemanja (Brazil), 159
Festival of Lights (India), 123–124
Festival of Lights (Jewish), 148–149
Festival of the New Bread (Celtic), 98–99
Festival of the Trays (Portugal), 136
Finland
    Independence Day, 150–151
    Pikkujoulu (Little Christmas), 149
    St. Knut's Day, 16–17
Fire Prevention Week, 122
Flag Day, United States, 78
Flores de Mayo, 60
Founding Day (Japan), 28
Fourth of July, 86–87
Fox Hill Day, 96–97
France
    Assumption Day, 101
    Bastille Day, 90
    Candlemas, 26–27
    Father's Day, 72
    Mardi Gras, 9–10, 22
    Mothers' Day, 55

G

H

Gambia
   Independence Day, 29
Gandhi Jayanti, 128
Germany
   Oktoberfest, 113
   Republic Day, 129
Ghana
   Independence Day, 35
   Yam Festival, 110–111
Girls' Day (Hina Matsuri), 34
Gokarne Aunsi, 97
Good Friday, 32
Greece
   Independence Day, 39
Greek, Ancient
   Birth of the Muses, 77–78
Green Corn Ceremony, 97–98
Green Monday, 23
Groundhog Day, 26
Guadalupe, Day of Our Lady of, 152
Guinea
   Independence Day, 128
Guru Gobind, Birth of, 158
Guru Nanak, Birth of, 143
Guy Fawkes Day, 140–141
Guyana
   Independence Day, 69

Hai Ba Trung, 20
Haile Selassie I, Birth of, 92
Haiti
   Independence Day, 13
   St. John's Eve, 79
Halloween, 133
Hanamatsun (Birth of Buddha), 47
Hanukkah (Jewish Festival of Lights), 148–149
Harvest festivals
   Corpus Christi (Mexico), 58–59
   Crop Over Festival (Barbados), 86
   Feast of Nganja (Angola), 42
   Feast of Okambondondo (Angola), 23
   Federal Thanksgiving Day (Switzerland), 119
   Gawai Dayak (Malaysia), 75
   Green Corn Ceremony (Native American), 97–98
   Htamane-hto (Myanmar), 136
   Kadazan Harvest Festival (Malaysia), 57–58
   Kwanzaa (African American), 156–157
   Moon Festival (China), 107–108
   Oktoberfest (Germany), 113
   Onam (Hindu), 109
   Pista Ng Anihan (Philippines), 66
   Shavuot (Jewish), 57
   Sukkoth (Jewish), 125–126
   Thanksgiving (Canada), 122
   Thanksgiving (United States), 137
   Vestalia (Ancient Roman), 75–76
   Yam Festival (Ghana), 110–111
   Zolla (Nigeria), 127
Higan-E (Fall), 119
Higan-E (Spring), 39
High Places, Festival of (China), 114–115

Hina Matsuri, 34
Hindu celebrations
    Bhau-Beez (Brother and Sister Day), 124
    Diwali (Dipavali), 123–124
    Holi, 32
    Navaratri, 122–123
    Onam, 109
Hispanic Heritage Month, 116–117
Holi, 32
Hong Kong
    Bun Hill Day, 55–56
    Moon Festival, 107–108
Htamane-hto, 136

I

Iban New Year (Gawai Dayak), 75
Iceland
    National Day, 78
Iemanja, Festival of (Brazil), 159
Independence Day celebrations (See also "National Day celebrations")
    Afghanistan, 103
    Australia, 13
    Bahamas, 88
    Bangladesh, 40
    Barbados, 145
    Botswana, 120
    Brazil, 114
    Cambodia, 141
    Cameroon, 13
    Central America, 116
    Chile, 118
    Colombia, 91
    Congo, 102
    Dominican Republic, 30
    Finland, 150–151
    Gambia, 29
    Ghana, 35
    Greece, 39
    Guinea, 128
    Guyana, 68
    Haiti, 13
    India, 100
    Indonesia, 102
    Israel, 57
    Jamaica, 99
    Jordan, 68
    Kenya, 151
    Lebanon, 144
    Lesotho, 129
    Liberia, 93
    Libya, 154
    Madagascar, 80
    Malaysia, 118
    Malta, 119
    Mauritania, 145
    Mauritius, 35
    Mexico, 118
    Myanmar (Burma), 14
    Nauru, 17
    Nepal, 29
    Nigeria, 127
    Pakistan, 100
    Panama, 140
    Paraguay, 66
    Peru, 94
    Poland, 142
    Sierra Leone, 51
    Singapore, 118
    Somalia, 80–81
    South Korea, 102
    Sudan, 13
    Swaziland, 114
    Syria, 49
    Tanzania, 151
    Togo, 51
    Trinidad and Tobago, 103
    Uganda, 130
    United States of America, 86–87
    Venezuela, 49
    West Samoa, 14

Zaire, 81
Zambia, 132
Zimbabwe, 50
India
    Baswant, 42
    Bhau-Beez (Brother and Sister Day), 124
    Children's Day, 142–143
    Divali (Festival of Lights), 123–124
    Gandhi Jayanti (Mahatma Gandhi's Birthday), 128
    Holi, 32
    Independence Day, 100
    Makra Sankrant (Winter Festival), 16
    Navaratri (Doll Festival), 122–123
    Onam (Harvest Festival), 109
    Pongal (Makra Sankrant), 16
    Republic Day, 17
Indonesia
    Independence Day, 102
International
    African Liberation Day, 68
    April Fools' Day, 46
    Arbor Day, 2
    Earth Day, 50–51
    Halloween, 133–134
    May Day, 61
    New Year's Day, 11–12
    New Year's Eve, 158–159
    Pan American Day, 49
    Red Cross Day, 132
    St. Martin's Day, 141
    St. John's Eve, 79–80
    Valentine's Day, 28–29
Iran
    No-Ruz (New Year), 37–38
Ireland, Northern
    Halloween, 133–134
    Orangemen's Day, 88–89
Ireland, Republic of
    Halloween, 133–134
    Saint Patrick's Day, 36
Isis, Birth of, 101
Israel
    Yom Ha'atzmaut (Independence Day), 57
    Yom Hasho'a (Martyr's and Heroes' Remembrance Day), 62
Italy
    Republic Day, 75

J

Jamaica
    Independence Day, 99
Japan
    Bean Throwing Day (Setsubun), 27
    Bird Week, 56–57
    Bon Festival, 89–90
    Festival of Amaterasu-o-Mi-Kami, 91
    Founding Day, 28
    Hanamatsuri (Birth of Buddha), 47
    Hina Matsuri (Girls' Day—Doll Festival), 34
    Kodomono-hi (Boys' Day), 63
    Kunchi Festival, 130
    Respect For the Aged Day, 115–116
    Sakura (Cherry Blossom Festival), 44
    Setsubun (Changing of the Seasons), 27
    Shichi-Go-San (Seven-Five-Three Festival), 143
    Shunki Korei, 39
    Sports Day, 131
    Tanabata Matsuri (Star Festival), 87–88
Jewish Holidays
    Hanukkah (Festival of Lights), 148–149
    Passover, 43–44
    Pesach (Passover), 43–44
    Purim, 21–22
    Rosh Hashanah (New Year), 110
    Shavuot, 57
    Simhath Torah, 126
    Sukkoth (Harvest Festival), 125–126
    Yom Ha'atzmaut, 57
    Yom Hasho'ah (Martyrs' and Heroes' Remembrance Day), 62
    Yom Kippur (Day of Atonement), 110
Jordan
    Independence Day, 68

Juneteenth, 79
Junkanoo, 156

K

Kadazan Harvest Festival, 57–58
Kadooment Day, 96
Karneval, 9–10
Kathin Ceremony, 109
Kenya
    Independence Day, 151
Kite Festival, 114–115
Kodomono-hi (Boys' Day), 63
Korea
    Childrens' Day, 64
    Independence Day, 102
    Kunchi Festival, 130
    National Foundation Day, 128
    Parents' Day, 64–65
    Tanabata Matsuri, 87–88
    Urini Nal, 64
Kunchi Festival, 130
Kuwait
    National Day, 30
Kwanzaa, 156–157

L

Labor Day (International), 61
Labor Day (United States, Canada), 106
Labour Day (Bahamas), 72–73
Lammas (Celtic), 98–99
Lantern Festival (China), 11
Lanterns, Feast of the, 89–90
Laos
    National Day, 66
    Pimai, 38–39
Latin America
    Día de los Reyes Magos, 15–16
    Independence Day, Central America, 116
    Nine Days of Posada, 153
    Pan American Day, 49
Leap Year Day, 30
Lebanon
    Independence Day, 144
Lesotho
    Independence Day, 129
Liberation Day, 65
Liberia
    Independence Day, 93
Libya
    Independence Day, 154
Lich'un, 43
Lights, Feast of (Myanmar), 125
Lights, Festival of (Diwali), 123–124
Lights, Festival of (Hanukkah), 148–149
Loy Krathong, 138–139
Lunar New Year, 8–9
Luxembourg,
    National Day, 79

M

Madagascar
    Independence Day, 80
Magha Puja, 24–25
Makra Sankrant, 16
Malaysia
    Gawai Dayak (Iban New Year), 75
    Independence Day, 118
    Kadazan Harvest Festival, 57–58
Mali
    Republic Day, 120
Malta
    Independence Day, 119–120
Mardi Gras, 9–10, 22
Martin Luther King Jr. Day, 10
Martinmas, 141
Martyrs' and Heroes' Remembrance Day, 62
Matatirtha Aunsi, 45–46
Mauritania
    Independence Day, 145
Mauritius
    Independence Day, 35
May Day, 61
Memorial Day, 55
Mexico
    Childermas, 158
    Cinco De Mayo, 62–63
    Corpus Christi, 58–59
    Day of Our Lady of Guadalupe, 152
    Independence Day, 118
    Nine days of Posada, 153
Midsummer Festival, 73
Mohammed, Birth of, 6
Monaco
    National Celebration, 144
Moon Festival, 107–108
Mormon
    Pioneer Day, 92–93
Morocco
    National Day, 35
    Youth Day, 88
Mother Night, 154
Mother's Day (France, Sweden), 55
Mother's Day (Nepal), 45–46
Mother's Day (United States), 54–55
Muharrum, 5
Muses, Birth of, 77–78
Muslim holidays
    Eid Milad-Un-Nabi (Birth of Mohammed), 6
    Eid-ul-Adhia, 5
    Eid-ul-Fitr, 3–4
    Muharram, 5
    Ramadan, 3
Myanmar (Burma),
    Feast of Lights, 125
    Htamane-hto, 136
    Independence Day, 14
    New Year, 48

N

Naganja, Feast of, 42
National Day celebrations (See also "Independence Day celebrations" and "Republic Day")
    Algeria, 78–79
    Argentina, 68
    Bahrain, 153
    Belgium, 91–92
    Bolivia, 99
    Brunei, 69
    China, 127–128
    Iceland, 78
    Kuwait, 30
    Laos, 66
    Luxembourg, 79
    Monaco, 144

Morocco, 35
New Zealand, 28
Philippines, 77
Portugal, 76
Senegal, 47
Sri Lanka, 27
Sweden, 75
Switzerland, 98
Tunisia, 37
Vietnam, 113–114
Yemen, 67
National Foundation Day (Korea), 128
Native American
    American Indian Day, 112
    Green Corn Ceremony, 97–98
    Sun Dance Festival, 74
Nauru
    Independence Day, 17
Nava Varsha, 48
Navaratri, 122–123
Nepal
    Gokarne Aunsi (Fathers' Day), 97
    Holi, 32
    Independence Day, 29
    Matatirtha Aunsi (Mother's Day), 45–46
    Nava Varsha (New Year), 48
Netherlands
    Bevrijdingsdag, 62
    Dodenherdenking, 62
    Remembrance Days, 62
    Sinterklaas Day, 150
    Tulip Festival, 45
New Year's celebrations
    Diwali (Hindu), 123–124
    Ethiopian New Year, 104
    Gawai Nayak (Iban New Year—Malaysia), 75
    Lunar New Year (Chinese), 8–9
    Muharram (Moslem), 5
    Nava Varsha (Nepal), 48
    New Year's Day, 11–12
    New Year's Eve, 158–159

No-Ruz (Iran), 37–38
Pimia (Laos), 38–39
Rosh Hashanah (Jewish), 110
San Khuda (Sierra Leone), 44–45
Songkran (Thailand, Myanmar), 48
Tet (Vietnam), 9
Yam Festival (Ghana), 110–111
Zolla, 127
New Zealand
    Anzac Day, 51
    Waitangi Day, 28
Nganja, Feast of, 42
Niger
    Republic Day, 154
Nigeria
    Independence Day, 127
    Zolla Festival, 127
Nine Days of Posada, 153
No-Ruz, 37–38
Norway
    Constitution Day, 67
    St. John's Eve, 80
    Walpurgis Eve (Feast of Valborg), 52

Okambondondo, Feast of (Angola), 23
Oktoberfest, 113
Onam, 109
One Hundredth Day of School, 23–24
Orangemen's Day, 88–89

P

Pakistan
   Baswant, 42
   Independence Day, 100
Palm Sunday, 32
Pan American Day, 49
Panama
   Independence Day, 140
Paraguay
   Independence Day, 66
Parents' Day (Korea), 64–65
Passover, 43–44
Pentecost, 58
Peru
   Independence Day, 94
   Spring Festival, 126
Pesach (Passover), 43–44
Philippines
   Constitution Day, 66
   Flores de Mayo, 60
   National Day, 77
   Pista Ng Anihan, 66
   T'Boli Tribal Festival, 111
Pikkujoulu, 149
Pimia, 38–39
Pioneer Day (Mormon), 92–93
Pista Ng Anihan, 66
Ploughing Ceremony, 59
Poland
   Corpus Cristi, 58–59
   Dyngus, 33
   Independence Day, 142
   St. Andrew's Day, 145
   St. Barbara's Day, 149–150
   St. John's Eve, 79
Pongal (Makra Sankrant), 16
Portugal
   Celebration of Our Lady of Fatima, 89

   Festival of the Trays, 136
   National Independence Day, 76
Posada, Nine Days of, 153
Presidents' Day, 21
Puerto Rico
   Constitution Day, 93
Purim, 21–22

R

Ramadan, 3
Rastafarian
   Birth of Haile Selassie I, 92
Red Cross Day, International, 132
Remembrance Day (Canada), 142
Remembrance Days (Netherlands), 62
Republic Day (see also "Independence Day" and "National
   Day")
   Czech Republic, 133
   Germany, 129
   India, 17
   Italy, 75
   Mali, 119
   Niger, 154
   Slovakia, 133
   South Africa, 69
   Turkey, 133
Respect for the Aged Day, 115–116
Ridvan, 50
Roman,
   Vestalia, 75–76
Rosh Hashanah (Jewish New Year), 110
Russia
   May Day, 61

S

St. Andrew's Day, 145
St. Barbara's Day, 149–150
St. Cecilia's Day, 144
St. Christopher's Day, 93
St. Francis of Assisi, Feast of, 129–130
St. John's Eve, 79–80
St. Knut's Day, 16–17
St. Martin's Day, 141
St. Nicholas Day, 150
St. Patrick's Day, 36
St. Stephen's Day, 156
St. Valentine's Day, 28–29
Sakura, 44
San Khuda, 44–45
Santa Lucia, Feast of, 152–153
Scandinavia
    Midsummer Festival, 73
Scotland
    Hogmannay (New Year), 11
Seker Bayrami (Candy Holiday), 4
Senegal
    National Day, 47
Setsubun (Changing of the Seasons), 27
Seven-Five-Three Festival, 143
Shaheed Dibash (Martyrs' Day), 29–30
Shavuot, 57
Shichi-Go-San, 143
Shunki Korei, 39
Sierra Leone
    Independence Day, 51
    San Khuda, 44–45

Sikh festivals
    Birthday of Guru Gobind, 158
    Birthday of Guru Nanak, 143
Simhath Torah, 126
Singapore
    Independence Day, 118
Sinterklaas Day, 150
Slovakia
    Republic Day, 133
    St. Nicholas' Day, 150
    St. Stephen's Day, 156
    Teachers' Day, 40
Somalia
    Independence Day, 80–81
Somhlolo, 114
Songkran, 48
South Africa
    Republic Day, 69
Splash Monday, 33
Sports Day (Japan), 131
Spring festivals and celebrations
    Baswant (India), 42
    Easter, 33
    Flores de Mayo (Philippines), 60
    Higan-E (Buddhist), 39
    Holi (India), 32
    Lich'un (China), 43
    May Day (Great Britain), 61
    No-Ruz (Iran), 37–38
    Peru, 126
    Pimai (Laos), 38–39
    Sakura (Cherry Blossom Festival—Japan), 44
    Setsubun (Japan), 27
    Shunki Korei, 33
    Tulip Festival (Holland), 45
    Vernal Equinox, 37
    Walpurgis Eve (Sweden), 52
Sri Lanka
    National Day, 27
Star Festival (Tanabata Matsuri), 87–88
Sudan
    Independence Day, 13
Sukkoth, 125–126
Summer festivals and celebrations
    Gawai Dayak (Malaysia), 75
    Midsummer Festival (Scandinavia), 73
    St. John's Eve, 79–80

Sun Dance Ceremony (Native American), 74
Vestalia (Ancient Rome), 75–76
Sun Dance Ceremony, 74
Swadhinata Dibash, 40
Swaziland
Somhlolo (Independence Day), 114
Sweden
Father's Day, 137
Feast of Santa Lucia, 152–153
Mother's Day, 55
National Day, 75
St. John's Eve, 80
St. Knut's Day, 16–17
Walpurgis Eve (Feast of Valborg), 52
Switzerland
Alp Feast, 84
Federal Thanksgiving Day, 119
National Day, 98
Syria
Independence Day, 49

T

Taiwan
Youth Day, 40
Tanabata Matsuri, 87–88
Tanzania
Independence Day, 151
Union Day, 51
T'Boli Tribal Festival, 111
T'Boli Tribal Festival, 111
Teachers' Day
China, 115
Czech Republic and Slovakia, 40
Tet Nguyen-Dan (New Year), 9
Tet Trung Thu, 108

Thailand
Chakri Day, 47
Constitution Day, 151
Loy Krathong, 138–139
Ploughing Ceremony, 59
Songkran (Buddhist New Year), 48
Visakha Puja Day, 73–74
Thanksgiving Day
Canada, 122
Switzerland, 119
United States, 137
Three Kings Day, 15–16
Togo
Independence Day, 51–52
Trays, Festival of the (Portugal), 136
Trinidad and Tobago
Independence Day, 103
Trinity Sunday, 58
Tulip Festival, 45
Tunisia
National Day, 37
Turkey
Republic Day, 133
Seker Bayrami (Candy Festival), 4

U

Uganda
Independence Day, 130
Umoja Karamu, 138
UNICEF Day, 134
Union Day (Tanzania), 51
United Kingdom
Boxing Day, 155
Guy Fawkes Day, 140–141
Halloween, 133–134
United States of America
American Indian Day, 112
Asian-Pacific Month, 60–61

Be an Angel Day, 103
Black History Month, 25
Brotherhood Week, 21
Columbus Day, 131–132
Emancipation Day, 12
Father's Day, 72
Fire Prevention Week, 122
Flag Day, 78
Groundhog Day, 26
Halloween, 133–134
Hispanic Heritage Month, 116–118
Independence Day, 86–87
Juneteenth, 79
Kwanzaa, 156–157
Labor Day, 106
Martin Luther King Day, 10
Memorial Day, 55
Mothers' Day, 54–55
Pan American Day, 49
Presidents' Day, 20
Saint Patrick's Day, 36
Thanksgiving Day, 137
UNICEF Day, 134
Valentine's Day, 28–29
V E Day, 65
V J Day, 99–100
Veteran's Day, 142
Women's History Month, 34
Urini Nal, 64

V

Valborg, Feast of, 52
Valentine's Day, 28–29
Venezuela
    Independence Day, 50
Vernal Equinox, 37
Vestalia (Ancient Roman), 75–76
Veteran's Day (United States), 142
Victoria Day, 54
Victory Day (Bangladesh), 153
Vietnam
    Hai Ba Trung, 20
    National Day, 113–114
    Tet Nguyên-Dan (New Year), 9
    Tet Trung Thu, 108
V-E Day, 65
V-J Day, 99–100
Visakha Puja Day, 73

W

Waitangi Day, 28
Walpurgis Eve, 52
Water festivals
    Dyngus (Poland), 33
    Holi (Hindu), 32
    Pimia (Laos), 38–39
    San Khuda (Sierra Leone), 44–45
Western Samoa
    Independence Day, 14
Whitsunday, 58
Winter festivals and celebrations
    Makra Sankrant, 16

Winter Solstice, 154
Winter Solstice, 154
Women's History Month, 34

Yom Kippur, 110
Youth Day (Morocco), 88
Youth Day (Taiwan), 40

Y

Yam Festival, 110–111
Yemen
    National Day, 67
Yom Ha'atzmaut, 57
Yom-Hasho'ah (Martyrs' and Heroes'
        Remembrance Day), 62

Z

Zaire
    Independence Day, 81
Zambia
    Independence Day, 132
Zimbabwe
    Independence Day, 49
Zolla Festival, 127

Index of Activities

A

Aerodynamics and flight, 114–115
Agriculture, 59, 77, 99, 111, 119, 136
Angels, 103
Animals, 16, 26, 33, 37, 48, 57, 63, 67, 101, 119, 129–130, 159
Architecture, 5, 89, 101, 124, 136
Art, 24, 32, 39, 42, 63, 64, 103, 143
Astronomy, 30, 73, 74, 88, 91, 107, 131–132, 154

B

Basket, 61
Boats and rafts, 123, 139
Bulletin boards, 33, 60, 62

C

Careers, 40, 103, 106, 115, 122, 130, 132, 144, 150, 155
Charts and graphs:
   data retrieval charts:

Asian-Pacific countries, 60
   effects of colonization of the Americas, 131
   Hispanic countries, 116
   religions, 3
   winter holidays, 150
   family members, 124
   twelve days of Christmas, 15
   moon phases, 107
Civil rights, 128
Climate, 16, 111
Colors, 32, 42, 126, 138
Communication, 12, 29, 98
Costumes, 22, 35, 96, 134, 136, 137
Crayon resist, 154

D

Dance, 9, 80, 113, 130
Dreidel, 148
Drums, 86, 89, 104, 112, 137
Dwellings, 125

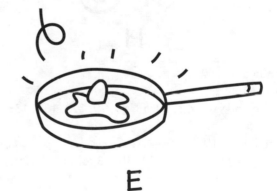

E

Ecology and environment, 2–3, 45, 50–51, 57, 80, 112, 122, 129, 149, 159
Education, 40, 109, 115

F

Family "gardens," 90
Farming, 59
Field trips, 23, 76, 99, 115, 118, 132

Fire safety, 76, 122
Flag, American, 78, 93
Folk tales and legends, 9, 10, 20, 25, 36, 61, 74, 88, 91, 112, 113, 155, 157
Food (See also Appendix B), 4, 16, 24, 27, 37, 43, 47, 55, 56, 64, 73, 96, 97, 98, 99, 103, 110, 111, 119, 123, 124, 125, 126, 127, 137, 152, 157
Foreign languages, 63, 90, 113, 116, 157, 159

G

Games, 117
Geography, 125, 151
Gifts, 4, 54–55, 64, 72, 124, 157
God's Eye, 116–117
Government, 21, 34–35, 39, 87, 141

H

Handicaps, 152
Hats, 136
Health and safety, 3, 29, 58, 89, 99, 122, 132, 133, 143, 157
Horns, 84, 110
Human Rights, 21, 30, 34, 39, 43, 62, 68, 74, 90, 92

I

Immigration, 36
Interviewing, 23, 34, 87, 115

K

Kimono, 35

Kinara, 157
Kites, 42, 115

L

Lanterns, paper, 11, 108, 125, 133

M

Machines, simple, 101, 131
Map skills, 38, 42, 66, 68, 122, 125, 126, 127. 131, 133, 151
Masks, 10, 111, 156
Math, 11, 14–15, 20, 22, 24, 30, 39, 49, 54, 78, 85, 86, 96, 104, 108, 127, 131, 134, 143, 148, 155
Menorah, 148
Mirrors, 91
Money, 24, 54, 63, 85, 86, 98, 136, 155
Monsters, 134
Mountains, 98, 119
Music, 10, 25, 36, 59, 84, 86, 89, 96, 104, 108, 109, 110, 112, 116, 138, 144, 153, 155, 156, 157
Musical instruments to make, 108, 110, 144
Mythology, 29, 40, 46, 76, 77, 88, 101

N

Natural disasters, 126, 132
Nature worship, 111, 154
Necklaces, 112
Notes, passing, 107
Nuclear weapons, 100

O

Opposites, 39
Ornaments, bread dough, 140

P

Painting, 87
Paper doll chains, 10
Paper mâché, 10, 117, 153, 156
Parades:
    Carnival, 10
    Chinese New Year, 9
    Pista Ng Anihan, 67
    Purim, 22
    Tet Trung Thu, 108
Performances, student, 35, 51, 52, 55, 63, 72–73, 77–78, 85, 87, 90, 96, 97, 104, 106, 143, 144
Personification, 17
Philosophy, 107
Physical activities, 63, 64, 67, 84, 97, 98, 109, 113, 117, 131
Pictographs, 112
Piñata, 117, 153
Plants, 3, 26, 27, 44, 45, 48, 73, 155
Poetry, 10, 28–29, 54, 55, 64, 109, 144
Potato prints, 36
Puppets, 4, 9, 26
Puzzles, 44
Pyramids, 101

R

Research projects, 10, 20, 25, 26, 34, 35, 38, 43, 46, 50, 54, 63, 87, 119, 122, 138, 150, 155
Role-playing, 10, 12, 89

S

Science, 25, 26, 27, 37, 43–44, 52, 80, 92–93, 143, 145
Seeds, 27, 33, 38, 42, 99, 134
Senses, 44, 110, 113
Shadows, 26
Soap, 54
Speakers, 50, 87, 106, 118, 132
Statistics, 21
Story bag, 112
Story elements, 36
Story telling, 90, 112
Sukkah, 125–126
Supernatural creatures, 134
Superstitions, 12, 26, 52, 59, 87, 91, 107, 145
Symbolism, 11, 16, 42, 56, 90, 101, 103, 141, 148, 156

T

Time, 12, 24, 28, 30, 33, 46, 127, 158–159
Timeline, 15, 20, 25, 54, 75, 110
Transportation, 15, 56, 77, 87, 101
Travel, 49, 73, 88, 93, 98, 110, 126

V

Vegetable prints, 36, 42, 134

W

War, 20, 55, 100, 112, 102
Water, 45, 109, 139, 159

Weather, 43, 48, 84–85, 110, 111
Weaving, 157
Wreaths, 65, 152
Writing, creative, 12, 17, 22, 23, 32, 36, 46, 52, 58, 59,
    63, 64, 73, 74, 77, 90, 114, 123, 124, 130, 131,
    138, 145, 155
Writing, letter or card, 20, 28, 40, 54, 103, 106, 115,
    123, 124, 155

Z

Zodiac, 9